REDISTRICTING

REDISTRICTING
The Most Political Activity in America

Charles S. Bullock III

ROWMAN & LITTLEFIELD PUBLISHERS, INC.

Lanham • Boulder • New York • Toronto • Plymouth, UK

Published by Rowman & Littlefield Publishers, Inc.
A wholly owned subsidiary of The Rowman & Littlefield Publishing Group, Inc.
4501 Forbes Boulevard, Suite 200, Lanham, Maryland 20706
http://www.rowmanlittlefield.com

Estover Road, Plymouth PL6 7PY, United Kingdom

British Library Cataloguing in Publication Information Available

Library of Congress Cataloging-in-Publication Data

Bullock, Charles S., 1942-
  Redistricting : the most political activity in America / Charles S. Bullock III.
    p. cm.
  ISBN 978-1-4422-0353-2 (cloth : alk. paper) — ISBN 978-1-4422-0354-9 (pbk. : alk. paper) — ISBN 978-1-4422-0355-6 (electronic)
  1. Apportionment (Election law) — United States. 2. Apportionment (Election law) —
  2. Political aspects — United States. I. Title.
  KF4905.B85 2010
  328.73'073455—dc22

                                                                              2009053911

Printed in the United States of America

To my four grandsons
Jason, Christopher, Daniel and Matthew Fern

Contents

Acknowledgments ix

1 Why Redistricting Is Important 1
2 Population Equality: How Equal Must Districts Be? 25
3 Minorities and Redistricting 49
4 The Populations Are Equal and Minorities Have Not Been
  Discriminated Against. Now What? 87
5 Partisan Gerrymandering: All's Fair in Love, War,
  and Redistricting 107
6 Gerrymandering Georgia: A Case Study 139
7 Looking to the Future 175

Notes 193

Index 215

About the Author 223

Acknowledgments

THIS BOOK IS THE RESULT OF TEACHING about redistricting—how it is done and its consequences—for four decades. Many people have contributed to my understanding of the topic. Most of those who have advanced my understanding were probably unaware of their role and none bear any responsibility for the lingering gaps in my knowledge. Much of my education has taken place in the context of the development of redistricting plans and then litigation challenging those plans. In some cases I have worked for the jurisdiction defending the plan while at other times I have helped those seeking to overturn the plan.

Those to whom I owe an intellectual debt include: John Alford, Steve Bickerstaff, Kim Brace, Kay Butler, Bruce Cain, David Canon, Dick Engstrom, David Epstein, the late Robinson Everett, Keith Gaddie, Bernie Grofman, Lisa Handley, Jerry Hebert, Sam Hirsch, Tom Hofeller, Bob Holmes, Paul Hurd, Gary King, Morgan Kousser, David Lublin, Susan MacManus, Doug Markham, Linda Meggers, Dick Murray, Tim O'Rourke, Andy Taylor, Bryan Tyson, Vince Fontana, Dave Walbert, Ron Weber, and Steve Zack. Kim Brace of Election Data Services has kindly permitted me to use some of the incomparable maps he has produced.

Completion of this manuscript would have taken much longer and might never have seen the light of day without the assistance of my secretary Bridget Pilcher. Wendi Finch also helped with preparation of the manuscript. Once the manuscript went into production, Elaine McGarraugh and Elisa Weeks at Rowman & Littlefield played critical roles that made my life much easier and the book much better.

1

Why Redistricting Is Important

The key concept to grasp is that there are no neutral lines for legislative districts.[1]

Gerrymandering is somewhat like pornography—you know it when you see it, but it's awful difficult to define.

—Rep. Abner Mikva[2]

IN 2000, GEORGE BUSH CARRIED TEXAS by more than 1.3 million votes. The Bush victory sparked little surprise since Bush came from Texas. The Lone Star State has voted Republican for president since 1952, except when another native son, Lyndon Johnson, was on the ballot and when it supported fellow Southerner Jimmy Carter in 1976. Moreover, by 2000, Republicans filled 28 of the 29 statewide elective partisan offices. Republican candidates also took 50.8 percent of the congressional vote. Thus at the onset of the twenty-first century, Texas seemed to be a red state. There was, however, a problem, at least from the Republican perspective. Although their nominees won most of the congressional votes cast in the state, this translated into only 13 of the 30 seats. The 2000 results continued a pattern that had begun with 1994, when Republican congressional candidates won a majority of the popular vote and yet failed to get even half of the state's congressional seats.

The explanation for the failure of popular support to translate into a commensurate share of the congressional seats lay with the districting plan. After the 1990 Census, Democratic Representative Martin Frost and a staffer devised a brilliantly effective gerrymander. Frost distributed Democratic supporters to maximize the number of districts his party could win. For the next decade, Democrats received a substantially larger share of the seats than their share of the popular vote.

Elections are essential to the legitimacy of any democracy. However, as the Texas example demonstrates, the way in which votes translate into seats depends upon the districting format. A districting scheme can make some votes worth more than others. As in Texas, the party that gets fewer votes overall (in this case, the Democrats) can win a majority of the seats in the legislature if the districting plan packs supporters of the losing party (here, the Republicans) into a minority of districts that are won by overwhelming majorities, while carefully distributing the supporters of the winning party (the Democrats) so that they win a greater number of seats by narrower margins. A less controversial result of a districting scheme, which would nonetheless be considered a gerrymander, enables the majority party to secure far more seats than it would receive under a less biased plan. By promoting or thwarting the ambitions of a political party, districting plans determine what interests in society will be best positioned to determine policy outputs. If the districting scheme favors rural voters, then the concerns of farmers may get more consideration than the needs of urban residents. A plan that gives Democrats a disproportionate share of the seats will likely enhance the influence of organized labor, environmentalists, and trial attorneys.

The impact of districting schemes is greatest in systems like those used in the U.S. House of Representatives and in most American state legislatures, where each district chooses one representative. With only one representative per district, parties compete under winner-take-all rules, so that the number of seats in the legislature held by a party can be maximized under a plan that allows it to win consistently with small majorities. In the most extreme hypothetical arrangement, if the majority party managed to win 51 percent of the vote in every district, then it would win all of the seats from a state even though it attracted only slightly over half of the votes. Of course, any plan that distributes votes in anticipation that a party will narrowly win a number of districts runs the risk of losing those competitive districts should partisan preferences shift even slightly.

In contrast with the single-member, plurality elections widely used in the United States, many nations have electoral systems designed to promote proportionality. At one extreme, the entire nations of Israel and the Netherlands serve as a single district and elect all members of their parliaments at-large with each party receiving a share of seats proportional to its share of the votes so that the ratio of seats to votes approximates 1:1. The approach used by the Israelis and the Dutch eliminates any problem of one party designing a districting plan to the disadvantage of its opponents—although it would not necessarily prevent some areas of the country or its interests being underrepresented. However, most nations that use proportional representation have multimember districts that represent states, regions, or other subdivisions within the nation. In these systems, districting can be important, as demonstrated in Japan where the party that has dominated its politics for most of the period since World War II draws great support from rural areas and therefore underrepresents urban interests.

The debate over the way in which votes should translate into seats predates the Constitution. Supreme Court Justice Antonin Scalia references a concern in North Carolina as early as 1732 that the governor might have manipulated boundaries in order to secure majority support in the lower chamber of the colonial legislature.[3] One of the most controversial issues at the Constitutional Convention involved the representation of states with populations of different sizes. The Great Compromise equalized state representation in the Senate regardless of population, while representation in the House reflected population differences.

Using population to distribute seats in the U.S. House of Representatives indicates a concern about fairness. Fairness has taken on many guises and is invariably invoked in the course of conflict over redistricting. While the Constitution is notable for its lack of specificity, which has allowed Congress and courts to expand federal authority through the "necessary and proper" clause, the document sets a lower limit with regard to the weighting of population in the House. Article 1, Section 2 specifies that "the number of representatives shall not exceed one for every 30,000 people." The Constitution also set the number of seats for each of the thirteen states in the first Congress. The Constitution called for a census within three years after Congress convened for its first meeting and then every ten years thereafter. After the initial census, adjustments would be made in the distribution of seats in the lower chamber.

Following the first census in 1790, eleven states gained seats, with the New York, North Carolina, and Virginia delegations almost doubling in size. Delaware remained with a single seat and only Georgia lost a seat, declining from three to two. After each census, from 1790 through 1910 with one exception, the House expanded. Despite a growing number of seats available, reapportionment following the census resulted in some states, particularly those in New England, gradually losing representation.

Although redistricting and reapportionment are often used synonymously, they have different meanings. Reapportionment is the redistribution of seats following the census, when seats in the U.S. House are allocated to states.

Redistricting involves the crafting of new districts from which those seats will be filled. When the states change their maps to reflect population shifts during the course of a decade, that is redistricting.

Seat Allocations to States

Until the 1960s, reapportionment and redistricting standards operated on very different bases. With one exception, reapportionment took place after each census, and while several different formulae have been used over time, the allocation of seats to states took place with great precision. Redistricting, however, occurred infrequently, even when rules were in place that called for it to be accomplished to reflect population shifts. Indeed, the general practice was to redistrict only when *absolutely* necessary. While equally populated districts have become the standard for all collegial bodies, for most of American history only the U.S. House reflected population changes among states—but even in that chamber, large population differences existed within states. We turn our attention now to the one instance in which population has always mattered, the distribution of congressional seats among states.

Table 1.1 shows the number of seats allocated to each state over time. The general trend has been for representation to move westward from the eastern seaboard. Another trend starting after World War II is the shifting of seats from the North to the South.

A snapshot taken following the 1900 Census would show the largest delegations to be New York (37 members), Pennsylvania (32), Illinois (25), Ohio (21), Missouri (16), Texas (16), and Massachusetts (14). A century later, California had the largest delegation (53 members), followed by Texas (32), New York (29), Florida (25), Pennsylvania (19), Illinois (19), Ohio (18), and Michigan (15). Of the seven largest states in 1900, all except Texas grew more slowly than the nation as a whole during the twentieth century and, consequently, lost seats. Pennsylvania, the nation's second largest state from 1820 until 1950, lost 13 seats. Proportionally, Missouri experienced the greatest loss, as its delegation declined by 44 percent to 9 members. While five of the seven largest states in 1900 remained in that exclusive category during the twentieth century, California exploded from 8 seats to 53, and Florida experienced an even greater percentage rate of growth since the 1900 Census allotted it only 3 seats.

Following the census taken at the dawn of the twenty-first century, California with 53 seats had the largest state delegation in the history of the nation, a distinction first achieved a decade earlier. Texas overtook New York during the previous decade for second place. Florida placed fourth, but projections

TABLE 1.1

U.S. House Apportionment, 1789–2002

State	1789	1792	1802	1812	1822	1832	1842	1852	1862	1872	1882	1892	1902	1912	1932	1942	1952	1962	1972	1982	1992	2002
Northeast																						
Connecticut	5	7	7	7	6	6	4	4	4	4	4	4	5	5	6	6	6	6	6	6	6	5
Maine				7	7	8	7	6	5	5	4	4	4	4	3	3	3	2	2	2	2	2
Massachusetts	8	14	17	13	13	12	10	11	10	11	12	13	14	16	15	14	14	12	12	11	10	10
New Hampshire	3	4	5	6	6	5	4	3	3	3	2	2	2	2	2	2	2	2	2	2	2	2
New Jersey	4	5	6	6	6	6	5	5	5	7	7	8	10	12	14	14	14	15	15	14	13	13
New York	6	10	17	27	34	40	34	33	31	33	34	34	37	43	45	45	43	41	39	34	31	29
Pennsylvania	8	13	18	23	26	28	24	25	24	27	28	30	32	36	34	33	30	27	25	23	21	19
Rhode Island	1	2	2	2	2	2	2	2	2	2	2	2	2	3	2	2	2	2	2	2	2	2
Vermont		2	4	6	5	5	4	3	3	3	2	2	2	2	1	1	1	1	1	1	1	1
North Central																						
Illinois				1	1	3	7	9	14	19	20	22	25	27	27	26	25	24	24	22	20	19
Indiana				1	3	7	10	11	11	13	13	13	13	13	12	11	11	11	11	10	10	9
Iowa							2	2	6	9	11	11	11	11	9	8	8	7	6	6	5	5
Kansas									1	3	7	8	8	8	7	6	6	5	5	5	4	4
Michigan						1	3	4	6	9	11	12	12	13	17	17	18	19	19	18	16	15
Minnesota								2	2	3	5	7	9	10	9	9	9	8	8	8	8	8
Nebraska									1	1	3	6	6	6	5	4	4	3	3	3	3	3
North Dakota												1	2	3	2	2	2	2	1	1	1	1
Ohio			1	6	14	19	21	21	19	20	21	21	21	22	24	23	23	24	23	21	19	18
South Dakota												2	2	3	2	2	2	2	2	1	1	1
Wisconsin							2	3	6	8	9	10	11	11	10	10	10	10	9	9	9	8
Pacific																						
Alaska																		1	1	1	1	1
California								2	3	4	6	7	8	11	20	23	30	38	43	45	52	53
Hawaii																		2	2	2	2	2
Oregon									1	1	1	2	2	3	3	4	4	4	4	5	5	5
Washington												2	3	5	6	6	7	7	7	8	9	9

TABLE 1.1
(Continued)

State	1789	1792	1802	1812	1822	1832	1842	1852	1862	1872	1882	1892	1902	1912	1932	1942	1952	1962	1972	1982	1992	2002
South																						
Alabama				1	3	5	7	7	6	8	8	9	9	10	9	9	9	8	7	7	7	7
Arkansas						1	1	2	3	4	5	6	7	7	7	7	6	4	4	4	4	4
Florida							1	1	1	2	2	2	3	4	5	6	8	12	15	19	23	25
Georgia	3	2	4	6	7	9	8	8	7	9	10	11	11	12	10	10	10	10	10	10	11	13
Louisiana				1	3	3	4	4	5	6	6	6	7	8	8	8	8	8	8	8	7	7
Mississippi				1	1	2	4	5	5	6	7	7	8	8	7	7	6	5	5	5	5	4
North Carolina	5	10	12	13	13	13	9	8	7	8	9	9	10	10	11	12	12	11	11	11	12	13
South Carolina	5	6	8	9	9	9	7	6	4	5	7	7	7	7	6	6	6	6	6	6	6	6
Tennessee		1	3	6	9	13	11	10	8	10	10	10	10	10	9	10	9	9	8	9	9	9
Texas							2	2	4	6	11	13	16	18	21	21	22	23	24	27	30	32
Virginia	10	19	22	23	22	21	15	13	11	9	10	10	10	10	9	9	10	10	10	10	11	11
Border South																						
Delaware	1	1	1	2	1	1	1	1	1	1	1	1	1	1	1	1	1	1	1	1	1	1
Kentucky		2	6	10	12	13	10	10	9	10	11	11	11	11	9	9	8	7	7	7	6	6
Maryland	6	8	9	9	9	8	6	6	5	6	6	6	6	6	6	6	7	8	8	8	8	8
Missouri					1	2	5	7	9	13	14	15	16	16	13	13	11	10	10	9	9	9
Oklahoma													5	8	9	8	6	6	6	6	6	5
West Virginia										3	4	4	5	6	6	6	6	5	4	4	3	3
Mountain West																						
Arizona														1	1	2	2	3	4	5	6	8
Colorado										1	1	2	3	4	4	4	4	4	5	6	6	7
Idaho											1	1	1	2	2	2	2	2	2	2	2	2
Montana											1	1	1	2	2	2	2	2	2	2	1	1
Nevada									1	1	1	1	1	1	1	1	1	1	1	2	2	3
New Mexico													1	1	1	2	2	2	2	2	2	3
Utah												1	1	2	2	2	2	2	2	3	3	3
Wyoming												1	1	1	1	1	1	1	1	1	1	1

show it surpassing New York before 2020. Pennsylvania, Ohio, Illinois, Michigan, New Jersey, and Georgia rounded out the top ten. Already, Georgia has overtaken New Jersey and moved into ninth place, and some projections show it passing Michigan as early as the 2010 Census. North Carolina will likely push New Jersey out of the top ten by 2010.

In the wake of widespread availability of air conditioning, the South, which (excluding Florida, Louisiana, and Texas) had lost representation in the middle decades of the twentieth century, became a major gainer, increasing from 106 seats in 1962 to 131 in 2002.[4] As in other regions, growth in the South has not been even. Growth has come to urban areas, with cities and their suburbs in Florida and Texas experiencing some of the most rapid expansion. The more rural states—Alabama, Mississippi, and Arkansas—saw their delegations decline from a total of 23 seats in 1942 to 15 seats as of 2002.

The other growth area in recent years has been the West, with California leading the way. As table 1.1 shows, at the end of World War II, California had 23 members of Congress, which tied it for the fourth-largest delegation. After gaining 30 seats, some projections indicate that it will not gain any more with the 2010 Census. Other major postwar gainers in the West include Arizona, which has grown from 2 to 8 seats; Colorado, growing from 4 to 7; and Washington, growing from 6 to 9. Nevada, the least populous state in 1940, now has 3 members of Congress. During the latter half of the twentieth century, only Montana among Mountain West and Pacific Coast states lost representation, while nine of the thirteen states gained seats.

Major losses have come in the Rust Belt. New York, Pennsylvania, Ohio, Indiana, Illinois, and Michigan had a total of 155 representatives in 1942. After the 2000 Census, these states' representation in the House shrank to 109. Every state in the North Central region has lost seats since 1942 and most have lost multiple seats. During the twentieth century, Iowa declined from a high of 11 to 5, Kansas from 8 to 4, Nebraska from 6 to 3, and the Dakotas from a high of 3 each to 1 apiece.

The shift in seats from the Rust Belt to the South contributed to a loss of influence by organized labor. Unions had great strength in the heavy industries found in the band of states from New York westward to Illinois. The South has right-to-work laws, which make union organizing much more difficult. Moreover, the independence of southerners has made them much less eager to join unions.

Taking seats away from the Northeast and upper Midwest has reduced the strength of the Democratic Party while enhancing that of Republicans. Of the ten delegations that lost seats after the 2000 Census, only three had GOP majorities in their delegations at that time. In five of the seven states that received additional seats following that census, a majority of the congressional delegation belonged to the GOP.

The decennial reapportionment of House seats also adjusts the numbers of presidential electors that the states have. Had the post-2000 reapportionment been in place at the time of the 2000 presidential election, George Bush would have won the Electoral College vote by seven more electors. Had the 2000 election been run using the distribution of House seats in place for the election as of 1960, rather than that for 2000, Al Gore would have become the nation's forty-third president even without the votes from Florida.

Stability and Leadership before the Redistricting Revolution

As will be discussed in the next chapter, for decades redistricting came infrequently and in some states almost never. As a consequence, legislative districts remained much the same for generations despite major population shifts. This continuity in district construction may help explain the startling phenomenon concerning the home districts of U.S. House leaders observed by Garrison Nelson.[5] In 1949, the Speaker of the House came from north Texas, the majority leader came from Boston, and the minority whip came from central Illinois. More than a generation later in 1976, the Speaker of the House came from Boston, the majority leader came from north Texas, and the minority whip came from central Illinois. More broadly, Nelson showed that more than 85 percent of the House leaders from the time of the Civil War until 1978 came from within five counties of another leader, indicating a remarkable continuity in the areas of the nation that produced the leadership of Congress—a phenomenon Nelson called "geographical propinquity."[6] Nelson hypothesized that these leaders sought to reproduce themselves by taking on as protégés individuals having similar backgrounds. The relevant background features were upward mobility, coming from a rural area, and having no sons. Although Nelson does not make this point, arguably the tendency to make few changes in district boundaries during most of the period he studied facilitated the desire of House leaders to pass on leadership positions to younger duplicates of themselves who were, to a degree, surrogate sons.

This phenomenon of House leaders sharing characteristics and coming from similar types of districts has now ceased. The change coincided with the increased emphasis on maximizing population equality among districts, which dramatically reduced the number of rural districts. Also contributing to the end of the practice on the Democratic side was the decision to have the Democratic Caucus elect the party whip, who usually advances to become party leader and still later, when Democrats organize the House, the Speaker. Until 1986 the majority leader in consultation with the Speaker tapped the new whip when that position became vacant, which made it easier to recruit replicas of the current leaders. Once the Democratic whip became an elected position, the entire caucus made the decision, and that has resulted in more variation in the geographic areas represented by Democratic leadership.

The recruitment of legislative leaders at the state level has not generated a study along the lines of Nelson's examination of House leaders. However, an example from one state indicates how a system where leaders are appointed helped rural interests maintain their influence even after redistricting reduced their numbers. As will be shown in chapter 2, Georgia had one of the most malapportioned legislatures in the nation. When the courts ordered that its districts be redrawn to reflect population, the makeup of the Georgia General Assembly underwent a major transformation, as it welcomed Republicans and African Americans as members of much enlarged urban delegations. However, even as more and more legislators came from urban and suburban areas, rural Democrats held on to a disproportionate share of influence within the legislature for another four decades. Since the leadership appoints committee chairs in Georgia, rural speakers promoted the careers of individuals who had similar backgrounds. In Speaker Tom Murphy's last term (2001–2002), no Democrat in a major leadership position came from metro Atlanta, although 45 percent of the Democratic legislators came from that part of the state. Four years later when Republicans won their first majority in the chamber in more than 130 years, the speaker came from the Atlanta suburbs, as did the speaker pro tempore and the chair of the powerful Rules Committee.

Who Does the Redistricting?

In most states (thirty-seven) the legislature has primary responsibility for designing the districts of its members, and in thirty-nine states with multiple districts the legislature draws the state's congressional districts.[7] As one might expect, these decisions have become more political as the relations between Democrats and Republicans in Congress and in many states have become increasingly testy. For a party to be fully in control of the process, it typically must have majorities in both chambers of the legislature and also control the governor's office (in all but two states, when the legislature draws district lines, the governor can veto plans). In some states, like Texas, having a majority is insufficient because the rules or norms of the legislature require an extraordinary majority.

A few states, with Iowa being the most prominent example, have reduced the role of the legislature in the districting process and have tried to make the process less partisan. Eleven states have followed Ohio's lead and give sole responsibility for redistricting of either the congressional or state legislative districts to an independent commission. In eight other states, including

Texas, a commission stands ready to draw the lines should the legislature fail to do so. Some commissions seek to minimize partisanship, while others do not. In Texas in 2001, each party controlled one chamber; the legislature deadlocked and, as a consequence, the five-member Legislative Redistricting Board redrew boundaries for the state house and senate. Four board members were Republicans and, not surprisingly, the plan they devised enabled their fellow partisans to seize control of the house. In five states, plans drawn by the legislature are reviewed by the state supreme court before implementation.

States must quickly redraw districts following release of new census figures. If the legislature fails to produce maps because it is riven by internal partisan rivalries or by partisan differences between the legislature and the governor, courts will carry out the task. Court-drawn maps remain in effect unless the legislature replaces them (as occurred in 2003 with the Texas congressional plan). Courts are also often brought into the redistricting process when the party that has lost before the legislature asks a state court, federal court, or both to replace the map.

While federal law usually takes precedence over state law, when it comes to redistricting, the state has the first opportunity to complete the process. Federal courts will not interfere with the state legislature's efforts so long as it appears that the legislature will meet the deadlines for having new districts in place in time for the next election. Nor can a federal court block the activities of a state court that is making adequate progress toward the development of a new plan.[8]

If a judicial challenge to an existing districting plan succeeds, the legislative body or commission responsible for redistricting has the first opportunity to take corrective action. If it appears that corrective action will not occur in timely fashion, then the court can draw a map on its own or, more likely, employ an outside expert to help with the process. Or, the court may adopt a plan offered by the litigant who successfully challenged the existing plan. When Florida failed to come up with a congressional plan in 1992, a law professor serving as consultant to the federal judge who heard the case stitched together a map using parts of plans urged by three of the parties in the litigation.

Members of Congress have no direct control over their fates when it comes to redistricting. About half the members of Congress have previously served in their state legislature and may be able to convince former colleagues to provide them with a secure district. However, when the majority of the legislature does not belong to the same party as the member of Congress, pleas from the Washington representative may go largely unheeded. In a worst-case scenario, a House member may even come under attack from an ambitious state legislator who connives to redesign the district in hopes of unseating the incumbent. To win favor with state legislators, members of Congress may host fundraisers, may attend meetings of the National Conference of State Legislatures, and will certainly return the phone calls of state legislators in the year or so leading up to a redistricting.[9]

In preparation for the 2000 Census and redistricting, both parties created organizations to promote their interests. Democrats had largely ignored state redistricting in 1990, probably because their party controlled the entire process in twenty-four states and their thirty-six years of continuous majorities in the House may have given them a false sense of invulnerability. In 2000, after six years in the minority in the U.S. House, Democrats formed an organization called IMPACT 2000 to promote their redistricting concerns. On the other side, the equivalent organization was the Republican Legislative Campaign Fund. Both of these organizations helped fund state legislative elections in critical states in the hopes of either winning complete control and therefore dominating redistricting or controlling at least one legislative chamber so they could block partisan plans coming from the other side. In Virginia, for example, in 1999 Republicans spent more than $400,000 in a successful effort to win control of both chambers.[10] The new maps paid off for the GOP, as it transformed Republicans in the state house from a narrow to a comfortable majority.

When Is Redistricting Done?

As will be explained in the next chapter, the Redistricting Revolution of the 1960s has required jurisdictions that elect legislators from districts to redraw the boundaries to reflect population shifts after each census. This is a marked departure from the past, when district lines might remain unchanged for generations, rather than being redrawn each decade.

Because getting approval for a new set of districts often inflames controversy, requires a great deal of time, and may leave deep wounds that are slow to heal, most states undertake the process only when necessary. That has meant that even after the Redistricting Revolution, states usually redo their congressional and state legislative districts only once in a decade. The major exception to this once-a-decade norm comes in the wake of a successful judicial challenge to the existing plan. Correcting problems identified by the courts may necessitate remapping the entire jurisdiction, although under some circumstances a less dramatic remedy may be possible. In both the mid-1990s and then a decade later after the Supreme Court identified problems with the Texas congressional districts, the legislature responded by redrawing only enough of the state to address the concerns raised by the Court.

In a break with tradition, the first decade of the new century saw three states redraw their congressional districts even though the current plans had *not* run afoul of a judicial decision. In the most controversial of these, U.S. House Majority Leader Tom DeLay convinced the Texas legislature to implement changes designed to defeat his Anglo Democratic colleagues.[11] DeLay hoped that eliminating some Texas Democratic colleagues would increase the slight Republican majority in the House.

The 2000 Census gave Colorado a seventh district. The new map, which was drawn by a judge, sought to create a Denver-area district in which Democrats and Republicans would have equal strength. The judge displayed a keen eye for political strength, coming up with a district that gave Al Gore a victory margin of less than 2,000. In the first congressional election, the district performed as expected, yielding the nation's most competitive result with Republican Bob Beauprez eking out a 121-vote victory. Republicans sought to make Beauprez safer by removing some Democrats.

The third example of a midterm redistricting not necessitated by a court order came in Georgia. Democrats had executed a viciously partisan gerrymander in an effort to increase their share of the congressional delegation from three to seven. After Republicans gained control of both chambers and the governorship, they created a new map to solidify the position of a junior Republican who had managed to win a district designed to elect a Democrat.

Democrats launched court challenges to all three of these plans, arguing in part that since the state had a legal plan in place changes could not be made until the next census. This argument prevailed in Colorado because the state constitution permits only one districting plan per decade unless a second one becomes necessary to meet court objections. Neither Texas nor Georgia had state laws nor constitutional provisions banning a new mapping effort, and federal judges found nothing in federal law that prevented drawing a new map. Critics worried that every time control of the redistricting forces in a state changed partisan hands, the victors would impose a new set of maps. These fears proved baseless; no state has significantly altered its congressional districts voluntarily since Georgia did so in 2005.

Not surprisingly, the party that gets to draw district lines usually comes out ahead. This is especially true if reapportionment gives the state an additional congressional seat.[12] In states that lose seats, the party drawing the districts does little better than hold its own. While it is not surprising that legislators will take care of their fellow partisans when drawing new maps, it may come as a shock to learn that judges also reveal partisan preferences when reviewing new maps. In an analysis of the plans drawn in the 1960s, Cox and Katz write: "Democratic dominance of the federal judiciary, combined with court decisions in deciding which plans were adequate in terms of malapportionment, meant that the pattern of reversions greatly facilitated, indeed, pushed, the adjustment of plans in a pro-Democratic direction."[13] While judges may have revealed partisan preferences in striking down existing plans, it is rare for a federal judge to come up with a distinctly partisan replacement plan. When judges must draw new districts, they rely heavily on the last legal plan rather than starting *de novo*. They may employ experts to help with the task. In explaining maps produced by or for courts, judges stress that they have sought to act in a nonpartisan manner.

Consequences of Districting Decisions

The distribution of seats in the legislative chamber goes a long way toward determining policy outcomes. Groups that are underrepresented have poorer prospects for setting the agenda and securing the policies that they prefer. In most legislatures, the majority party exercises disproportionate control over the issues that come to the floor and the timing for issues to be considered. Some legislatures, like Tennessee and Texas, have a tradition of allowing members of either party to chair committees, but many other states follow the practice in Congress in which only members of the majority party chair committees.

Districting plans affect not only the representation of parties but also the extent to which minorities will serve in the legislature, and diversity in a chamber can affect the agenda. Research has shown that having members of racial and ethnic minorities in a collegial body results in issues being introduced that are not brought forward in their absence. David Canon has shown that African Americans in Congress are more likely than white legislators to introduce legislation that has a racial component, even when the white legislator represents a district with a sizable minority population.[14] According to Canon, black members are more likely to put out press releases dealing with racial issues and to insert racially oriented materials into the Extension of Remarks portion of the *Congressional Record* than are white legislators.

As they have accrued seniority, African American state legislators have achieved leadership positions in the Democratic Party. In chambers in which Democrats have majorities, African Americans increasingly chair committees and fill chamber leadership posts like California's former speaker Willie Brown and North Carolina's former speaker Dan Blue. Case studies of black influence in southern state legislatures report variation in the success of legislative black caucuses in achieving their policy objectives, but the mere presence of a black caucus ensures that African American concerns are aired.[15]

Case studies at the local level also document the ability of minorities to at least inject their concerns into the policy debate. Success in achieving minorities' objectives hinges on the ability of minorities to form coalitions with the dominant group of the governing body.[16] Districting practices that ensure the presence of minorities in governing bodies result in decisions that distribute a larger share of public benefits to the minority community.[17]

Gerrymandering Techniques

Until the 1960s, many of the inequities within legislative chambers stemmed from what might be called "sins of omission" rather than "sins of commission." Differences in district populations resulted largely from inaction, or what has been labeled the "silent gerrymander." Seats in the U.S. House were redistributed after each census, but states that maintained the same number of seats rarely made adjustments to their congressional districts. Those favoring changes found it impossible to overcome inertia. Incumbents, not surprisingly, liked the arrangement under which they had succeeded. As has become readily apparent in the wake of the Redistricting Revolution, when changes have to be made, they unleash frenetic political ambitions that can divert the attention of the legislature from all other tasks and inflict wounds that may never heal. Therefore unless necessary, many legislatures thought it far better to leave existing congressional districts in place even as populations among the districts became increasingly unequal. Changing districts' boundaries occurred even less often for state legislatures, where the number of seats rarely changed. Legislatures failed to reallocate their seats even as the population of states underwent dramatic changes (a topic to be explored in detail in the next chapter).

Once the Supreme Court mandated the adjustment of legislative district lines after each census in order to reflect population shifts, gerrymandering became increasingly a "sin" of commission rather than omission. Four tactics have been widely used by those seeking to secure a disproportionate share of the legislative seats. These tactics have been used to disadvantage political parties as well as racial and ethnic minorities.

One tactic is to *crack* the opposition by dividing a population that if put into a single district would be sufficient to determine the outcome of elections in that district. Dividing a group into two or more districts, so that it is less than a majority in any district, denies the party or group an opportunity to elect its preference. Figure 1.1 shows Mississippi's congressional districting plan adopted in the immediate aftermath of the Voting Rights Act of 1965. Historically the majority-black counties along the state's western boundary

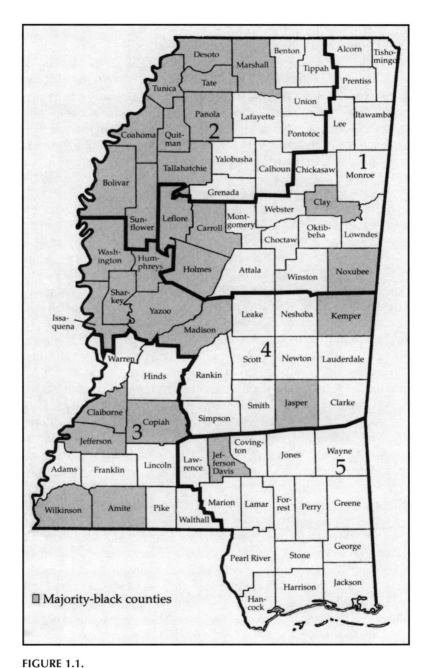

FIGURE 1.1.
Cracking Mississipppi's black vote in the 1966 congressional plan.
Source: Frank R. Parker, Black Votes Count: Political Empowerment in Mississippi after 1965
(Chapel Hill, NC: University of North Carolina Press, 1990), 49.

from Issaquena north to the Tennessee border had constituted a single district, the Delta District. Every county in the Delta District, which existed from 1882 until 1956, had a black majority, and once African Americans could vote without impediment they would be able to send their preferred candidate to Congress. The cracking of the African American population (displayed in figure 1.1) put portions of the old Delta District in three different districts (Districts 1, 2, and 4). As a consequence, in none of Mississippi's districts did blacks constitute as much as 45 percent of the adult population.[18] As a result of cracking the black population, Mississippi, the state with the highest black percentage in the nation, did not send an African American to Congress until 1986, following the creation of a 58 percent black district.

The second technique *packs* a district when the minority is too large to be denied representation. Those in charge of redistricting set out to minimize the number of seats that the minority can win by placing as many members of the minority as possible into a single district (as shown in table 1.2). Although Party B accounts for 48 percent of the votes in the community, the packed plan gives it only a single seat, District 3, which it wins with 90 percent. To the right of table 1.2 is an alternative plan in which Party B's supporters have been unpacked. Party B still wins District 3 comfortably and under normal circumstances would also win District 1. Party A continues to have commanding margins in Districts 4 and 5 and has a slight advantage in District 2, although Party B is competitive in that district under the unpacked plan.

Stacking, the third tactic, involves including the minority party or ethnic group as part of a much larger district that elects multiple legislators. If single-member districting were used, the minority party or group could dominate one district; however, by including it in a district that elects multiple members, its preferences can be voted down by the predominant party or ethnic group. Figure 1.2 provides an example of stacking carried out by the Georgia General Assembly in 2001. As part of an effort by Democrats to maximize the number of seats they could control in the state house, they combined some single-member districts to form multimember districts. In the example in figure 1.2, Districts 70 and 73 in DeKalb County, which had elected black Democrats before redistricting, were combined with District 108 in Henry County, which had elected a white Republican. The new district, District 60, had three seats; in 2002, African American Democrats won all three, thereby eliminating one Republican.

A fourth gerrymandering technique, *incumbency gerrymandering*, disadvantages incumbents of the opposing party. This can be done by separating incumbents from the population that they have represented. In more extreme cases, multiple incumbents are forced to compete against each other. One type of incumbency gerrymandering pairs an incumbent of the majority party

TABLE 1.2
**Example of an Effective Plan to Pack
One Party into a Single District and an Alternative**

	Packed		Unpacked	
	Party A	*Party B*	*Party A*	*Party B*
District 1	600	400	425	575
District 2	600	400	525	475
District 3	100	900	350	650
District 4	650	350	650	350
District 5	650	350	650	350
Total votes	2600	2400	2600	2400

with one of the minority party in a district in which the electorate favors the majority party. This may be done to punish a member of the minority party who has been a particularly aggressive partisan. In some instances, the new map places two or even more incumbents from the same party in a single district. Figure 1.3 shows a corner of southwest Georgia. The only two Republicans from this part of the state in 2001 represented Districts 163 and 180. District 163 contained the white, Republican-leaning population of northwest Dougherty County. Fifty miles and two intervening districts to the south lay District 180 in Thomas County. The new map managed to combine the homes of the representatives of these two districts. Republican areas of Dougherty County were extracted, as was the northern portion of Thomas County. Uniting this district shaped something like a seahorse were the suburban Republicans in southern Lee County and then selected precincts in Worth and Colquitt counties. By combining the homes of the Republicans representing Districts 163 and 180, one would surely lose. Since southwest Georgia had grown very slowly, the area was scheduled to lose a seat and by combining the two Republicans into a single district, Democrats ensured that the loss came from the opposition party.[19] Another benefit for the majority from eliminating some members of the minority party is to remove minority leaders who have the experience, skill, and insight to maximize their party's influence within the legislature.

Wasted Votes

Each of the first three tactics identified above is sometimes discussed in the context of "wasted votes." The idea behind wasted votes is that the disadvantaged group will get less in return for its votes than does the majority group.

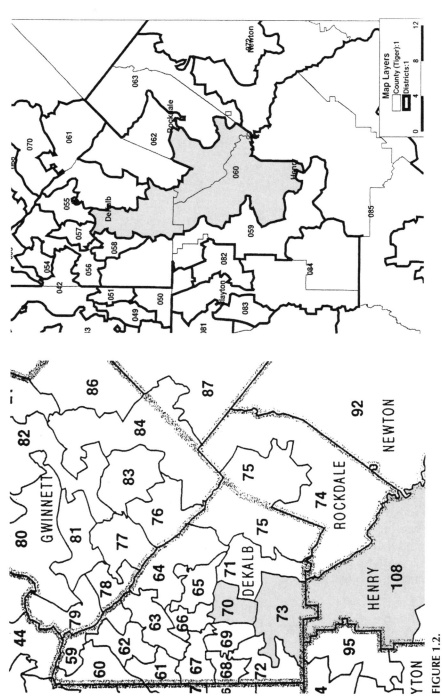

FIGURE 1.2.

Example of stacking. Districts 70 and 73, which elected black Democrats, are configured with District 108, which elected a white Republican, to form District 60, which elected three black Democrats.

Source: Prepared by the Carl Vinson Institute of Government, University of Georgia.

For example, in cracking, the minority group may win as much as 49 percent of the vote in multiple districts and yet none of its nominees win. Consider a chamber that included ten seats and the majority party won each of these by a 51–49 percent margin. Obviously the majority made very effective use of its votes, while the minority party won nothing despite attracting almost half the votes. In stacking, like cracking, the minority group party wins no seats despite having a substantial share of the vote.

With packing, wasted votes work in the following fashion. Since all that it takes to win is a majority, by concentrating the minority in a district that it wins, it spends far more votes by perhaps winning the district with 80 or 90 percent of the vote where only 50.1 percent would be necessary; even with a comfortable margin of 55 percent of the vote, the district contains far more of a party's supporters than necessary. In the hypothetical packed example in table 1.2, Party B wins District 3 with 90 percent of the vote, far more than needed, and loses the other four districts.

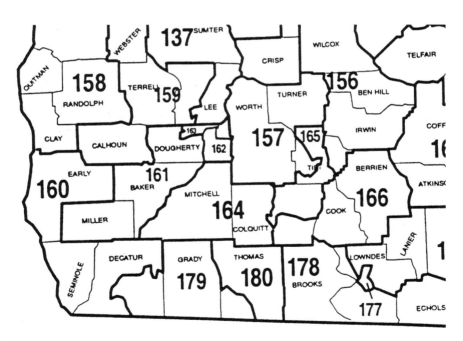

FIGURE 1.3.
Maps showing how the houses of Republicans in old Districts 163 and 180 were combined in new District 137.
Source: Prepared by the Carl Vinson Institute of Government, University of Georgia.

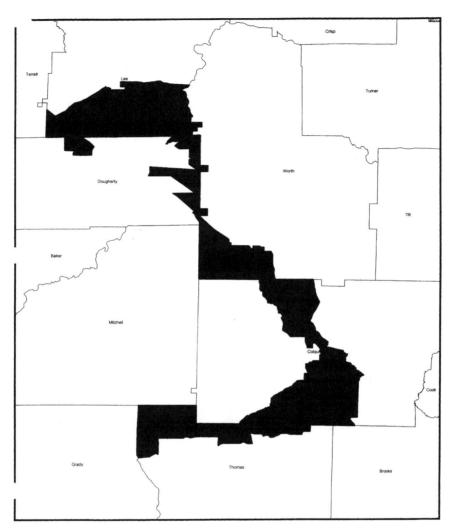

FIGURE 1.3.   (*Continued*)
Source: Plaintiff's demonstrative exhibits *Larios v. Cox* 300 F Supp. 2d 1320 (N.D. Ga. 2004).

Majority Party Payoff

Single-member districts are not designed to achieve proportional representation of political parties. The winner-take-all nature of single-member districts makes it extremely unlikely that each party will get a share of seats proportional to its share of the votes. Systems designed to achieve proportional representation use multimember districts for at least some of the seats, and the designers of these systems want to see parties achieve a proportion of the seats roughly equal to their share of the vote.[20] Even in the absence of aggressive gerrymandering, single-member district systems typically reward the majority party with a larger share of the seats than its share of the vote. The majority party is more likely than the minority party to have districts in which its electors have a slight advantage, and therefore the majority party will have fewer wasted votes. The advantage enjoyed by the majority party has been dubbed the Matthew Principle, based on the New Testament passage "For whosoever hath, to him shall be given, and he shall have more abundance: but whosoever hath not, from him shall be taken away even that he hath."[21] In a similar vein, the advantage of the majority party has been referred to as the Sheriff of Nottingham phenomenon, after the sheriff who, in contrast to Robin Hood, stole from the poor to give to the rich.

In a single-member, plurality system, the relationship between votes and seats is not a straight line running at about a 45-degree angle, as one might expect in a proportional representation system. Instead, in an unbiased single-member system, the relationship between votes and seats will be curvilinear, with the line passing through the point at which 50 percent of the vote translates into half of the seats. The mere fact that the majority party gets more seats than its vote share need not indicate a gerrymander. Andrew Gelman and Gary King explain that an apportionment scheme is free of *bias* if the reward given to one party should it achieve a majority of the vote is comparable to the bonus given to the other party should it receive the same share of the vote.[22] Thus if Democrats get 57 percent of the legislative seats when they poll 52 percent of the vote in the state, the system would be free of bias if Republicans also won 57 percent of the seats in return for a 52 percent vote share. Gelman and King have developed a free software program that assesses the degree of bias in an apportionment system.[23]

A phenomenon related to bias in a districting plan is *responsiveness*, which refers to the degree to which changes in the partisan preferences of the electorate result in changes in the makeup of the legislature. Many criticize the current congressional districting schemes for reducing responsiveness by making most districts either safely Democratic or overwhelmingly Republican. When districts have been packed with members of a particular party, then even if a substantial minority of the population changed its preferences and voted for the opposing party that would fail to shift partisan control of many districts. For example, in the packed arrangement in table 1.2, even if Party B gained an additional 9 percent of the vote in each district, it would still win only in District 3. The unpacked plan has greater responsiveness; if Party B won an additional 3 percent of the vote in District 2, it would gain another seat.

Since incumbents are unlikely to change their policy preferences dramatically, getting a legislature to adopt different policies requires the replacement of incumbents with new members who have different preferences. The greater the number of marginal districts, the greater the potential for achieving policy change. The smaller the shift in the electorate needed to replace one party with another, the more responsive the system.

Journalists and academics have long argued the desirability of having competitive districts. Until recently, about the only dissenters were incumbents, who (not surprisingly) preferred electoral systems that returned them to office with comfortable margins. Recently Thomas Brunell has presented the case for having legislators represent districts comprised overwhelmingly of supporters of one party.[24] Brunell relies on survey data showing that individuals who support winning congressional candidates are more likely to approve of the job being done by Congress and to believe that their representative attends to the needs of the constituency. Additionally, voters whose choice won election have a greater sense of political efficacy. Based on these findings, Brunell argues that districts should pack in voters of the district's majority party to eliminate competition, since in competitive districts greater numbers of voters will have backed the unsuccessful candidate. Brunell's recommendation therefore is to draft a plan in which Democrats have overwhelming majorities in some districts while Republicans enjoy insurmountable majorities in the remaining districts.

Importance of the Census

Since the apportioning of seats in the Congress and the distribution of benefits under some programs rest on the census, states have become increasingly interested in ensuring an accurate count. States join the Census Bureau in sponsoring public service announcements to encourage residents to return the census forms. Census takers are trained to go to out-of-the way homes to tally as many people as possible and to seek out the homeless by going to shelters and checking under bridges, in wooded camps, and in abandoned buildings. No matter how conscientious census takers and local communities are in encouraging a full count, some people, such as undocumented aliens, do not want to be found and counted. Undocumented aliens have been particularly difficult to enumerate since, despite promises from the Census Bureau that they will not be reported to the Immigration and Naturalization Service, those who are in the country illegally fear that federal agents may report them and they will be deported.

At the margins, it may not take too many individuals to win or lose a seat for a state. In 2000, Utah failed to get an additional seat by a margin of 857 individuals.[25] In 1981, poor jobs of counting residents cost Georgia and Indiana seats that went to California and New York.[26] A more accurate count might have netted California, Georgia, and Montana each an additional congressional seat following the 1990 Census, while Oklahoma, Pennsylvania and Wisconsin would have each received one fewer seat.[27]

The other side of the coin for achieving accurate enumeration is overcounting some people. This tends to involve the more affluent, who may have multiple homes, but can also involve students counted both at their parent's home as well as at their campus address.

Even though states have become increasingly concerned about getting a full count, critics contend that an accurate count is impossible. The American Statistical Association and the Census Bureau itself both recommend sampling to ensure a more accurate enumeration of the population, rather than actually trying to locate every person living in the United States. The supporters of sampling note that despite efforts at encouraging a full count, the number of households failing to return the census forms has increased. Leaders of some immigrant organizations as well as some conservative organizations have threatened to boycott the 2010 Census.

States with large numbers of undocumented residents urged use of sampling for the apportionment following the 2000 Census. These states hoped to maximize their number of seats in Congress, which would enhance their political influence. Moreover, since some $180 billion a year in federal programs is based on population, having a more complete count would also advantage states in which finding all of their residents may be particularly difficult. The Census Bureau estimates that the undercount in Georgia in 1990 amounted to 142,425 people, which cost Georgia $2 billion in federal dollars during the decade.[28] One estimate put New York City's loss at $850 million because of the undercount in 2000.[29] The loss of federal funds because of an undercount becomes especially painful as states try to balance their budgets during a period of economic downturn.

Arguments over the advantages of sampling versus a census quickly took on partisan overtones in the late 1990s. Democrats believed that, since the census disproportionately misses the poor while double-counting the wealthy, a more accurate figure would increase the number of people who could be used to draw Democratic districts while reducing the number of Republican districts. In the course of drawing new plans, some individuals in Democratic districts would be shifted to districts represented by Republicans, which might result in Democrats winning some of what had been Republican districts.[30] This explains why the Republican Speaker of the U.S. House characterized sampling as "a dagger aimed at the heart of the Republican majority."[31]

Resolution of this increasingly partisan debate fell to the Supreme Court, which required the use of the census counts and not sample estimates to apportion seats among the states.[32] Since the Constitution designates the census as the basis for allocating seats, the Court rejected arguments that it could be done using a sampling technique, even if statisticians were correct in their contention that a sample would be more accurate. The Court did say, however, that the estimates based on sampling could be used for other purposes such as allocation of funds or the actual drawing of districts.

The intensity of the congressional debate over whether to fund sampling in addition to the full count that the Supreme Court demanded sprang from the narrowness of the Republican majority in the House. As Congress debated what to do during the first half of 1999, Republicans outnumbered Democrats by only 222 to 211. Both parties recognized that the census count and the redistribution of seats might determine which party would control the House after the 2002 election. If a fuller count resulted in a few more Democratic seats, they might supplant Republicans and take control of the House. Because minorities were more likely to be missed by census takers, the ranking Democrat on the Government Reform Census Subcommittee in the House sought to place her party's position on a higher plain by contending that the need for an accurate count "is truly the civil rights issue of the decade."[33]

Despite the claims of the statisticians, the 2010 Census will again be an effort at a full enumeration. Difficulties in getting families to return their census forms contribute to the rising costs, which are estimated to run as high as $14.5 billion.[34] A decade earlier, the census cost $8 billion, double the cost for the 1990 Census. To track down delinquent households, the Census Bureau hires and trains 140,000 additional workers.

Plan of the Book

The next four chapters will examine items that influence the drawing of district maps. Chapter 2 focuses on what has become the most important criterion: equalizing populations among districts. Chapter 3 looks at the second most important factor, which is treating ethnic minorities fairly. Chapter 4 considers multiple traditional districting principles such as compactness and respect for existing political boundaries.

Partisanship is the topic for chapter 5. While the initial gerrymander sought to disadvantage a political party and much of today's gerrymandering is designed to enhance the strength of one party at the expense of the other, courts have yet to establish operational criteria for determining what constitutes an unacceptable partisan gerrymander.

One of the states that has experienced repeated challenges both in the courts and in its dealings with the Department of Justice is Georgia. Chapter 6 provides a case study of the application of districting standards to this state.

Chapter 7 looks forward to the changes that the 2010 Census may require for the apportionment of congressional seats. It also reviews the rules likely to guide the redistricting that will take place early in the next decade.

2

Population Equality:
How Equal Must Districts Be?

To the extent that a citizen's right to vote is debased, he is that much less a citizen.[1]

IN A DEMOCRACY AS PRACTICED STILL IN A FEW New England towns, the citizenry comes together and sets policy for the community. Each participant has a single vote. In representative democracies, citizens choose representatives who make decisions for them. Each representative has one vote. But what if the representatives come from constituencies that have dramatically different numbers of people? The idea behind a citizen democracy suggests that these representatives who have equal votes should represent roughly equal numbers of constituents.

Questions about the weight to be given the population go back to the earliest days of the Republic. A stumbling block at the Philadelphia convention that drafted the federal Constitution involved allocation of representatives. The larger states thought their greater population entitled them to more influence in the legislature. The less populous states, fearing that their interests would be made subservient to those of the more populous states, wanted equal representation for each state as had existed under the Articles of Confederation. The Great Compromise provided something for both the large and the small states, with each state having equal representation in the Senate in order to address the concerns of the small states while the House allocated representation on the basis of population as demanded by the larger states.

The Constitution established each state's initial representation in the U.S. House. The two smallest states, Delaware and Rhode Island, each received one representative. The most populous states got greater numbers of seats; Virginia got ten, while Massachusetts and Pennsylvania got eight each. These allocations based on best guesses as to relative population size were adjusted after the first census, taken in 1790. The Constitution underscored the importance of linking representation to population, since it provided for a decennial census and reassessment of a state's number of House seats following the census.

The early interest in linking population to seats in the House did not extend to concern about the population per seat in state delegations. Not until the 1960s did courts review population deviations and strike down plans that allowed vast disparities in the number of people per district. Until the Supreme Court held that population deviations in congressional districts violated Article I, Section 2, states rarely redrew district lines unless the size of their delegation changed. And even a change in a state's number of seats did not always immediately lead to new maps. The failure to address population deviations also characterized state legislatures and local collegial bodies. Even when the state constitution called for periodic adjustments to reduce population deviations, the legislators responsible for drawing new maps often ignored the requirement since reallocation would result in some of their number losing their seats. Only recently has having districts with equal populations become the most important requirement when creating a new plan.

America began as an agrarian nation, with cities developing slowly. Consequently, shifts in population that produced districts having unequal numbers of residents resulted in urban districts having far more people than rural districts. Rural legislators saw no reason to cede influence to their urban rivals, especially if giving cities and suburbs more seats would strengthen the opposition party.

A History Lesson

The concerns of rural America were so great that after the first census reporting that most Americans no longer lived in rural communities Congress failed to reapportion its seats. Following the 1920 Census, Congress declined to increase the number of seats as it had done after every census except for 1840, when it eliminated ten seats. With the size of the House fixed, Congress ignored the census rather than reduce the representation of rural states located primarily in the Midwest and South. For the first and only time in history, the size of a state's congressional delegation was divorced from the state's share of the national population.

Members of Congress ultimately felt guilty about the failure to carry out reapportionment in 1920 and the willful violation of the constitutional directive
that "Representatives . . . shall be apportioned among the several states . . . according to their respective numbers." Recognizing its own weakness in failing
to carry out its duty, Congress gave up the power to determine the number
of seats for each state and transferred the responsibility to the Census Bureau.
Not surprisingly, after failing to reallocate seats following the 1920 Census,
the reapportionment carried out in the next decade had a dramatic impact.
Almost half of the states, twenty-one of the forty-eight, lost seats following
the 1930 Census. While most only lost a single seat, Missouri, which had been
the seventh largest state in the nation in 1910, saw its delegation shrink from
sixteen to thirteen members.

The trauma of losing seats proved so great that Missouri (along with Kentucky, Minnesota, and Virginia) failed to adopt plans for its shrunken delegation and instead elected all members at-large in 1932. In each of these states
except Minnesota, statewide elections coupled with Franklin Roosevelt's
coattails resulted in the defeat of Republican incumbents, so that the entire
delegation became Democratic. Alabama adopted the same ostrich-like approach when it lost a seat following the 1960 reapportionment. In each of
these instances, before the next election, the state drew single-member districts around the homes of the surviving legislators.

Reluctance to draw new maps was not limited to states that experienced
loss. At times, states reacted slowly to the good fortune of gaining a second
seat. Idaho, Montana, and Utah, each of which gained a seat following the
1910 Census, elected both of their members at-large in 1912 before creating
single-member districts prior to the 1914 election. When Arizona received
a second seat following the 1940 Census, it did not get around to drawing
single-member districts until the 1946 election. After gaining seats in 1932,
1952, and 1962, Texas filled the new seats through at-large elections before
creating a new district around the home of the winner. Following the 1940
reapportionment, three of the seven states that gained seats did not redistrict
in time for the 1942 election. From 1912 when Illinois gained two seats until
1942 when it lost a seat, it elected two at-large members. Four states that
gained seats following the 1932 reapportionment were slow to draw districts.
Both Ohio and New York elected some members at-large throughout that
decade, and the Connecticut delegation had one at-large seat up until the
Redistricting Revolution hit in 1964. Following the 1930 reapportionment,
twelve of forty-two states with multimember delegates elected at least one
at-large member.

Prior to the 1960s, the U.S. House was the one institution in which an attempt was made to base representation on population—and even there the

1920s constituted a notable exception. While each state's House delegation reflected its share of the national population, states made little effort to see that each of their members of Congress represented roughly equal constituencies. In the past, Congress had enacted legislation requiring the rough equalization of populations among a state's districts, but that legislation had never been enforced and had lapsed well before the 1960s. Indeed, the condition under which each member of a state's House delegation had constituencies of the same size occurred in the anomalous situation of electing all members at-large. In those few situations, each of the state's representatives had exactly the same number of constituents since each represented the state's entire population. While some people who lived in districts whose representatives had far more constituents than the representatives from other parts of the state fretted that they were underrepresented, no serious challenge to the status quo came until the 1940s.

Unsuccessful Challenge to Population Deviations

The 1940 Census showed Illinois to be the third most populous state, a position it had held for half a century. Most of the population lived in Chicago, which accounted for 51.5 percent of Illinois's population. In apportioning its twenty-five districts for the 1940s, six districts lay wholly within the city of Chicago, with another six partially in the city.[2] Of these dozen districts, all but three had more people than the average for the state. Of the thirteen districts that did not include part of Chicago, all but three were underpopulated, and one of the overpopulated districts was located in suburban Cook County (the county in which Chicago is also located). Illinois's district lines had not changed since 1901. Over the next four censuses, populations shifted so that after the 1940 Census, the least populous district had 112,116 people, only one-eighth the number of the most populous district. Seven districts had fewer than 200,000 people.

The state legislature's persistent failure to address the underrepresentation of the Windy City prompted a judicial challenge that reached the Supreme Court. Chicago residents wanted more influence in the congressional delegation, and that could be achieved if their share of seats approximated their share of the state's population. In the opinion of the Court, which attracted only two other justices, Felix Frankfurter dismissed the complaint because of a lack of justiciability. That is, the Court said it lacked jurisdiction over what it saw as a political question.[3] According to Frankfurter, Congress, not the courts, had the authority to supervise the districting policy of states. Frankfurter saw the question presented to the Court in *Colegrove v. Green* as a political thicket that he warned the judiciary not to enter. Frankfurter naively observed, "Of course no court can affirmatively re-map the Illinois districts so as to bring them more in conformity with the standards of fairness for a representative system." As we shall see, courts now regularly carry out redistricting when legislatures fail to act. Frankfurter recommended that the plaintiffs turn to the legislature, advice which had already proven fruitless. He also observed that Congress has responsibility for overseeing the makeup of its membership and therefore could intervene—another suggestion that has never helped those aggrieved by an unequal districting system.

The Supreme Court had also indicated its unwillingness to become embroiled in challenges to the districting arrangements of state legislatures. It refused to overturn the arrangement used by Georgia that severely limited the influence of urban areas by restricting even the most populous counties to no more than three seats in the state house and, under an arrangement somewhat analogous to the Electoral College, gave individual urban counties the Electoral College, gave individual urban counties no more than 6 of the 410 unit votes used to determine winners in statewide Democratic primaries.[4]

Conditions on the Eve of the Revolution

Justice Frankfurter's advice that those unhappy with population inequalities should look elsewhere for help did nothing to improve the situation for underrepresented portions of states. Table 2.1 shows several measures of population inequality for state legislative chambers calculated shortly before the Supreme Court launched the Redistricting Revolution. With rare exceptions, the districts within each chamber had wide differences in their populations.

The first measure, calculated by Paul David and Ralph Eisenberg, presents the ratio of the population for the most and least populous districts within a legislative chamber.[5] In state lower chambers, the most extreme values come from New England states, which gave representation to every township. Districts in the larger cities had hundreds of times more people than did the districts of tiny rural townships. Connecticut and Vermont also had the oldest plans in place, with Vermont not having redistricted since it became a state in 1793 and the most recent map for the Connecticut house dating from 1876.[6] Outside of New England, the Florida and Georgia houses had the largest values, with some districts having populations approximately a hundred times that of the least populous district.[7] Even in the most equitably apportioned chambers, the most populous house districts had three, four, or five times the population of the smallest districts. Hawaii, the nation's newest state, had the least skewed districting arrangement, but even there some districts had more than twice as many people as others.

TABLE 2.1
Measures of Malapportionment prior to the Redistricting Revolution

State	David and Eisenberg*		1955 Apportionment**		Measuring Malapportion***
	Lower	Upper	Lower	Upper	Schubert-Press
Alabama	15.6	41.2	27.15	28.26	13.8
Alaska	6.4	10.8	N/A	N/A	41.5
Arizona	5.3	85.8	N/A	19.3	27.2
Arkansas	6.4	2.3	37.52	46.95	66.1
California	6.2	422.5	44.7	11.88	20.2
Colorado	8.1	7.3	34.67	36.12	45.5
Connecticut	424.5	6.4	9.59	36.5	27.1
Delaware	35.4	16.8	19.4	22.7	50.6
Florida	108.7	98	17.19	17.67	10.2
Georgia	98.8	42.6	26.3	26.89	-4
Hawaii	2.2	5.9	N/A	N/A	48.9
Idaho	25.5	102.1	41.53	19.05	50.1
Illinois	3.6	9.4	46.02	29.42	47.2
Indiana	5.4	4.4	36.95	39.25	-4.3
Iowa	17.8	15	29.34	33.94	7.8
Kansas	33.2	21.3	22.59	33.67	10.9
Kentucky	6	2.9	37.59	45.19	13.9
Louisiana	17.4	8	25.61	34.07	40.9
Maine	6.6	2.8	39.12	37.91	80.3
Maryland	12.5	31.8	27.57	15.52	29.8
Massachusetts	13.9	2.3	42.15	48.76	96.3
Michigan	4	12.4	42.29	32.34	43.7
Minnesota	13.3	5.8	31.56	35.93	1.3
Mississippi	16.7	8.8	32.67	34.59	42.1
Missouri	22.2	2.8	23.71	47.37	46.2
Montana	14	88.4	40.8	18.4	44.7
Nebraska	unicameral	2.7	N/A	41.88	80.9
Nevada	31.4	223.6	28.82	12.36	16.6
New Hampshire	1,081.3	3	37.4	44.75	71
New Jersey	4.6	19	43.95	17.01	58.9
New Mexico	15.5	139.9	35.67	20.07	23.2
New York	14.8	4	37.06	40.91	69.2
North Carolina	19	6	30.16	40.09	56.6
North Dakota	7.5	9.9	39.02	35.36	41.8
Ohio	14.5	2.2	29.19	20.68	81.2
Oklahoma	14	26.4	33.38	29.45	9.5
Oregon	3	3.5	45.42	42.18	86.5
Pennsylvania	31.1	10.7	41.63	35.44	70.8
Rhode Island	39	141	34.17	13.53	42
South Carolina	3.1	25.1	46.72	26.57	55.6
South Dakota	4.7	5.8	38.73	40.85	44.2
Tennessee	23	6	30.13	33.26	11.8
Texas	6.7	9.4	39.85	36.8	26.6

TABLE 2.1
(*Continued*)

State	David and Eisenberg*		1955 Apportionment**		Measuring Malapportion***
	Lower	Upper	Lower	Upper	Schubert-Press
Utah	27.8	6.9	38.99	26.75	43.2
Vermont	987	6.4	12.58	45.67	44.8
Virginia	7.1	5.5	43.69	43.93	47.6
Washington	4.6	7.3	33.87	35.44	62.6
West Virginia	9	3.4	38.87	45.68	65.2
Wisconsin	3.9	2.8	38.87	46.53	58.5
Wyoming	3.4	9.8	39.92	28.77	62.3

*David and Eisenberg calculate the ratio in the population in the most and fewest people represented by a member in the legislative chamber at the time of the 1960 Census.
**Minimum percentage of the population needed to elect a majority of the chamber using the apportionment plan in place following the 1950 Census. "Unrepresentative States," *National Municipal Review* (1955): 571–575, 587.
***This measure is the Schubert and Press measure of apportionment fairness based on skewness and kurtosis of the distribution of legislators.
Sources: Paul T. David and Ralph Eisenberg, *Devaluation of the Urban and Suburban Vote* (Charlottesville: Bureau of Public Administration, University of Virginia, 1961), 3; Gordon E. Baker, *Rural versus Urban Political Power* (New York: Random House, 1955), 16–17; Glendon Schubert and Charles Press, "Measuring Malapportionment," *American Political Science Review* 58 (June 1964): 325–326.

In state senates, the upper range was not as great as in the house, although in five states some districts had more than a hundred times as many people as others. California was the least equitably apportioned; Los Angeles County had a senator for its six million people, while at the other extreme one rural district had only fourteen thousand people. Eight states apportioned their senators in such a way that the range between the largest and smallest districts was less than a factor of three, with Ohio having the fairest distribution—although even there the largest district had more than twice the population of the smallest district.

The second measure in table 2.1 reports the smallest share of the state's population that could elect a majority within a legislative chamber. In a perfectly apportioned legislative chamber, it would take just over 50 percent of the population to elect a majority of the chamber. However, in the Alabama house, if one began with the least populous district and then added the next least populous until the 53 least populous of the 105 districts in the house had been aggregated, based on the apportioning system used in the 1950s, this would account for just over 27 percent of the state's population. In the most extreme situation, less than 10 percent of the population of Connecticut could elect a majority of that state's lower chamber. In four states, less than 20 percent of the population could elect a majority of the house. In the eleven states that had the most equitable systems, it would require more than 40 percent of the state's population to elect a majority of the chamber. In South Carolina 46.72 percent of the population would be the minimum to elect a majority in its house, while in Illinois just over 46 percent of the population provided the minimum to elect a majority of that state's lower chamber.

In nine states, a majority of the senate could be elected by less than 20 percent of the population. In California and Nevada, approximately 12 percent of the population sufficed to elect a majority of the senate, while in Rhode Island, as little as 13.5 percent of the population could elect a senate majority. At the more equitable end of the distribution, it would take the districts accounting for almost 49 percent of the Massachusetts population to elect a majority of the senate in the Bay State. Seats in the upper chambers were more equitably distributed than in lower chambers, with at least 40 percent of the population required to elect a majority of the senators in fourteen states. In seven of these states it would have required more than 45 percent of the population to elect a majority of the senate.

The final equality measure, which was developed by Glendon Schubert and Charles Press, is a more sophisticated effort and looks at the shape of the distribution of legislative districts in terms of population using two measures of distribution, skewness and kurtosis.[8] Unlike the other measures, which provide a separate score for each chamber, Schubert and Press calculate a single score for a state. On their measure, a perfectly apportioned legislative chamber in which areas got a share of seats equal to their share of the population would score 100. While no state achieved perfect proportionality, Massachusetts with a score of 96.3 comes closest. Maine, Nebraska, Ohio, and Oregon each received scores above 80. At the other extreme, Georgia and Indiana had negative scores, while Oklahoma, Iowa, and Minnesota each had positive scores of less than 10.

Back to Court

Early in the 1960s the Supreme Court received another invitation to enter the political thicket, and this time the Court met the challenge. A 1960 voting rights case served as a bridge. *Gomillion v. Lightfoot* challenged an action by the Alabama legislature that transmogrified Tuskegee from a square to a 28-sided polygon in order to remove all but four or five African American voters.[9] Justice Frankfurter, who wrote the majority opinion, strove to distinguish the Tuskegee plan from the one the Court avoided in *Colegrove v. Green.*

While the *Colegrove* plaintiffs complained of vote dilution, the new maps *denied* most Tuskegee blacks a vote in municipal elections. The racial discrimination here made this case appropriate for relief under the Fifteenth Amendment rather than it being a political issue (which Frankfurter would not have touched). Coming to the aid of the *Gomillion* appellants in a complaint about district fairness served as a halfway step toward repeal of *Colegrove*.

Baker v. Carr involved the Tennessee state legislature, which, like the Illinois congressional districts, had not been redrawn since 1901.[10] As a result of legislative inaction, often called the silent gerrymander, by the 1960s huge disparities in representation existed among Tennessee's counties, which (as in most states) provided the basis for legislative seats. These disparities existed even though the state constitution required that counties' representation in the legislature be based on the number of registered voters. As an example of the inequity, two counties had two representatives each, even though one county had more than ten times the population of the other. As the measures of equality presented in table 2.1 show, Tennessee does not score well. On the Schubert and Press Index, it scored 11.8, and the majority of the house could be elected by less than a third of the population. The range between the largest and smallest districts in Tennessee was a factor of 23. While the state did not score well, it was far from the worst-apportioned state in the Union.

Brushing aside Justice Frankfurter's concerns, the Court plunged into the "political thicket" and cited the Equal Protection Clause of the Fourteenth Amendment as the basis for requiring greater equality in the population of the districts. The Fourteenth Amendment, ratified in the immediate aftermath of the Civil War, focuses on the actions of states with its admonition that, "No state shall . . . deny to any person within its jurisdiction the equal protection of the laws." The Court perceived denial of equal protection in districts that had differences in their populations. Voters in overpopulated districts had less influence in the political system than did those living in districts with fewer people. The Court did not indicate how much variation would be tolerated in district populations, but in a concurring opinion, Justice Clark observed that "No one . . . contends that mathematical equality among voters is required by the Equal Protection Clause." As we shall see, Justice Clark failed to anticipate subsequent pressures that have prompted ever smaller deviations in the populations of a jurisdiction's districts. The Clark concurrence did, however, demonstrate greater political sophistication than Frankfurter had in *Colegrove*. Clark recognized that the plaintiffs had no other recourse, since the legislature and the governor of Tennessee had ignored calls for adherence to the requirement of the state constitution.

The Supreme Court ruling in the Tennessee case resolved the issue of justiciability of equal population challenges in state legislatures, and within a year thirty-six similar suits challenged legislative plans across the nation.[11] These challenges prompted many states to redraw districts to eliminate the grossest inequalities. Relying on the federal analogy, states initially took steps to equalize district populations in only one chamber. Since every state has two senators, states assumed that if the seats in one chamber reflected population differences, seats in the other chamber could be based on other considerations such as geography, which might allow them to continue allocating one seat per county or some other geographic grouping.

Two years after *Baker*, the Supreme Court addressed the federal analogy and found it inappropriate for states. Seats in the Alabama legislature had not been reallocated since the beginning of the twentieth century, despite a requirement in the state constitution for a decennial redistricting. Birmingham and other cities were underrepresented, while rural areas had more seats than their population would justify. Jefferson County (Birmingham) had 600,000 people; Bullock County had 13,000. Each had one senator. In requiring population as the basis for seat distribution in *both* chambers, the Court observed that "people, not land or trees or pastures, vote." Chief Justice Earl Warren saw the right to an equally weighted vote as a critical right of citizenship. To the extent that some people's votes had greater influence than others, it amounted to a form of disfranchisement. Voters who lived in overpopulated districts had less opportunity to shape the makeup of the government, which in turn might mean less opportunity to influence its policy decisions. As in *Baker*, the *Reynolds v. Sims* decision did not require exact equality in the population of districts but speculated:

> So long as the divergences from a strict population standard are based on legitimate considerations incident to the effectuation of a rational state policy, some deviations from the equal-population principle are constitutionally permissible with respect to the apportionment of seats in either or both of the two Houses of a bicameral state legislature.[12]

The *Reynolds* decision set off another round of litigation. By the mid-1960s, cartographers were busy redrawing legislative chambers in forty-seven states.[13]

Shortly before rejecting the federal analogy, the Supreme Court had revisited the question of congressional districting, which had lain dormant since 1946. While the Court relied on the Equal Protection Clause to require that states equalize populations among their legislative districts, that portion of the Constitution could not be used to challenge disparities in congressional populations. Despite the inapplicability of the Equal Protection Clause to the federal Congress, the Supreme Court extended its call for greater population equity, to congressional districts. To justify its congressional ruling, the Court turned to Article I, Section 2, of the Constitution, which states that, "The House of Representatives shall be composed of members chosen every second year by the people of the several states, and the electors in each state. . . ." The Court interpreted this provision as banning irrational population differences among a state's congressional districts. The leading case, *Wesberry v. Sanders*, involved Georgia's congressional districts redrawn when the state lost two seats in the 1930 reapportionment. [14] By 1960 the Fifth District had the nation's second largest population, with more than 800,000 people. At the other extreme, the Ninth District had fewer than a third as many people.

As table 2.2 shows, when *Wesberry* was filed only three of Georgia's ten congressional districts were overpopulated (had populations more than 100 percent of the ideal),[15] with the range being from a low of 69 percent of the ideal in the Ninth District to 209 percent of the ideal in the Fifth District. After the state redrew its districts following the *Wesberry* decision, six districts were overpopulated and four remained underpopulated. After redistricting the least populated had 84 percent of the ideal, while the most populous had 116 percent of the ideal. This amounted to a difference of about 125,000 people. The new plan divided the Fifth District, and the part that remained in the Fifth District came closest to having the ideal population with a score of 101 percent. The remainder of the old Fifth District became the new Fourth District, which had a population 108 percent of the ideal. The mountainous Ninth District remained the most underpopulated with only 84 percent of the

TABLE 2.2
Population of Georgia Congressional Districts before and after *Wesbury v. Sanders*

District	Before		After	
	Population	% of Ideal	Population	% of Ideal
1	379,933	96	420,354	107
2	301,123	76	358,133	91
3	422,198	107	340,110	86
4	323,489	82	424,917	108
5	823,489	209	398,763	101
6	330,235	84	455,575	116
7	450,740	114	450,740	114
8	291,185	74	338,948	86
9	272,154	69	329,738	84
10	348,379	88	408,823	104

Sources: U.S. Bureau of the Census, *Congressional District Data Book (Districts of the 88th Congress)* (Washington, DC: U.S. Government Printing Office, 1963); *Congressional Directory*, 89th Congress, 1st Session (Washington, DC: U.S. Government Printing Office, 1965).

ideal population. While Georgia's ten districts came nowhere close to having exactly the same number of people, redistricting substantially reduced the range.

As happened with state legislative districts, once the courts demanded equal populations in congressional districts, similar challenges became widespread. In the first two years after *Wesberry*, congressional districts in twenty-six states were challenged.[16] Another seventeen suits were filed during the next biennium, and in 1969–1970 six more suits were filed. As we will see shortly, some states had to defend not only old plans that suffered from the silent gerrymander but also some of the corrective efforts they took.

In time, the Supreme Court extended its ruling involving state legislatures to include local collegial bodies that elected representatives from districts.[17] Members of school boards, county commissions, city councils, and other local bodies elected by districts must be chosen from districts with equal populations. The sole exception to the requirement that legislative districts have equal populations remains the U.S. Senate. To change the districting arrangement for the Senate would, of course, require a constitutional amendment.

Equality Requirements Become More Precise

The Supreme Court follows a minimalist approach and decides only what it must in order to resolve the specific fact situations in the cases before it. While the three decisions discussed above made quite clear that the status quo would no longer be tolerated, the Court did not provide precise details for what would be necessary to meet the "one person, one vote" standard first enunciated by Justice William Douglas.[18] Although these decisions became characterized as requiring population equality among districts, perfect equality was not Clark's standard in the *Baker* concurrence. The amount of acceptable variation gradually became clearer and narrower as courts ruled on additional challenges and struck down smaller and smaller deviations between the most and least populous districts.

The Congressional Standard

The Supreme Court's reluctance to establish a precise guideline for congressional districts resulted in states having to pay repeated visits to the cartographers. Hiring mapmakers was not the only cost. Since the maps go a long way toward determining who will continue to serve in the legislature, the fights over redistricting are some of the most vicious and evoke some of the most duplicitous behavior. Moreover, frequent shifting of district lines can cause confusion among voters and weaken their relationships with their legislators.

In the 1960s Missouri paid the highest price for unclear standards for acceptable population deviations. The "Show-Me State" had to redraw its districts three times between 1960 and 1970. The plan in place after the 1960 Census had districts that ranged in population from 378,499 to 506,845 (as reported in table 2.3). Obviously, districts in Missouri were not as unequal as those in Georgia had been. While the largest Georgia district had about 550,000 more people than the smallest, in Missouri, the largest district had only 128,000 more people than the smallest. Nonetheless, Missouri, like Georgia, placed its largest city at a disadvantage. The three most overpopulated districts in 1962 contained St. Louis and its immediate suburbs. In terms of deviations from the ideal population, the range extended from 88 to 117 percent.

In the first remap (1966), Missouri reduced the range in populations to 390,240 to 475,667. Note that the deviations in the 1966 plan for Missouri are smaller than in the post-*Wesberry* plan for Georgia. Nonetheless, the Missouri plan included a 10 percent overpopulated district and another one that

TABLE 2.3
Population of Missouri Congressional Districts in Plans from 1962 to 1970

	1962 Plan		1966 Plan		1968 Plan		1970 Plan	
District	Pop.	% of Ideal	Pop.	% of ideal	Pop.	% of ideal	Pop.	% of ideal
1	466,482	108	475,667	110	439,648	102	431,210	99.8
2	506,854	117	460,501	107	437,456	101	432,535	100.1
3	480,222	111	469,888	109	449,743	104	432,449	100.1
4	418,981	97	402,526	93	420,180	97	432,254	100.1
5	378,499	88	406,067	94	430,412	100	431,178	99.8
6	388,486	90	394,236	91	440,145	102	432,130	100.0
7	436,933	101	425,820	99	453,000	105	432,215	100.1
8	452,385	105	443,747	103	444,695	103	431,630	99.9
9	409,369	95	451,121	104	427,841	99	431,811	100.0
10	381,602	88	390,240	90	423,868	98	432,007	100.0
Range	88–117		90–110		97–105		99.8–100.1	

Sources: *U.S. Bureau of the Census, Congressional District Data Book (Districts of the 88th Congress)* (Washington, DC: U.S. Government Printing Office, 1993); *Supplement to Congressional District Data Book: Missouri* (Washington, DC: Bureau of the Census, August 1966); *Congressional Directory, 91st Congress, 1st Session* (Washington, DC: U.S. Government Printing Office, 1969); *Congressional Directory*, 92nd Congress, 1st Session (Washington, DC: U.S. Government Printing Office, 1971).

was 10 percent underpopulated. This triggered a second challenge, which the state also lost, and led to the 1968 map, which had a range in populations of 420,180 to 453,000. The second remap reduced the population deviations in eight districts, added fewer than 1,000 people to the Eighth District, and left the Seventh District further from the ideal than it had been. The range in population as measured in terms of the ideal had now been narrowed to 97 to 105 percent. The St. Louis districts were no longer the most overpopulated in the state, although each had slightly more people than the ideal for Missouri. The range in population, which had been 128,000 in 1963, had been reduced to 33,000.

Despite these improvements, urban residents prevailed on yet another challenge, which prompted the state to devise a plan that reduced the population range to 1,357 people. The third redistricting, done in time for the 1970 election, had almost completely eliminated population deviation, bringing it down to 0.3 percent based on the 1960 Census. The 1970 plan that reduced the population deviations did so by breaking with tradition and splitting counties other than those in the St. Louis and Kansas City areas.

Of course, a critic might look at the figures used to assess the 1970 plan and point out that this plan was drawn a decade after the population enumeration on which it was based. Consequently, the effort at eliminating population deviations had something of an artificial ring to it. Indeed, the best estimates suggested that the range in the 1970 populations in these districts went from 380,047 in Kansas City's Fifth District to 576,117 in the Eighth District, extending from the Missouri River to the Arkansas border.[19] Consequently, while the plaintiffs in the prolonged litigation could take pride in having achieved almost absolutely equal populations in Missouri's districts based on the 1960 Census, in reality the deviation in these new districts exceeded that for the state in the 1962 plan. Of course, Missouri along with other states redrew its congressional districts prior to the convening of the 93rd Congress in 1973. The new plan had a total range in population of 2,109 based on the 1970 Census.

By the time states adjusted their congressional districts to reflect the population shifts during the 1960s, most had brought the range in their populations down to less than 1 percent. Almost 300 congressional districts had population deviations within 1 percent of the ideal for their state, a dramatic change from a decade earlier when only nine districts in the entire nation came that close to the ideal population.[20]

After almost a generation of ever-constricting limitations on population deviation, the Supreme Court enunciated what has become its final statement on population variations in a state's congressional districts. *Karcher v. Daggett* involved the New Jersey redistricting following the 1980 Census. In the challenged plan, the range between the largest and the smallest districts was just under 0.7 percent, or 3,674 people. Nonetheless, when confronted with a plan that had even smaller deviations, the Court rejected the state's plan, observing that "there are no de minimis population variations, which could practically be avoided, but which nonetheless meet the standard of Article I, Section 2 without justification."[21] Justice William Brennan recognized the artificiality of the push for absolute equality, since the census undoubtedly fails to count some people and even if absolutely accurate when taken, by the time that a legislature draws districts and the Court rules on a challenge, population shifts will have occurred. Nonetheless, Brennan pushed for equality in district populations, since he feared that setting an acceptable standard as anything other than absolute equality would be treated by states as a license to have that much deviation. He feared that what a court might think of as a ceiling for acceptable deviation states would treat as the floor.

States learned through bitter experience and at the cost of millions of dollars in litigation fees that a plaintiff who produces a map with less population deviation than that adopted by the state usually wins in court and has the cost of litigation absorbed by the state. In 2002, a federal court struck down Pennsylvania's congressional map that had a population range of only 19 people when plaintiffs provided a map that zeroed out the differences.[22]

By 2001, a number of states had taken the *Karcher* ruling to heart and, hoping to stave off delays and costly litigation, produced plans that reduced population deviation to the absolute minimum of 1 person.[23] Seventeen states achieved minimum deviations and another six reduced the range in population to less than 10 people. The largest range was right at 1 percent.

Eliminating all deviations had become feasible thanks to geographic information system software (GIS), which links population to geography. These computer programs facilitate drawing numerous alternative plans in quick succession. In the past, redistricting involved drawing lines on large maps and then calculating district population by manually adding up figures for numerous counties, precincts, and census blocks. With this labor-intensive procedure, time constraints limited the number of iterations that a map could be put through, and consequently, mapmakers worked with larger geographic units, concentrating on counties in most states, in order to make their tasks manageable. In larger cities, mapmakers in the days before GIS worked with precincts, the smallest political units, which frequently contain 1,000 to 2,000 voters.

With the GIS software, the population for a proposed district can be obtained with a few clicks of a mouse by indicating which counties, precincts, or census blocks to include. This allows cartographers to work quickly, trying alternatives with smaller and smaller pieces of geography as they seek to eliminate population differences among a state's districts. The census block is the smallest available unit and typically contains less area than an electoral precinct. In an urban area, a census block would likely be defined by four streets and be what one generally thinks of as an urban block. In a rural area, a census block may contain many square miles and might be defined by highways, railroad tracks, rivers, streams, or political boundaries like state, county, or city lines. Census blocks must have visible boundaries, with the only exception occurring when a portion of a block is in a city and the other part lies outside of the corporate limits. In those instances, the city boundary divides a block, often along lines not visible to the naked eye. When trying to even out the population of a district, mapmakers will frequently have to go census block by census block, making slight adjustments in the district's population as they substitute a block with slightly more or less population as needed to eliminate population deviations.

A consequence of demanding smaller population deviations is to split a larger number of cities and counties. Working with smaller bits of geography can also make it easier to gerrymander.

Note that the quote from *Karcher* above suggested that states might be able to justify deviations from absolute equality. One potentially acceptable factor would be to minimize splitting precincts or counties. Iowa law prohibits splitting counties when drawing congressional districts. Nonetheless, its five-district plan for 2001 had a range in populations of only 134 people. The largest deviation in the post-2000 plans also occurred in a state that did not split any counties. The Arkansas plan had a total deviation of 1 percent.

Population Deviations below the Congressional Level

Courts have viewed the constitutional basis for requiring equality among congressional districts as setting a more demanding standard than the Equal Protection Clause establishes for other collegial bodies. At about the same time that the Supreme Court concluded that states should aim for zero deviation in congressional plans, it seemingly gave the nod to permitting a 10 percent total deviation in plans for other jurisdictions.[24] Following numerous cases in which the courts required smaller and smaller population deviations, the Supreme Court adopted a standard widely interpreted as permitting deviations of 5 percent above and below the ideal population for a jurisdiction. For the next twenty years, the +/–5 percentage point deviation rule was widely accepted as a safe harbor. If a jurisdiction devised a plan in which no districts fell outside of the +/–5 percentage point range, many doubted whether the plan could be successfully attacked on population grounds.

The Georgia General Assembly was among those that accepted the +/–5 percent rule as a safe harbor. As will be described in greater detail in chapter 6, the Georgia legislature devised plans in 2001 in which the range in population from the ideal totaled 9.98 percent. In a desperate effort to maintain their legislative majorities, the Democrats overpopulated Republican districts by 4, 4.5, and even 4.99 percent, while underpopulating Democratic districts by comparable amounts.

When Republicans challenged the Democratic gerrymander, the state answered that since all districts conformed to the +/–5 percent rule, they were not subject to attack. The trial court rejected the idea that plans which limited deviation to +/–5 percent enjoyed some kind of immunity. [25] The testimony of state witnesses whose rationale for the plan was to underpopulate districts in south Georgia and Atlanta in order to maintain more seats in these slow-growing portions of the state left the judges unconvinced. The court pointed back to the *Reynolds* decision handed down forty years earlier, which had invalidated plans that gave disproportionate influence to certain parts of states. The Supreme Court upheld the decision of the lower court. [26]

When the Georgia legislature failed to come up with new plans, the three trial court judges who had heard the case employed law professor and redistricting expert Nathaniel Persily to produce new maps. [27] The court's plan reduced the range in population to less than 2 percent in each chamber.

While the court plan in Georgia now has little deviation in district populations, it remains possible for states and localities to have plans with more variation if they provide an acceptable explanation. For example, a state might justify population deviations as necessary to avoid splitting racial groups, counties, precincts, or communities of interest between districts or to avoid pairing incumbents. Another possible rationale would be that the deviations resulted from drawing districts that followed natural boundaries such as rivers or mountain ranges. Yet another justification for a plan would be that it produced more compact districts. The Georgia defendants cited none of these possible explanations.

Problems with the Equal Population Standard

Critics of the emphasis on having equal populations point out that equalizing populations among districts need not produce the "one person, one vote" called for by Justice Douglas. If the objective is for each *vote* to have equal weight, registered voters or at least prospective voters rather than population should be equalized among districts. [28] After all, children cannot vote, nor can noncitizens or those in prison. Nonetheless, the courts have focused on the total population counts and sought to equalize those numbers. As a consequence, voters in districts with large numbers of children and/or noncitizens have a greater influence in the policy process than do voters living in districts with few children and/or noncitizens.

An effort to equalize numbers of registrants would exclude noncitizens, children, and others who had not registered to vote when designing districts. Even equalizing numbers of registrants would leave voters in some districts with greater influence than in others because of differences in turnout rates. If the standard really became equal numbers of voters, then districts comprised of low-income areas or heavily populated by young adults would have far more people than districts in affluent areas or having an older population.

Political scientist James Campbell has demonstrated that the differences in participation rates bear a relationship to partisanship, with districts that elect Democrats frequently having far fewer active participants than districts that elect Republicans.[29] Campbell shows that during the 1990s, the ratio between the most and fewest votes in a congressional district went as high as 8.48:1. Ronald Weber, in an extensive analysis of differences in turnout in state legislative elections from 1968 through 1998, finds ratios for the most to least votes in a state legislative district as high as 20:1.[30] A quick look at the David and Eisenberg ratios in table 2.1 shows that the disparity in numbers of actual voters exceeds the differences in districts' total population in many states prior to *Baker*. Weber finds that districts having the lowest turnout are ones with heavy concentrations of African Americans or Latinos and that it is in these districts that competitive elections least often occur. In the absence of uncertainty about the electoral outcome, fewer voters bother to turn out.

Using some measure other than total population, such as adults, registrants, or voters, would have political implications. Selecting any basis other than total population for allocating legislative seats would likely result in more Republican and fewer Democratic districts.

While equalizing voters among a jurisdiction's districts might be more in keeping with the "one person, one vote" concept, it would introduce another set of problems. First, turnout is at least partially driven by competition, with more voters mobilized by interest in the outcome of a high-profile election. While interest in the result of a presidential or statewide contest for governor or senator may push up turnout, a fiercely contested congressional seat or even sheriff's office can also bring voters to the polls. Consequently, if turnout became the basis for drawing districts, there might be an accompanying obligation to make districts equally competitive.[31]

Second, as the enthusiasm surrounding Barack Obama's candidacy demonstrated, numbers of registrants and turnout can increase dramatically in a short period of time. Figures from the 2009 New Jersey and Virginia gubernatorial elections show that participation rates can also fall precipitously, as African Americans and young voters inspired by Obama failed to turn out. In light of the political bloodletting that invariably accompanies redistricting and the time often required to pass a plan, legislators would have to redistrict after each election, or at least after each presidential election, to adjust for variations in participation. If adjustments came only once a decade, as they currently do, then (to return to the first point) districts that had hotly contested elections—perhaps triggered by the death or retirement of the incumbent—in the election year used as the basis for redistricting would be advantaged (be drawn to include fewer people), while those in which an established incumbent ran unopposed would be penalized as they expanded to include more people.

Initial Consequences on "One Person, One Vote"

As noted at the outset of this chapter, the Illinois plaintiffs brought the *Colegrove* case because voters living in different parts of a state had unequal influence. Those who lived in underpopulated, rural districts had greater influence than those who lived in overpopulated, urban districts, since each vote in an underpopulated district was more significant in determining electoral outcomes. Since urban districts were overpopulated, they elected fewer legislators than they would get with a fairly apportioned plan and therefore had less ability to pass legislation that would benefit cities and their suburbs.

An important consequence of urban underrepresentation was thought to be receipt of state funds. A leader in the Florida house, which for decades was run by and for the benefit of the rural north Florida Park Chop Gang, justified his legislature's allocation formula. "I believe in collecting taxes where the money is—in the cities—and spending it where it's needed—in the country."[32]

The requirement that states equalize populations among districts after what had frequently been decades of inaction produced dramatic changes in the makeup of most legislatures. Immediately following the early redistricting decisions of the 1960s, the number of rural legislators declined and the number from urban areas increased. Now, suburban areas increasingly benefit from decennial redistricting, with rural areas continuing to lose representation and many cities also getting fewer legislators. Those changes have resulted in fewer farmers and small-town merchants serving in the legislature, often being replaced by owners of small businesses and community activists.

Critics of the inequities that resulted from the silent gerrymander had high expectations for the Redistricting Revolution. They anticipated that as metropolitan areas gained seats, legislatures would pass more progressive legislation. Early research done on the consequences of equalizing populations among legislative districts threw cold water on those hopes. Studies that used equity of apportionment as an independent variable generally found that a fairer distribution of legislative seats did not correlate positively with more spending on public schools or welfare programs or the needs of large cities.[33]

While the general thrust of the early research suggested that equitable apportionment had little effect, some researchers did identify consequences of redistricting. Not surprisingly, reapportionment increased the frequency with which urban legislators appeared on the winning side of roll calls and led to the adoption of more progressive policies.[34] States with more equitably apportioned legislatures tended to spend more on higher education and housing programs.[35] Redistricting resulted in legislatures becoming more supportive of consumers, the environment, and civil rights.[36]

A correlate of more equal distribution of representation was a more equal distribution of state funding. Not surprisingly, before the Redistricting Revolution rural counties overrepresented in the state legislature received a disproportionate share of state funding, as the Florida legislator cited above believed they should.[37] Recent scholarship has shown that following redistricting, counties that received additional representation began getting a more proportionate share of the state's dollars. The amount of money redistributed was far from trivial. "The cumulative effect was to shift approximately $7 billion annually towards counties that had been under-represented prior to the imposition of the one-person, one-vote."[38] Not only did redistricting shift the allocation of state funds, federal funds also flowed more generously to urban areas at the expense of rural areas.[39] The authors summarized, "Equal votes produced equal distribution of money." Crop supports for farmers became less of a congressional priority, while Congress increasingly turned its attention to the concerns of consumers and environmentalists. As McCubbins and Schwartz emphasize: "In transferring political power from rural to metropolitan areas, redistricting was the enzyme for the organization of consumer and environmental interests."[40]

In the South, shifting seats from rural counties to urban areas opened the way for the election of the first African American legislators in recent times. When legislators had represented entire counties, urban voters sent whites to fill their few seats, while in rural areas, obstacles to participation such as literacy tests, poll taxes, and intimidation sufficiently reduced the black electorate so that even in majority-black counties, whites won the legislative seats. But when urban areas got their proportionate share of the seats in single-member systems, African Americans dominated some districts, and with fewer obstacles to participation in urban areas they began to win seats.

Note that the Voting Rights Act, initially passed in 1965, coincides with the onset of the Redistricting Revolution. The protections extended by the federal government in much of the South removed the literacy, good character, and understanding tests that had minimized black registration. Once African Americans could register and vote, it proved relatively easy to translate their new political activism into legislative seats. The last struggle in the effort to secure fair representation for urban areas often involved a switch to single-member districts rather than electing all legislators from multimember, countywide districts. That issue was resolved at different times in different southern states. Mississippi was the last state to make single-member districts widespread; once it did so, the number of black members in the state house jumped from four to fifteen.[41]

The introduction of minorities into state legislatures resulted in new issues appearing on the policy agenda. Even if minority legislators could not attract enough allies to adopt their preferences, their views and concerns often differed from those of the white, frequently rural legislators of the past.[42]

A third change from redistributing seats to reflect population promoted the political party that had greater strength in the cities than in the countryside. Redrawing congressional districts outside the South eliminated what had been a Republican bias. The causes for this change were twofold. First, Democrats enjoyed exceptional political success in winning state legislative seats in 1964 when Barry Goldwater's presidential bid proved unpopular even with many traditional Republican voters. Thus the legislatures responsible for reacting to suits filed pursuant to *Wesberry* were much more likely to be Democratic than if the Redistricting Revolution had come earlier.[43] Second, the courts that passed on the constitutionality of districting plans disproportionately had judges with Democratic leanings, and the partisan orientation of the judge influenced how he or she reacted to challenges to the existing plans.

While the 1964 election with the Lyndon Johnson coattails helped Democrats win state legislative seats, two years later a reaction favoring Republicans occurred. The swing back toward the GOP in 1966, along with continued redrawing of state legislative districts, resulted in the 1966 elections recording the greatest number of state legislative chambers changing partisan hands at least since 1940.[44] Thirty of seventy-four non-southern, partisan legislative chambers underwent a change in their majority. Outside the South, increasing representation for urban areas frequently advantaged Democrats, but not in all states, as Persily and his collaborators point out.[45] In the North and West, farmers and small-town merchants tended to vote Republican. While Republicans might also have substantial strength in urban areas, Democrats were relatively stronger there than in the rural parts of the state and consequently benefited from the new urban districts.

In the South, Republicans tended to be the beneficiaries. While Democrats maintained overwhelming majorities in southern legislatures into the 1990s and beyond in a few states, Republican presidential candidates began attracting urban voters in the 1950s. With reapportionment, additional seats went to suburbs where a white-collar labor force fresh from the Midwest or Northeast had recently settled. These imported voters, who had brought their Republican loyalties along with their household goods, enthusiastically sent Republicans to the legislature.

The *Reynolds* decision that both of a state's chambers must be based on population eliminated an alternative rationale for legislative districts. Indeed, some states nested house districts within senate districts. As Persily and his colleagues show, following implementation of *Reynolds* changes, the legislative chambers within a state came to look much more alike in terms of their partisan composition.[46]

Controversy

In this and the next three chapters, each of which deals with standards considered for redistricting, the chapter concludes with continuing arguments over the standards that have been adopted. To some extent this reviews the reason for the standards that have been imposed by courts and juxtaposes against those rationales the arguments that have come from opponents.

Arguments For

Population equality has been the foremost consideration in redistricting ever since the federal judiciary stepped in to regulate what had been exclusively a matter for state legislatures. Ensuring that each voter has an equal influence in selecting legislators has an obvious appeal. Each vote counts equally when electing executives from president to governor and down to mayor, so why should votes not count equally when selecting those who pass the laws?

The consequences of the silent gerrymanders that distorted most states' congressional delegations and state legislatures resulted in rural areas exercising inordinate influence. Rural dominance meant that urban and suburban interests got short shrift, even as they became home to an increasing share of states' populations and had growing needs for state and federal aid.

While the drafters of the federal Constitution had to allow small states greater influence than large states in the Senate in order to devise a plan acceptable as a replacement for the Articles of Confederation, no such compromise had been required in the individual states. Consequently, the Supreme

Court could assert that all state legislators should represent people and not acres, trees, or farm animals.

Arguments Against

If the objective is for each district to have equal influence, then focusing on populations misses the mark. Because of differences in the concentrations of noncitizens, children, felons, and the politically apathetic, voters in some districts have much greater influence than in other districts even immediately after equalizing populations among districts. For example, in 2002 in the newly drawn districts of New York, the number of votes cast ranged from 50,527 in the Twelfth District to 214,854 in the Twenty-First District. If the objective is for voters to have equal influence, then at a minimum it is citizen, voting-age populations and not total populations that should be equalized. Drawing districts with equal numbers of registrants would come still closer to equalizing the weight of each vote. The closest approximation might come from drawing districts with little deviation in the numbers of votes cast in the most recent presidential election.

The *Karcher* decision's push for minimal population deviations among a state's congressional districts rests on an untenable assumption. The failure to count all Americans, with the poor and minorities especially susceptible to being overlooked, means that districts actually lack equal numbers of people even in plans that have zeroed out population differences. Even if districts have equal numbers of people when counted in the census, by the time states get the census data and draw districts, the figures are outdated; new housing has sprung up on what had been vacant lots or farmland at the time of the census, and some dwellings inhabited at the time of the census have been abandoned. Think of the devastation wrought by Hurricane Katrina on the housing stock of New Orleans and other low-lying areas along the Gulf Coast. Judicial demands for miniscule population deviations have an artificial ring and carry costs. Efforts to eliminate population deviations prolong redistricting sessions, and even the smallest population differences provide the basis for judicial challenges that can cost jurisdictions millions of dollars in attorneys' fees.

The emphasis on eliminating trivial population differences necessitates dividing counties, cities, and communities of interest that would much prefer to remain united in a single district. Splitting a community among two or more districts may reduce its influence in the legislature, as it plays a smaller role in the electoral fortunes of the legislators who represent parts of it than it would in one legislator's constituency. An alternative argument that a community split between two legislators may have two people who will promote its interests may be correct for populous cities or counties, but is unlikely to hold true for small communities.

The demand that the plan approach zero population deviation creates new opportunities to gerrymander. Software facilitates separating Democratic from Republican precincts or white from minority census blocks. Calling for districts with equal populations has opened the way for mischief that was much harder to achieve when working with whole counties to build districts.

At least during the early days of the Redistricting Revolution, people living in counties that no longer had a local resident representing them expressed alienation and frustration.[47] They doubted whether their new legislator who lived in a neighboring county would look out for their interests, and they began plying the governor with requests for assistance. Residents of small counties who can never send one of their own to the legislature because of the electoral dominance of a larger neighbor may be more likely to question whether the government responds to the needs of people like them.

Conclusions

In less than two generations, the population standards for districting plans have gone from tolerating as wide a variation in district populations as a state chose to permit to pressing toward zero deviation. The gross disparities such as those cited early in this chapter gave rural voters a disproportionate influence in legislatures and over the shaping of public policy.

Courts gradually forced jurisdictions to minimize the deviations in district populations. For congressional districts, the perspective of the Supreme Court has been that all citizens should have equal representation, and that value has made it increasingly difficult to justify deviations from absolute equality. Courts have pressed toward this standard of absolute equality even while acknowledging that problems in getting a full and accurate census count coupled with population shifts make absolute equality more myth than reality. The problem of the census missing some residents, particularly poorer ones, is widely acknowledged. The explosive growth in some suburban areas means that from the taking of the census in April until legislatures get around to drawing districts more than a year later, underrepresentation of some suburban voters in the new plans will likely result.

The courts have continued to accept more population deviation for collegial bodies below the U.S. House. For years it appeared that these districts could deviate from the ideal population by as much as +/−5 percent. Drawing districts with that level of population deviation, however, does not make them immune to a challenge, as Georgia learned in 2004. The next round of redistricting may force additional states and localities to reduce the population deviations in their districts. The software available makes that task relatively easy, even as it opens the way for new adventures in gerrymandering.

3

Minorities and Redistricting

A redistricting plan violates the Voting Rights Act if it simply has a discriminatory result.[1]

Within the Division, the failure to maximize came to be regarded as evidence of purposeful discrimination.[2]

THE CONSEQUENCES OF DISTRICTING PLANS FOR minorities and their reactions to the districting process have varied greatly over time. This chapter takes a largely chronological approach to organizing the materials relating to the relationship between minorities and districting plans. In the days before the "one person, one vote" court decisions, plans in most states, especially in the South, disadvantaged minorities. In some instances the disadvantage was not based on an intention to discriminate against minorities but stemmed from the failure to adjust boundaries to reflect population shifts. As America became less reliant on agriculture for its economic success, the nation's black population moved to the cities. Some share of this migration combined a move to the city with a departure from the Jim Crow South to northern cities like Detroit, Chicago, and New York, which provided greater opportunities for better jobs and better schools. To the extent that districting plans disadvantaged urban America, they resulted in fewer districts in the areas where minorities concentrated when leaving the rural South.

In the wake of *Baker v. Carr* and *Wesberry v. Sanders* and the allocation of legislative seats based on population, some southern legislatures and communities split minority concentrations in an effort to eliminate or at least minimize the likelihood that a black could be elected. Some jurisdictions that had utilized single-member districts shifted to at-large elections at the local level, which made it harder for minorities to win office. In southern state legislatures, the allocation of larger numbers of seats to urban areas witnessed the election of the first blacks in decades. In large urban areas with substantial minority concentrations, single-member district plans resulted in some majority-black districts, and these elected African Americans.

Implementation of Section 5 of the Voting Rights Act ensured that districts that had become majority black would not be redrawn to eliminate the black majority. Later this provision, which covers all of nine states and portions of seven others, forced the creation of additional minority districts. In the early 1990s, the Department of Justice (DOJ) demanded that jurisdictions subject to Section 5 maximize the number of districts in which a racial minority would constitute a majority of the electorate. Affirmative action gerrymandering generated an unprecedented number of new majority-minority districts. These new districts sent record numbers of African Americans to Congress.

By the turn of the twenty-first century, a number of black political leaders had embraced new objectives. Into the 1990s, their top priority had been to maximize the number of districts likely to be won by a minority candidate. By 2001, the top priority in some states shifted to protecting the Democratic majority in the legislature, even if that meant reassigning minority voters to bolster the electoral prospects of white Democrats. This overview highlights the topics that will be developed in the course of this chapter.

Impact of "One Person, One Vote"

For decades African Americans left the South for the greater freedom and opportunities in northern cities. In 1960, the black population had reached 23 percent in Chicago, 14 percent in Los Angeles, 29 percent in Detroit, and 14 percent in New York. Among African Americans who remained in the South, many had sought better-paying jobs in cities. The 1960 Census showed Atlanta to be 38 percent black, while New Orleans was 37 percent black and Birmingham's black population approached 40 percent.

The pervasive underrepresentation of urban areas reduced the number of legislative seats that might be placed in heavily black neighborhoods, and consequently, reduced opportunities—in the South it eliminated opportunities—for African American representation in the state legislature. While the Latino population in 1960 was heavily concentrated along the Mexican border and still largely rural, had the Redistricting Revolution not taken place, this group would in time also have suffered from the failure to redraw legislative districts to reflect urbanization.

Shifting legislative seats to metropolitan areas provided the first opportunities for African Americans to elect members of their race to southern legislatures since the massive disfranchisement that took place around the turn of the twentieth century.[3] While each southern state had one or more majority black counties, meaning that a county-based apportionment scheme might result in the election of black legislators, Jim Crow barriers proved so insurmountable that no rural blacks had won legislative seats in half a century. Conditions in the rural South prior to the civil rights revolution fit with the "black threat hypothesis" from V. O. Key.[4] Based on his extensive study of southern politics in the middle of the twentieth century, Key observed that white resistance to black political and economic progress varied directly with the proportion of blacks in the local population, so that African Americans had the fewest rights in the most heavily black areas. Consequently, it was in the majority-black counties that barriers to political participation proved most impenetrable. White opposition stemmed from a realization that should political rights be extended to African Americans, the jurisdiction would likely be governed by blacks or at least by the candidates for whom blacks voted. Consequently, in the county-based districting schemes, overwhelmingly black counties elected white legislators.

With the onset of equally populated districts, minorities faced new challenges. The same tactics used to disadvantage a minority party can be and have been employed to limit the influence of racial or ethnic minorities. District lines can split or crack minority concentrations so as to deny them any representation.[5] Alternatively, where minority concentrations are too large to deny them any representation, the number of legislative seats they are likely to win can be reduced by packing the minority population into one or a few districts rather than adopting alternative plans that, by distributing the minority population more broadly, would likely result in a greater number of seats being controlled by those voters. Finally, the widespread use of multimember plans at the time of the Redistricting Revolution often stacked the decks against the minority population so that its candidates lost in each of a series of head-to-head contests; if single-member districts were drawn, the minority population would stand a good chance of electing its preferred candidate in at least one of those districts.

An early challenge to multimember districts involved Marion County, Indiana, which includes Indianapolis. The eight senators and fifteen representatives from Marion County all ran countywide resulting in twenty-three head-to-head contests, forcing each candidate to campaign throughout the county. This arrangement frequently resulted in a one-party sweep. Although the county had a substantial black population, African Americans rarely won seats to the legislature because they ran as members of the minority (Democratic) party, which consistently lost countywide.[6] A single-member system would have anchored some seats in black neighborhoods where black Democrats could have won. While the trial court found for the plaintiffs and threw out the multimember plan, the Supreme Court allowed it to stand because partisanship and not race explained the electoral outcomes. The Supreme Court acknowledged that when racial or partisan minorities compete countywide they are less likely to win than if the county had a series of single-member districts, some of which would be dominated by the minority.

A couple of years later, in another opinion written by Justice Byron White, the Supreme Court reached a very different conclusion from its Indiana holding.[7] The High Court upheld a lower court decision that required replacing at-large districts in two Texas counties with single-member districts. The Court pointed to the infrequency of victories by African Americans in Dallas County or Latinos in Bexar County. The opinion reviewed examples of discrimination that had confronted blacks and Latinos in these counties before concluding that while partisanship accounted for the defeat of African Americans in Indianapolis, discrimination thwarted minorities' political ambitions in Texas.

At almost exactly the same time that the Supreme Court launched the Redistricting Revolution, Congress passed the Voting Rights Act (VRA). This 1965 legislation, which has been renewed four times, most recently in 2006, authorizes federal officials to serve as guardians of black political interests during redistricting in selected states. Amendments to the VRA in 1975 extended protections to language minorities, as will be described later. A subsequent amendment in 1982 broadened the scope of the federal protection against racial gerrymandering so that it applies nationally. The next section explores how federal law has invalidated efforts to minimize minority influence through redistricting.

Section 5

The 1965 Voting Rights Act came after three attempts to facilitate black registration. The Civil Rights Acts of 1957, 1960, and 1964 had produced only modest improvements in black registration rates in the region.[8] A frustrated President Lyndon Johnson directed his attorney general, Nicholas Katzenbach, to draft "the goddamnedest toughest voting rights law you can devise."[9] Katzenbach's design froze existing practices relating to registration and participation in selected states and required that any changes in the laws regulating registration or voting in those jurisdictions receive federal approval before implementation. He anticipated that requiring federal preapproval for changes would prevent southern jurisdictions from designing new obstacles to black participation, thus avoiding the dilatory practices that had thwarted school desegregation during the previous decade.

The VRA involved an unprecedented intervention of the federal government in what had been exclusively a state responsibility. Aside from the constitutional guarantees of the right of women and African Americans to vote, conduct of voter registration activities had been left to the states and, in reality, typically to local officials who operated registration offices. Given the intrusion of federal authority into what had been a local responsibility, the scope of jurisdictions to be covered was carefully drawn. The jurisdictions that would need to get federal approval prior to changing their laws relating to registration or voting, a procedure called "preclearance," had long records of discriminating against prospective black voters. The preclearance provision is also frequently referred to as Section 5 because it appears in that part of the VRA.

Section 4 of the VRA set forth a two-part test to identify jurisdictions needing preclearance. Jurisdictions had to obtain preclearance if less than half of their voting-age population had registered or voted in the 1964 presidential election *and* they had a test or device as a prerequisite for voter registration. The tests or devices included a literacy test, an understanding test, or a good character test. The legislation did not include poll taxes as a test or device. The two-part test made Alabama, Georgia, Louisiana, Mississippi, South Carolina, Virginia, and a little more than a third of North Carolina's counties subject to preclearance.

Preclearance of laws relating to voting or registration can be pursued in either of two ways. A jurisdiction can submit proposed changes to the attorney general, who has sixty days in which to review the matter. If the attorney general objects to the proposal, the jurisdiction must go back to the drawing board and redesign the proposal to meet the federal objections. The alternative approach allows jurisdictions to ask the district court of the District of Columbia for a declaratory judgment that the proposed change does not discriminate against African Americans. If the attorney general rejects a jurisdiction's proposal, it can appeal to the court in the District of Columbia. No changes can be implemented until approval has been secured through one of these two approaches.

During the latter half of the 1960s as the "one person, one vote" revolution got under way, the need for preclearance did not apply to redistricting. The covered jurisdictions and, seemingly, the Department of Justice applied the preclearance requirement only to proposals that changed the conditions

under which prospective voters went about registering or voting. Since drawing districts did not directly affect registration or turnout, jurisdictions did
not need to secure preclearance for their new plans.

DOJ became more aggressive after 1969, when the Supreme Court gave a
broad interpretation to the VRA preclearance requirement. In *Allen v. State
Board of Elections*, the Court held that Mississippi jurisdictions needed to
secure preclearance before changing the electoral structure of county su-
pervisors from districts to at-large, before making the position of county
superintendent of education an appointive rather than an elective office, and
before changing the criteria that must be met for a candidate to run as an
Independent.[10] None of these changes related to requirements for individuals
seeking to register or cast votes and, therefore, the Mississippi jurisdictions
had not sought preclearance. These changes did, however, affect the ability
of minorities to elect their preferred candidates. In explaining its decision,
the Court took language from the redistricting cases that had discussed the
importance of having a "meaningful" vote. Drawing on *Reynolds v. Sims*, the
Court observed: "The right to vote can be affected by dilution of voting power
as well as by the absolute prohibition on casting a ballot." The Court took an
expansive view of Section 5, observing:

> We must reject a narrow construction that appellees would give to Section 5.
> The Voting Rights Act was aimed at the subtle, as well as the obvious, state
> regulations that have the effect of denying citizens their right to vote because of
> their race.

While the *Allen* decision broadened the scope of the VRA, it did not specifically address the issue of redistricting, which came up in 1973. The DOJ
rejected Georgia's state house redistricting plan. DOJ also found Georgia's
remedial effort to be wanting. At that point, Georgia refused to submit any
further plans, arguing that Section 5 did not apply to redistricting since the
legislation made no mention of that activity. Moreover, the state contended
that even if Section 5 did apply to redistricting, a plan could be rejected only if
DOJ found it to be discriminatory and DOJ had not reached that conclusion.
The Supreme Court rejected Georgia's contentions.[11] The Court referred to
Reynolds v. Sims, which had discussed vote dilution in the context of urban
votes often having less weight or influence than those of rural voters. Moreover, the Court pointed out that Congress had not objected to the Supreme
Court decision in *Allen* when renewing Section 5 in 1970 and thus had given
tacit consent to the Supreme Court's ruling broadening the applicability of
Section 5. The Court also rejected the state's claim that a plan had to be approved unless DOJ showed it to be discriminatory. The Court noted that had
Georgia followed the judicial route and sought a declaratory judgment from

the court in Washington, D.C., the state would have had the burden of proof. This burden of proving that its actions did not discriminate also extends to administrative submissions to DOJ.

Retrogression

The Supreme Court set forth the standard for assessing the impact of new plans on minority political strength. The Supreme Court clarified that while Congress designed Section 5 to prevent harm to minorities, it could not be used as an affirmative tool. DOJ had rejected a plan for New Orleans that drew two districts majority black by population where previously there had been none. DOJ objected to the new plan because blacks did not constitute a majority of the registered voters in both of these districts. The Supreme Court held that Section 5 prohibits only *retrogression*, meaning that as long as a new plan did not leave black voters worse off than the *status quo*, DOJ must approve the proposal.[12] Even though an alternative plan might result in African Americans having greater political influence, *Beer v. United States* held that Section 5 creates no obligation to maximize the political influence of minorities. In the 1980s, the first redistricting round after *Beer*, efforts to protect seats currently held by minorities frequently helped the Democratic Party.[13]

Consequences of Early Redistricting

Even though jurisdictions had no obligation to draw additional minority districts, the consequences of the initial implementation of districting plans equalizing populations had a dramatic impact on black representation in most southern legislatures. After decades of failing to adjust for population shifts, the first equal-population plans often increased black representation. Placing additional seats in urban areas promoted black office holding because some of the new urban districts had black population majorities. In states subject to Section 5, a dramatic increase occurred as the number of blacks serving in lower chambers more than tripled from nineteen to sixty, as shown in table 3.1. Excluding Georgia, where Atlanta's black concentration coupled with the region's largest legislature and adoption of single-member districts in urban areas had facilitated the election of African Americans in the previous decade, the increase in Section 5 states is even more impressive. In the Alabama house, the number of black legislators jumped from two to thirteen following redistricting. Redistricting saw the first dozen African Americans elected to the South Carolina house, and in Louisiana the number grew from one to eight. In states not subject to Section 5 as of 1972, the number of black representatives grew from nine to twenty-three. The need to secure preclearance

TABLE 3.1
The 1970s Redistricting and the Increase in the Numbers of
African Americans Elected to Lower Chambers of Southern Legislatures

State	1969	After 1970 Redistricting
Section 5 states		
Alabama	0	13
Georgia	12	19
Louisiana	1	8
Mississippi	1	4
North Carolina	1	3
South Carolina	0	12
Virginia	2	1
Total	19	60
Non–Section 5 states as of 1972		
Arkansas	0	3
Florida	1	3
Tennessee	6	7
Texas	2	8
Total	9	23

Source: Prepared by author.

also increased black representation on many city and county collegial bodies.[14]

Section 5 of the VRA came up for renewal in 1975. Latinos, who had monitored the effectiveness of Section 5 in increasing the numbers of black officeholders, used the opportunity for renewal to press Congress to expand the scope of the legislation to include language minorities. The 1975 amendments to the VRA included a new trigger that extended coverage to jurisdictions in which less than half of the voting-age citizens had registered or participated in the 1972 presidential election and in which registration and election materials had been available only in English where at least 5 percent of the adult citizens belonged to a single language minority group. Thus, for example, if at least 5 percent of the adult citizens in a county or state primarily spoke Spanish and the election-related materials had not been published in Spanish, and fewer than half of the adults had voted in 1972, the jurisdiction now had to comply with Section 5 preclearance. This amendment extended Section 5 coverage to all of Alaska, Arizona, and Texas along with five Florida counties, two New York counties, three California counties, and selected counties in South

Dakota and Michigan. Jurisdictions covered by the 1965 trigger continued to have to secure preclearance.

Once jurisdictions with substantial Latino populations subject to Section 5 had to secure preclearance, the numbers of districts likely to elect Hispanics increased. In the Texas house, immediately following the 1982 redistricting, the number of Latino members rose from seventeen to twenty-one.

Section 2

In 1982, in addition to extending Section 5 for a quarter of a century, Congress added a new provision to the VRA that applied nationwide. Congress rewrote Section 2, which had previously been nothing more than a restatement of the Fifteenth Amendment. The objective of the rewrite reduced the evidentiary burden on plaintiffs challenging *existing* electoral systems. Recall that Section 5 applied only to selected jurisdictions seeking to make changes and, consequently, when no changes were attempted, Section 5 had no role. For example, Section 5 did not help minorities unable to elect their preferred candidates in a city that had used at-large elections prior to congressional adoption of the VRA. Of course, if plaintiffs could prove that a jurisdiction had intended to discriminate against minorities, then the jurisdiction could prevail under either the Fourteenth or Fifteenth amendment to the Constitution. Section 2 eliminated the requirement that plaintiffs prove an intent to discriminate in order to force a change in an existing electoral structure. All that plaintiffs needed to demonstrate under Section 2 was that an electoral system provided minorities less opportunity to participate in the political process and to elect their preferred candidates than whites had. While a caveat warned that Section 2 did not require that minorities be represented on governing bodies in proportion to their share of the population, wide disparities between the minority percentage in the electorate and holding elective office frequently triggered litigation.

The impetus for rewriting Section 2 came from a Supreme Court decision that allowed Mobile, Alabama, to elect all commissioners citywide.[15] Although Mobile's population was almost 40 percent black, no African American had won a seat on the city commission. The Supreme Court ruled against the plaintiffs because they failed to prove that the at-large electoral system, which dated from 1911, had been adopted or maintained for discriminatory purposes.

Since the jurisdiction had no obligation to have minorities serving in roughly the same proportion as in the population, Congress identified a set of factors for judges to consider when hearing suits brought under Section 2. The seven major factors and two subsidiary ones constituted what became known as the totality-of-the-circumstances test. The seven elements of the totality of the circumstances are the following:

1. Has there been a history of official discrimination in the jurisdiction that makes it harder for minorities to register or vote?
2. Is there evidence of racially polarized voting?
3. Have members of the minority community won elections in the jurisdiction?
4. Have slating groups discriminated against minorities when backing candidates?
5. Are there lingering consequences of past discrimination such as school segregation?
6. Have candidates made racial appeals in previous elections?
7. Has the jurisdiction made use of factors that may have enhanced the impact of other elements and made it harder for minorities to succeed politically? (Among the enhancing factors are unusually large electoral districts, majority vote requirement, and a prohibition on single-shot voting.)

Two secondary factors that the courts might consider in a Section 2 suit are these:

1. Whether local elected officials had been responsive to the policy requests coming from the minority community.
2. Whether the political practice being challenged is standard for the state or is something extraordinary.

Congress specified that judges should not simply count up the number of items on which the plaintiffs prove their case and the number on which the defendants' evidence is more compelling. Nor need the courts give equal weight to each of the items. Finally, courts could also consider additional evidence; the items in the totality-of-the-circumstances test should not be considered as exhaustive.

Immediately after the enactment of Section 2, voting rights attorneys began challenging at-large and multimember electoral systems across the nation. In *Thornburg v. Gingles*, the first case to work its way through the judicial system and come before the Supreme Court, the majority opinion established a three-part test that plaintiffs must meet in order to prevail.[16] The first prong of the *Gingles* test requires that plaintiffs demonstrate that the minority group seeking relief is sufficiently large and compact to form a majority of the adult population in a single-member district that could be carved out of the existing arrangement. In meeting this test, the plan offered by the plaintiffs can have no more districts than the number of officials currently elected at-large or from a multimember district.[17] If it is impossible to create a district in which the minority group would dominate, then the Court saw no way in which relief could be provided. The second prong requires that the plaintiffs prove political cohesion, which means that the group bringing the suit usually unites behind the same candidates. If the plaintiff minority group is not politically cohesive, then it may be losing elections because it fails to coalesce behind particular candidates. The third prong requires a showing that when the minority group has united behind candidates, those individuals usually lose as a result of a bloc vote by whites. If the plaintiffs successfully meet the three prongs of *Gingles* test, then the Court will review the seven factors in the totality-of-the-circumstances test.

The Supreme Court set forth the three-prong *Gingles* test in a challenge to North Carolina's multimember legislative districts. Seven years later, the Court extended the test to efforts to reconfigure existing single-member arrangements.[18] As a consequence of the literally hundreds of challenges filed pursuant to Section 2, the number of local collegial bodies that have single-member districts has increased, which necessitates adjusting their boundaries to equalize population after each census. Multimember districts that once dominated state lower chambers have now become rare and, except in areas where minorities are too scarce to be able to meet the first *Gingles* prong, have disappeared altogether.[19]

Section 2 and Section 5 Reviews

Section 2 proved useful beyond challenging at-large and multimember districting systems. DOJ incorporated Section 2 into reviews of plans submitted by jurisdictions subject to Section 5 following the 1990 Census. With Section 2 available, DOJ could enforce affirmative action gerrymandering designed to promote descriptive representation—that is, creating heavily black districts that would be represented by an African American. DOJ reasoned that it made no sense to approve a plan that might later be attacked under Section 2 for not providing an equal opportunity for minorities to elect their preferred candidates. Avoiding retrogression no longer sufficed to secure DOJ approval. DOJ even rejected plans that increased the number of majority-minority districts, if additional minority districts could be drawn. Section 2 gave DOJ the leverage to force the creation of majority-minority districts (districts in which most adults belonged to a minority group).

David Lublin demonstrated the link between racial concentrations and the election of minorities to Congress. From 1972 to 1994, African Americans won all but 19 of 219 elections in majority-black districts but only 72 of 5,079 in districts lacking a black majority.[20] Latinos won 82 of 105 contests in districts in which they constituted a majority but only 29 of 5,190 in districts where they were in the minority. While Lublin's book appeared after DOJ's push for majority-minority districts, it had long been recognized that these offered the surest way to increase the minority presence in legislative bodies.

White southern Democrats objected to the creation of majority black districts. While some of the opposition may have stemmed from racism, white and black Democratic politicians often found themselves competing in a zero-sum game. As Republican support grew among southern white voters, white Democratic politicians became increasingly dependent on black votes. As the black percentage in a district's electorate declined, so did prospects for a Democratic victory. Since majority black districts invariably elect African Americans while overwhelmingly white districts in the South elect Republicans, the most optimal districts for white Democrats had 50 to 90 percent white populations. In time as more whites became Republicans, white Democrats needed higher concentrations of blacks, with districts in the 30 to 50 percent black range providing relatively secure bases.[21]

North Carolina illustrates what happened in the early 1990s when DOJ incorporated Section 2 into Section 5 reviews. North Carolina, which had not elected a black member of Congress since 1898, created a majority black district in its 1991 plan. Despite the absence of retrogression, DOJ refused to preclear the plan because the state could have drawn a second majority black district. While not guilty of retrogression, one black district among a dozen fell far short of the 22 percent black in North Carolina's population, and alternative plans contained two majority-black districts.

Georgia and Louisiana encountered similar rejections from DOJ, even though in Georgia's case the plan enhanced black representation by creating a second majority-black district. With two majority-black districts among eleven, African Americans would be in a good position to elect 18 percent of Georgia's members of Congress. However, forcing Georgia to develop a plan with three majority-black districts created the potential to elect 27 percent of the delegation would match the black percentage in the state's population.

Relatively early in the redistricting process, DOJ warned jurisdictions that did not have to get preclearance that they must now comply with the Department's interpretation of Section 2. The assistant attorney general for civil rights announced, "We plan to exercise our authority under Section 2 and examine plans adopted in states not subject to Section 5 review."[22]

In order to maximize the number of majority-minority districts, jurisdictions often had to link geographically separated minority concentrations. The requirement that districts have equal populations meant that a cartographer connecting pockets of minority voters would have to avoid including too many whites lest the population become too large. These plans produced some exceptionally convoluted districts, as shown in figure 3.1, where a 620-mile-long Louisiana congressional district combined black populations in five urban areas along with majority black rural parishes bordering the Mississippi River. The weirdly shaped Fourth District followed the entire length of the Mississippi River as it separates Louisiana from Mississippi, and almost the entire state boundary between Louisiana and Arkansas to the north. This district became christened the "Zorro" district after a 1950s television show featuring a Robin Hood–type character named Zorro, whose trademark was a "Z" slashed with a sword on a piece of fabric.

Once DOJ had established its expectation that jurisdictions submit plans designed to maximize the number of districts likely to elect minorities, other

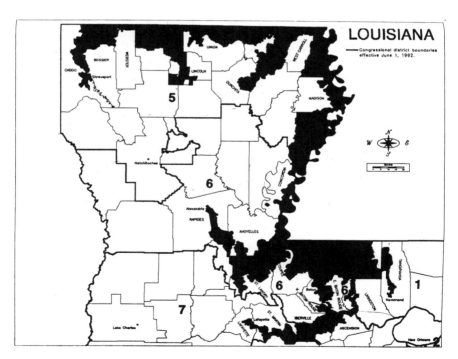

FIGURE 3.1.
Louisiana's Second District, the Zorro district.
© Election Data Services, Inc. (www.electiondataservices.com)

states took the cue and submitted plans that enhanced minority representation. The affirmative action gerrymanders that resulted from DOJ's incorporation of Section 2 expectations into its Section 5 reviews produced the first majority-black districts in Alabama, South Carolina, and Virginia. North Carolina drew two and Florida created three black districts. Georgia added two majority-black districts, raising its number to three, while Louisiana and Texas each added a second black district. As table 3.2 shows, each of the new black districts drawn in Section 5 states had a black majority population. Districts in Alabama, Louisiana, South Carolina, and Virginia and Georgia's Eleventh District all had populations more than 60 percent black.

TABLE 3.2
New Majority-Minority Districts Created after the 1990 Census

Black Districts	In 1992	Percent Black before 1992	After Challenge
AL-7	67	33	unchallenged
FL-3	55	27	50
FL-17	59	27	unchallenged
FL-23	52	new	unchallenged*
GA-2	57	37	39
GA-11	64	new	37
LA-4	67	new	31**
NC-1	57	35	50
NC-12	57	new	36
SC-6	62	41	settled***
TX-30	50	new	45
VA-3	64	28	54

Hispanic districts	In 1992	Percent Hispanic before 1992	After Challenge
FL-21	70	new	unchallenged
IL-4	58	new	unsuccessfully challenged
NY-12	57	new	49
TX-28	60	new	unchallenged
TX-29	60	new	45

*Challenge dismissed for being filed too late.
**When redrawn following a successful challenge, this became LA-5.
***SC-6 was challenged but resolved before a trial and was not redrawn.

Sources: Racial percentages for the districts used in 1992 come from Michael Barone and Grant Ujifusa, *The Almanac of American Politics, 1994* (Washington, DC: National Journal, 1993). The before-1992 racial figures come from Alan Ehrenhalt, ed., *Politics in America: The 100th Congress* (Washington, DC: Congressional Quarterly Press, 1987). The racial figures for districts redrawn after successful challenges come from Michael Barone and Grant Ujifusa, *The Almanac of American Politics*, 2000 (Washington, DC: National Journal, 1999).

The DOJ reviews in the early 1990s prompted Florida to create a second Latino congressional district, while Texas added two districts with heavy Latino concentrations as shown in table 3.2. New York added a 57 percent Hispanic district, which sent the state's second Latino to Congress. Illinois, although not subject to Section 5, drew a 64 percent Latino Chicago district, dubbed the "earmuff district" because of the shape it took to link two Hispanic neighborhoods separated by a black concentration.

The 1992 elections produced results in line with DOJ expectations. The number of African American members of Congress from the South increased from five to seventeen, and Latinos won House seats in four of the five new Hispanic districts. The one exception, Texas 29, saw an Anglo Democrat defeat a Latino in a contested runoff that featured racially polarized voting.[23] Although Latinos constituted 55 percent of the adults in Texas 29, only 31 percent of the voters had Spanish surnames, indicating that efforts to mobilize Latinos met with little success. Ben Reyes, the first Latino to represent a Houston district in the Texas house, led in the initial primary but lost the runoff when the eventual winner, Gene Green, made an issue of Reyes's bankruptcy and failure to pay taxes. Reyes failed to consolidate the supporters who had backed the Latino candidates eliminated in the first primary.

Some of the gains by minority candidates came at the expense of Anglo incumbents. In Alabama, South Carolina, and North Carolina, long-time white representatives chose not to run. Another white Democratic incumbent lost a reelection bid in southwest Georgia. In New York, Stephen Solarz, a leading House foreign policy expert who had the largest campaign war chest of any House member, nonetheless lost the Democratic primary to Nydia Velázquez in the new Hispanic district.

Impact below Congress

Each round of redistricting has facilitated the election of additional African Americans to southern state legislatures, and DOJ's standards for the early 1990s made an additional contribution. Table 3.3 shows pickups by African Americans of southern state house seats in the elections held immediately after a state adopted new maps. While more intensive research would be required before attributing all of these gains to the new maps, the table reports a striking coincidence. In eight states more than half the number of seats held by blacks in 2007 were initially won in the immediate aftermath of a redistricting. Only in Virginia did a substantial majority of African American gains come during the course of the decade and not right after implementation of new districts. The numbers of black-held seats in 2007 does not constitute the high-water mark in all states, and that explains why Alabama shows twenty-seven seats having been initially won by blacks immediately after a redistricting although African Americans held only twenty-six seats in 2007.

TABLE 3.3
Increases in African American House Members Following Redistricting

	1960	1970	1980	1990	2000	# Blacks 2007
AL	0	13*	6*	8	0	26
AR	0	3	0	5*	0	11
FL	1	1	7	0	0	19
GA	7	6*	0	4	3	44
LA	1	7	3	9	1	22
MS	1	14*	3	9	1	35
NC	1	1	8	4	0	21
SC	0	9*	0	7*	1	27
TN	6	1	1	2	1	16
TX	2	6	0	1	0	14
VA	2	0	0	0	1	11

*Figures from two redistrictings during the decade are combined.

DOJ's demands that states create more black districts in the early 1990s led to additional black-held seats in nine states. Arkansas and Louisiana experienced their greatest increases in African American representatives in that decade. Five other states had their second largest post-redistricting boost in the 1990s. The 1990s saw major increases even in states that had sizable black caucuses. Mississippi, South Carolina, and Alabama, which follow Georgia in terms of numbers of black representatives, each elected at least seven additional African Americans under the 1990s plans. Nationwide, the number of black legislators grew from 438 to 523 between 1991 and 1993. The new plans sent one more Latino to the Texas senate and four to the house, while Florida Latinos added two state house seats.

The number of blacks serving on county commissions jumped by more than 10 percent, while the number serving on city councils increased by approximately 200 following the 1990 round of redistricting. While it would be inaccurate to attribute all of the increase in minority public officials to redistricting, rearranging boundaries to form majority-minority districts played a major role. In the early 1990s, DOJ rejected 183 redistricting plans,[24] and while the cause for some of these may have been retrogression, the problem with others was their failure to increase the number of districts likely to elect minorities.

Courts React to DOJ's Use of Section 2

Some observers found the emphasis on creating heavily minority districts offensive. Robinson Everett, a Duke University law professor, went to court challenging North Carolina's Twelfth District. That district, which appears

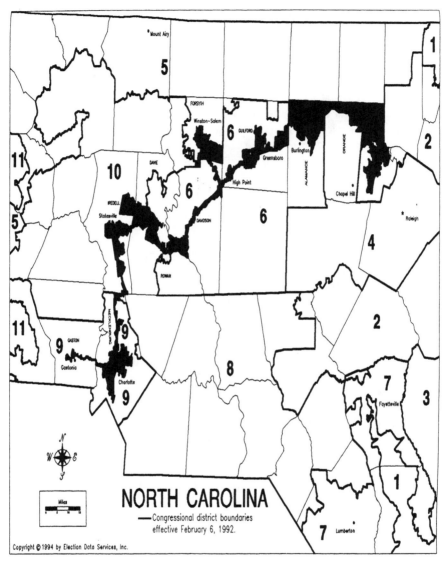

FIGURE 3.2
North Carolina's Twelfth District as of 1993 (shown in black).
© Election Data Services, Inc. (www.electiondataservices.com)

in figure 3.2, stretched from Gastonia, west of Charlotte, then northward in an arc through High Point and Greensboro to Durham, with an arm extending up to the northwest to include the black population of Winston-Salem. Connecting the black neighborhoods in seven cities made a 57 percent black district possible. As it went about linking black concentrations, at some points the district narrowed to include only I-85, thereby avoiding whites and giving the district its popular name, the "I-85 District." As a black legislator observed, the district was so narrow that if someone drove the length of that interstate highway with doors open on both sides of the car it might kill a large share of the district's population. As shown in the previous chapter, at several points the I-85 District had only touch-point contiguity.

Although the trial court in North Carolina dismissed Everett's complaint, the North Carolina map troubled five members of the Supreme Court. Justice Sandra Day O'Connor in her opinion for the Court in *Shaw v. Reno* observed:

> We believe that reapportionment is one area in which appearances *do* matter. A reapportionment plan that includes in one district individuals who belong to the same race, but who are otherwise widely separated by geographical and political boundaries and who may have little in common with one another but the color of their skin, bears an uncomfortable resemblance to political apartheid. It reinforces the perception that members of the same racial group—regardless of their age, education, economic status, or community in which they live—think alike, share the same political interests, and will prefer the same candidates at the polls. We have rejected such perceptions elsewhere as impermissible racial stereotypes.[25]

When courts concluded that districts have been drawn predominantly on the basis of race, they invalidated the districts.[26] This holding builds on earlier cases that found race to be a suspect category, which resulted in the courts' applying strict scrutiny. To withstand a challenge, the jurisdiction must prove that the plan had been narrowly tailored and furthered a legitimate state interest. Absent such a showing, the map would fail as a violation of the Equal Protection Clause previously used to invalidate racial segregation in the workplace, schools, and public facilities generally. Since DOJ had led jurisdictions to believe they must draw predominantly minority districts, those who challenged the districts had no difficulty demonstrating that considerations of race dominated the mapping decisions. In short order, some of the newly created majority-minority districts in other states came under attack.

North Carolina 12, which touched off challenges to racially gerrymandered districts in *Shaw*, continued to be litigated throughout the decade. A new version drawn in 1997 extended no farther east than Greensboro and no farther west then Charlotte. This shorter district nonetheless reached out to pick up the black population of Winston-Salem, for an overall black percentage of 47.

This district was challenged for giving predominance to racial considerations. The state responded that in drawing this district the legislature had relied primarily on party voting preferences and not race. To counter the state's claims, plaintiffs introduced an e-mail sent from the staff member responsible for the new districts to the chair of the senate redistricting committee. The staffer explained: "I have moved Greensboro Black community into the Twelfth District and now I need to take bout [sic] 60,000 out of the twelfth. I await your decision on this."[27]

While that e-mail convinced the trial court that race remained the primary consideration in drawing the new version of the district, the Supreme Court disagreed and upheld the legality of the district.[28] By accepting the state's claim that partisan considerations, in this case the effort to draw a district likely to elect a Democrat, had guided its actions, the Supreme Court sent a clear signal to jurisdictions preparing to equalize populations in the wake of the 2000 Census. The Court acknowledged that the most heavily Democratic districts would also often be the ones with the largest concentrations of African Americans. Nonetheless, so long as most of the rationales offered for a map emphasized partisanship and not race, the Supreme Court seemed likely to uphold the plan.

When plaintiffs succeeded in proving that a plan had been drawn predominantly on the basis of race, jurisdictions had to redesign their maps, and invariably this lowered minority concentrations. The final column in table 3.2 shows the percentage of relevant minorities in new districts following successful challenges to the racially gerrymandered districts created at the beginning of the decade. The least change in majority-black districts occurred in Florida, where the Third District went from 55 percent down to 50 percent, and in North Carolina, where the First District in the eastern part of the state dropped from 57 percent to 50 percent black. Virginia's Third District remained majority black, although it experienced a 10 percentage point decrease to 54 percent black. Both districts in Georgia, North Carolina 12, and Louisiana 4 ended up with black percentages below 40 percent.

Voting rights attorney Laughlin McDonald expressed the fears of many in the civil rights community when he said about *Miller v. Johnson,* "I really fear this court is sending us back to the dark days of the 19th century."[29] Despite concerns that adding whites to these districts would make it impossible for the minority legislators to win reelection,[30] only one black legislator left Congress following successful *Shaw* challenges. Cleo Fields (LA-4) believed that with a population less than one-third black and the prospect of facing a Republican incumbent he had such poor prospects for winning that he did not seek another term but instead ran for governor. Although he made it into the runoff, he polled only 37 percent of the vote in the second round against Republican

Mike Foster.[31] In the other redrawn districts, black incumbents continued to win reelection throughout the remainder of the decade by putting together biracial coalitions. Black incumbents' ability to replace black supporters who had been removed from the districts with white votes indicates that growing numbers of southern white voters will support the candidacy of a minority candidate.[32]

The one Latina whose district was changed, Nydia Velázquez, won additional terms with overwhelming majorities even though the Hispanic percentage in her district declined by 8 percentage points. In Texas's Twenty-Ninth District, the Anglo Democrat continued to win as the district lost a quarter of its Hispanic population.

Toward the end of the 1990s, the Supreme Court addressed DOJ's requirement that jurisdictions making Section 5 submissions devise plans that would withstand a Section 2 challenge. The police jury (the equivalent of county commission in other states) of Bossier Parish, Louisiana, submitted a new plan for its twelve districts in 1991. DOJ approved the plan even though none of the districts had a black majority. About fifteen months later, the Bossier Parish school board submitted a plan identical to that of the police jury, but by this time the local chapter of the National Association for the Advancement of Colored People (NAACP) had come up with an alternative that had two majority-black districts. DOJ rejected the school board plan, citing the new information provided by the NAACP chapter. The school board challenged DOJ's authority to reject a plan that was not guilty of retrogression. The previous plan had no majority-black districts and neither did the new one. When the case reached the Supreme Court, the Court reasserted the *Beer* nonretrogression standard from a generation earlier.[33] All that jurisdictions need do to secure preclearance was to avoid making the situation for minorities any worse in the new plan. Congress had not added Section 2 considerations to Section 5 reviews when it renewed the Voting Rights Act in 1982, which led the Court to believe that the standard from *Beer* remained unchanged. The DOJ argument that it made no sense to approve a plan that could then be successfully challenged under Section 2 did not convince a majority of the Court.

Is Proportionality Sufficient?

DOJ had used Section 2 to force some states to maximize the number of heavily minority districts. In *Johnson v. DeGrandy*, the Supreme Court rejected a lower court decision that called on Florida to maximize the number of Hispanic districts in the state house.[34] Although, as noted earlier, Section 2 did not require jurisdictions to have a number of minority districts roughly proportional to the minority's share of the population, the Supreme Court relied heavily on proportionality in supporting the plan from the state legislature rather than that of the minority plaintiffs. Even though plaintiffs' alternative plans would have created an additional predominantly Hispanic district, the Court ruled that unnecessary since both Latinos and blacks dominated a number of districts roughly proportional to their share of the Dade County population. Justice Souter's opinion observed: "One may suspect vote dilution from political famine, but one is not entitled to suspect (much less infer) dilution from mere failure to guarantee a political feast."

In *DeGrandy*, the Court also had to wrestle with the problem of two sizable minorities. One way in which to create an additional Latino district would have divided an African American concentration. The Court found the state's plan, which did not subdivide blacks, acceptable.

Gingles's First Prong

The discussion thus far of Section 2 has involved efforts to link geographically disparate concentrations of a single minority. Underlying the *Shaw*-type challenges has been the first prong of *Gingles*, which requires that the minority group be sufficiently *compact* and numerous to form the majority in a district. With the *Shaw* cases restricting state efforts to combine geographically dispersed concentrations of a single minority, a question that has arisen is whether geographically proximate populations of *differing* ethnic groups can form the basis for a Section 2 suit challenging a districting plan. For example, assume that neither African Americans nor Latinos are sufficiently numerous to constitute a majority within a district but if united the combined population of the two minorities would be a majority. Would a jurisdiction be obligated to draw a district in which the combined minority groups constituted a majority?

Courts will not assume that diverse minority groups share common interests; plaintiffs must prove that they do. For plaintiffs to prevail they must demonstrate that the two (or more) minorities do indeed share political preferences in elections.[35] Proof of shared candidate preferences is easier in general elections than in primaries or nonpartisan contests. With the major exception of Cuban-Americans in south Florida, most Latinos join African Americans and Asian Americans in supporting Democratic candidates in general elections. However, in primaries and non-partisan elections such as are often used in municipalities, Hispanic voters often support an Anglo who is running against an African American.[36] This phenomenon appeared repeatedly during the 2008 Democratic presidential primaries, in which Hillary

Clinton typically attracted heavy support from Latinos in her unsuccessful contest against Barack Obama.

Jose Garza, an attorney with the Mexican-American Legal Defense and Education Fund, noted the differences between blacks and Latinos, warning: "I think public-interest applicants have to be cognizant of the fact that our goals will not always be in lock step."[37] A number of factors influence the degree to which African American and Latino voters join forces.[38] Interethnic conflicts become particularly fierce when two groups share living space, especially if the population will sustain the creation of a district dominated by one group or the other but not two districts in which each ethnic group could dominate one. The example of Houston's Twenty-Ninth District as drawn in the early 1990s demonstrates the difficulty of separating Latino and black residents even when the population is sufficiently large. The plan created a 60 percent Hispanic origin population Twenty-Ninth District along with an Eighteenth District in which blacks constituted a slight majority. As shown in figure 3.3, the black district wrapped around much of the Twenty-Ninth District and neither district had readily identifiable boundaries.[39]

Section 5 Revisited

The evidence that reducing minority concentrations in congressional districts did not result in the defeat of minority incumbents encouraged some minority state legislators to rethink how heavily minority district populations needed to be. Back in the 1970s, many believed that for African Americans to control an election outcome their share of the population needed to be around 65 percent.[40] The rationale for this belief was that the minority population tended to be younger than the white population, that minority adults registered to vote at lower rates than whites, and that among registrants minorities turned out at lower rates than whites. By the early 1990s, DOJ did not push to have minorities constitute approximately two-thirds of a district's population but instead required that minorities make up a majority of the voting age population in order to satisfy *Gingles*'s first prong. In 2001, DOJ sought unsuccessfully to force Georgia to beef up the minority percentage in three senate districts, as will be discussed later.[41]

In 2009, the Supreme Court had to deal with a different aspect of the numerosity standard. The North Carolina constitution forbids the splitting of a county. When this "whole-county provision" was applied to District 18, it resulted in a district 35.33 percent black in its voting age population (VAP). Prior to the 2001 redistricting, the district had a black majority, but population shifts made it impossible to avoid lowering the black percentage. Plaintiffs wanted a 39.36 percent black VAP, but that would have necessitated split-

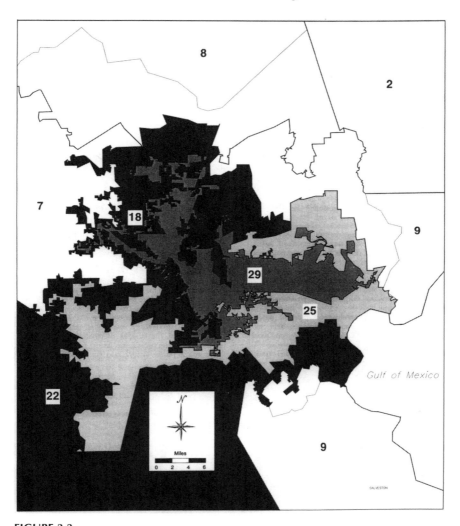

FIGURE 3.3.
Texas Districts 18 and 29 as drawn in 1992 to separate blacks and Hispanics.
Source: Congressional Districts in the 1990s: A Portrait of America. Washington, DC: CQ Press, Inc., 1993,
    p. 715. Reprinted with the permission of CQ Press Inc.

ting a county. The plaintiffs argued that Section 2 of the Voting Rights Act
took precedence over the "whole-county provision." The state split Pender
County to create the blacker district, and that led to the challenge heard by
the Supreme Court. The trial court considered District 18 at 39 percent black
to be a *de facto* majority-black district, since enough whites would support
the candidate preferred by African Americans to elect that individual. While

the Supreme Court acknowledged that states could create districts in which a coalition of blacks and whites would elect the black-preferred candidate, it refused to find that Section 2 *required* the creation of such districts.[42] The Court observed: "Section 2 does not impose on those who draw election districts a duty to give minority voters the most potential or the best potential to elect a candidate by attracting crossover voters."

When Party Trumps Race

Following the 1990 Census, many minority group leaders had as their top priority maximizing the number of districts in which their preferences had a high probability of winning. Both the career civil servants and the political appointees at DOJ supported those ambitions.[43] The careerists in DOJ's Voting Rights Section charged with conducting Section 5 reviews wanted to see minorities elected and eagerly enforced calls for higher minority concentrations in preclearance jurisdictions, as described earlier. Bush administration political appointees had a different motivation. They recognized that creating additional majority-minority districts could promote Republican ambitions, and the top Republican appointee acknowledged that some of his decisions were politically motivated. John Dunne, assistant attorney general for civil rights, acknowledged:

> You know, I can't tell you that I was sort of like a monk hidden away in a monastery with only the most pure of intentions. I am a Republican. I was part of a Republican administration. And to tell you that at no moment during the course of my [career], the discharge of my responsibilities, was I totally immune or insensitive to political consideration, I don't think would justify anybody's belief.[44]

To design heavily minority districts necessitated aggregating minorities from surrounding districts and, especially in the South, as districts adjacent to new black ones became whiter they also became more Republican.[45] In southern legislatures, Republicans frequently joined African American members to push plans maximizing the number of majority black seats. For this reason the Louisiana district shown in figure 3.1 was characterized as "the illegitimate child of an illicit political love affair between blacks and Republicans."[46]

As already shown, African Americans increased their share of congressional and state legislative seats in the South following the 1990 round of redistricting. Their partners in pushing for plans that maximized the number of districts having black majorities also benefited. Most estimates place the number of congressional seats gained by Republicans because of the racial gerrymandering at between nine and seventeen. Both minorities and

Republicans gained from the race-based new plans, while white Democrats lost seats.[47] By 1995, all five southern congressional districts represented by Democrats in 1991 that lost 10 percent or more of their black population had elected a Republican.[48] David Lublin goes so far as to say, "The most telling criticism of racial redistricting may be that it undermines the representation of minority interests even as it assures the election of more racial minorities to the U.S. House of Representatives."[49] The conservative Republicans who replaced moderate white Democrats rarely supported items of the African American political agenda.

The creation of a majority-black district in Alabama demonstrates how that action helped Republicans in adjoining districts. The legislature more than doubled the black percentage in the Seventh District so that it became 67 percent African American and elected a black member of Congress. District 7, shown in figure 3.4, extended a long arm into Jefferson County to reach Birmingham's African Americans. The new Seventh District shared a boundary with all of Alabama's other districts except the Fifth. As table 3.4 shows, with the creation of District 7 the black percentage in District 6 dropped by 28 percentage points, while in District 2 it fell by 8 percentage points. In the first election held in the new districts, moderate white Democrat Ben Erdreich, who saw critical black support removed from the Sixth District, lost to a Republican challenger by a 52 to 45 percent margin. In 1990, senior Republican William Dickinson had eked out a 4,426-vote victory in District 2. When he retired, Democrats saw this as a potential pickup and nominated George Wallace Jr. The son of the former four-term governor might have won the open seat had the district remained roughly one-third black. He lost by fewer than 3,600 votes in the substantially whiter district, which had lost Montgomery's black population.

The impact of bleaching surrounding districts in order to concentrate African Americans in districts in which they would constitute a majority had an even greater impact on the partisan makeup of Georgia's congressional delegation. Before the 1992 redistricting, Georgia had eight white Democrats, one black Democrat, and a single Republican. After gaining a seat and going through the redistricting process, which required three submissions before the DOJ gave its approval, Georgia had three majority-black districts; in 1992 each of these elected an African American. The 1992 election also saw Republicans gain three seats. As table 3.5 shows, Republicans picked up the First District, where the black population dropped from 32 percent to 23 percent. They also won District 3, where the black population fell by 17 percentage points, and District 4, where it was cut in half down to 12 percent. The 1994 election, which produced the first Republican majority in the House since 1954, saw Republicans win the Eighth District, where the black population

FIGURE 3.4.
Alabama's congressional districts as of 1993.
© Election Data Services, Inc. (www.electiondataservices.com)

TABLE 3.4
Racial Makeup and Partisanship of Alabama
Congressional Districts before and after 1992 Redistricting

District	% Black	1991 Incumbent	% Black	1993 Incumbent
1	30	Republican	29	Republican
2	32	Republican	24	Republican
3	28	White Democrat	26	White Democrat
4	7	White Democrat	7	White Democrat
5	15	White Democrat	15	White Democrat
6	37	White Democrat	9	Republican
7	30	White Democrat	67	Black Democrat

Source: Prepared by author.

had been reduced by 15 percentage points, and the Tenth District, where it had been cut by 5 percentage points. Republicans also defeated the Democratic incumbent in the Seventh District—although not because of racial change, since the black population inched up from 9 to 13 percent.

Political scientists John Petrocik and Scott Desposato offer a different explanation for why racial gerrymandering hurt Democrats.[50] They explain that white Democratic members of Congress became vulnerable as a result of the new plans swapping out large numbers of their constituents. The negative

TABLE 3.5
Changes in the Racial Makeup of Georgia
Congressional Districts Following the 1992 Redistricting

District	% Black	1991 Incumbent	% Black	1993 Incumbent
1	32	White Democrat	23	Republican
2	37	White Democrat	57	Black Democrat
3	35	White Democrat	18	Republican
4	25	White Democrat	12	Republican
5	67	Black Democrat	62	Black Democrat
6	20	Republican	6	Republican
7	9	White Democrat	13	Republican*
8	36	White Democrat	21	Republican*
9	5	White Democrat	4	Republican**
10	23	White Democrat	18	Republican*
11	new district		64	Black Democrat

*Changed from Democrat to Republican in 1994.
**Incumbent elected as a Democrat but changed parties in 1995.

Source: Prepared by author.

evaluations of the Democratic Party in 1992 and 1994 coupled with many voters lacking familiarity with their Democratic incumbents wiped out a number of these Democrats whom redistricting had made marginal. The Petrocik-Desposato explanation concurs with research showing that incumbents usually do less well with voters newly added to their districts than with those whom they have previously represented and with whom they have cultivated a personal attachment.[51]

The loss of support whether from white or black Democratic voters proved especially devastating to their party in the Deep South. As table 3.6 shows, in the late 1990s the five Deep South states had only four white Democrats in Congress. In 1990 these states had sent twenty-four white Democrats to Congress. After the next redistricting, when Georgia Democrats gerrymandered the state in hopes of gaining four seats, they managed to add two white Democrats. In 2008, white Democrats won open seats in Alabama and Mississippi. In 2009 the Deep South had eight white Democrats along with seven black Democrats, the first time since 1995 that black Democrats had not outnumbered white Democrats in this subregion.

Creation of additional minority districts had less impact outside the South. David Lublin attributes the difference to the presence of liberal whites available to replace blacks removed from a district, so that bleached districts in the

TABLE 3.6
Composition of Deep South White Democratic Districts

District	% Black
Democratic in 1997	
AL-5	15
LA-7	24
MS-5	20
SC-5	31
Democratic after 2004	
GA-8	32
GA-12	45
Democratic gains in 2008	
AL-2	33
MS-1	26

*Democrat Donald Cazoyoux won a special election in May 2008 in LA-6 but lost to Republican Bill Cassidy in November.

Source: Created by author.

North continue to elect Democrats.[52] Liberals are in too short a supply to be substituted for blacks in the South.

Racial redistricting exacted a cost on southern Democratic state legislators. Lublin estimates that of 105 seats lost by Democrats between 1990 and 1994, 45 could be attributed to redistricting.[53] These losses cost Democrats control of some southern legislative chambers that had been majority Democratic for generations. Lublin and Voss estimate that redistricting cost Democrats the control of both the South Carolina and Virginia houses and enabled Republicans to hold on to their majority in the North Carolina house longer.[54] In some other states redistricting kept Democrats from making gains in 1992 in the state legislature. Another consequence of the racial gerrymandering which resulted in more Republicans winning state legislative seats was to help the GOP develop a farm team of experienced officeholders who, in time, could successfully compete for higher offices.[55]

Not All Bleaching Helped Republicans

Texas provides an exception to the general proposition that newly bleached districts elected Republicans. In the Lone Star State, Representative Martin Frost (D) designed a plan that extracted blacks from Republican districts rather than Democratic districts, and Democrats maintained control of the delegation throughout the decade.[56] Table 3.7 shows the changes in the black percentage in Texas districts exclusive of the heavily Hispanic ones. The table also shows the race and ethnicity of incumbents in 1991 and two years later, once the Frost plan took effect. Of eight Republican districts, all but one saw its black percentage decline while in District 21, the black percentage remained constant at 3 percent. In District 8 the black percentage dropped by 15 points, while District 2 experienced a 9-point decline in its black population. Of thirteen districts with white Democrats, six saw their black percentage increase, while two held constant. Only four of the districts with white incumbents experienced a loss in black percentages. While the increases tended to be very small, the fact that most white Democrats found themselves no worse off in terms of their percentage of black constituents contrasts sharply with the experiences in Alabama and Georgia.

A major factor in Frost's ability to protect most of his fellow white Democrats was the presence of a number of Republican districts from which blacks could be removed.[57] Recall that Georgia had only one district with a Republican in 1991, and while the black percentage there dropped from 20 to 6 percent that could not possibly meet DOJ's demands for the creation of two new majority-black districts. Similarly, in Alabama, while both districts represented by Republicans gave up some black voters, that alone would not have sufficed to create the new majority-black Seventh District.

TABLE 3.7
Changes in Percent Black in Selected Texas Congressional Districts, 1991 to 1993

District	% Black	1991 Districts Incumbent	% Black	1993 Districts Incumbent
1	18	White Democrat	18	White Democrat
2	15	White Democrat	17	White Democrat
3	7	Republican	4	Republican
4	13	White Democrat	8	White Democrat
5	22	White Democrat	16	White Democrat
6	9	Republican	5	Republican
7	7	Republican	6	Republican
8	20	Republican	5	Republican
9	22	White Democrat	22	White Democrat
10	10	White Democrat	11	White Democrat
12	16	White Democrat	8	White Democrat
13	5	White Democrat	8	White Democrat
14	10	White Democrat	11	White Democrat
17	3	White Democrat	4	White Democrat
18	35	Black Democrat	51	Black Democrat
19	6	Republican	2	Republican
21	3	Republican	3	Republican
22	17	Republican	8	Republican
24	29	White Democrat	19	White Democrat
25	24	White Democrat	27	White Democrat
26	7	Republican	4	Republican
30	New district		50	Black Democrat

Source: Prepared by author using data from *The Almanac of American Politics*. Michael Barone and Grant Ujifusa, *The Almanac of American Politics, 1992*, and *The Almanac of American Politics, 1994*. (Washington, D.C.: National Journal, 1993 and 1995, respectively.)

Changing Racial Composition and Roll-Call Voting

Not only did the affirmative action gerrymanders imposed by DOJ in the early 1990s change the composition of legislative chambers, they may have affected the voting choices made by sitting legislators. While bleaching districts in order to create new majority-minority ones wiped out some white Democrats, others survived. With fewer black constituents, these white Democrats confronted a more conservative constituency and may have shifted to the right to better represent the median voter in their new district. If white Democrats who lost some of their black constituents became less responsive to African American policy concerns, that plus the new Republicans could result in a loss in substantive representation that could offset gains in descriptive representation attributable to the creation of majority-minority districts. Former Congressional Black Caucus member Craig Washington registered his concern about the potential trade-off: "I would rather have three white representatives who vote with me and one who votes against me, than one black who votes with me and three whites who vote against me."[58]

Scholars have found evidence to bolster the concerns articulated by Washington. Overby and Cosgrove, who examined all members of Congress and not just southerners, report a strong relationship between changes in a district's racial composition and the roll-call behavior of Democrats and rural legislators.[59] Sharpe and Garand find that white members of Congress who got much whiter districts following redistricting became significantly more conservative.[60] Modest changes in the racial makeup of a district did not trigger a change in legislator behavior. Southern members became significantly more liberal as the percent black in their districts increased. On the other hand, Bullock observed no change in the voting behavior of southern white members of Congress that could be linked to changes in the racial makeup of their districts.[61] Shotts contends that the injection of new minority legislators more than offset any shifts to the right by white members of Congress, so that delegations transformed by affirmative action gerrymanders emerged as more liberal than before.[62]

New Decade, New Approach

By the beginning of the twenty-first century, minority priorities in some southern states had shifted. During the course of the 1990s, Democrats, who had controlled every southern legislature for decades, lost both chambers in Florida, South Carolina, and Virginia, and the Texas senate, and Republicans controlled the North Carolina house for two terms. Since, with rare exceptions, African American legislators belong to the Democratic Party, when Democrats lose control of a chamber, black legislators lose influence and their ability to achieve the policy preferences of their constituents suffers. In many chambers only members of the majority party chair committees. Even in chambers with a tradition of allowing minority party members to chair some committees, the majority party's leadership controls the agenda. Stark trade-offs had accompanied the gains of the early 1990s in descriptive representation. "What after all, was the point of increasing black representation only to tip control of the legislature to an opposing party openly hostile to almost any remedy to past and present discrimination?"[63]

Shifts in political control to the GOP, loss of political influence by black legislators, and greater willingness among whites to vote for African Americans came together to alter black legislators' strategy following the 2000 Census. Previously, blacks had objected to seeing African American concentrations split to bolster the political fortunes of white Democrats.[64] Now black caucuses no longer sought to maximize the number of seats likely to elect African Americans. Even the inducement of a new district likely to elect an African American to Congress from Houston failed to win the support of most members of the Texas Legislative Black Caucus for the DeLay plan. In Texas and elsewhere the priorities became (1) to maintain African American incumbents and (2) to redistribute excess black voters so as to bolster the political fortunes of white Democrats.

That African American legislators accepted smaller black concentrations in their districts may stem in part from scholarly work showing that districts could be less heavily minority without endangering the ability of black voters to elect their preferences. The lower threshold for a secure black district varies. Representative Melvin Watt (D-NC) explains that he can win in a less heavily black district than would be needed by his colleague in North Carolina's other black district because whites in Watt's urban district are more likely to support an African American candidate than are the whites in the rural First District.[65]

David Epstein has contributed to multiple publications making the point that African Americans have a better-than-even chance of electing their choices in districts less than 50 percent black VAP. To have a better-than-even chance of electing a black to Congress from the South, districts need be only about 40 percent black adults.[66] To have at least a 0.5 probability of electing a black to the South Carolina senate, the district needed to be only 47 percent black.[67] In the Georgia General Assembly, Epstein estimated that just over 44 percent black adults in a district sufficed for African Americans to have at least an even chance of winning open seats.[68] At 50 percent black VAP, the probability of African Americans electing a preferred candidate in Georgia rose to 75 percent.[69] The experiences following *Shaw v. Reno* reinforced Epstein's estimates. As reported in table 3.2, whiter districts continued sending African Americans to Congress.

African American legislators approved decreasing the black VAP in Georgia's twelve majority-black senate districts by an average of 10 percentage points. DOJ objected to three 51 percent black VAP districts, when Georgia sought a declaratory judgment for its 2001 redistricting plans. When this case came before the Supreme Court in *Georgia v. Ashcroft*, the Court initiated a dramatic departure from the nonretrogression standard, and in so doing adopted the approach suggested by Bruce Cain, which indicated two acceptable ways for minority influence to come into a legislative chamber.[70] "Indeed, the state's choice ultimately may rest on a political choice of whether substantive or descriptive representation is preferable," wrote Justice O'Connor.[71] The Court said that jurisdictions could pursue either of two paths. One was the traditional approach of maintaining or increasing racial concentrations. Alternatively, jurisdictions could have fewer districts that had overwhelming concentrations of minority populations in conjunction with a number of "influence" districts having minority populations between 25 and 50 percent. An influence district, while unlikely to elect a member of the minority group, nonetheless would have a sufficient minority population to determine the outcome of the election. Consequently the winner, probably a white Democrat, would be responsive to minority concerns. In support of the proposition that white Democratic legislators would support black policy goals, Carol Swain, a professor of law and political science at Vanderbilt University, has shown that after controlling for the percentage of blacks in a constituency, white and black Democrats had very similar votes on roll calls.[72]

Ashcroft had the potential to prevent the ratchet effect produced by *Beer*'s nonretrogression standard. If Section 5 is interpreted to mean that the minority percentage can never be reduced by a new plan, then at a minimum minority concentrations will remain constant in each majority black or Latino district and, more likely, will increase. Table 3.8 shows the ratchet effect as the percent African American tends to increase over time in the four southern congressional districts covered by Section 5 that elected black members of Congress prior to 1992. The first two African Americans elected to the House in 1972 both represented districts less than 45 percent black. DOJ demands boosted Georgia's Fifth District to 65 percent black prior to the 1982 election. Texas's Eighteenth District remained virtually unchanged with 41 percent black population, although its Latino percentage increased. The Texas district then became 10 percentage points blacker with the 1990s redistricting, while the Fifth District in Atlanta dipped slightly to 62 percent black. During the 1980s, African Americans won seats in Louisiana and Mississippi. The Louisiana district was 45 percent black, but when it was redrawn in the early 1990s its black population rose to 61 percent. The Second District of Mississippi was drawn to be 54 percent black at the beginning of the decade; litigation prompted a remapping that boosted the black percentage to 58 percent, at which point Mike Espy, an African American, won the seat. This district also became blacker in the 1990s, as its black percentage went to 63 percent. The 2003 districts saw Mississippi-2 remain at 63 percent black, while Louisiana-2 increased to 64 percent black. John Lewis's district lost some of its black population in the plan drawn in 2001 and litigated in *Ashcroft*. Lewis supported the reduction in his district's black percentage. The black population in Texas-18 increased to 42 percent from the 40 percent that the district had following *Bush v. Vera*, which found the 51 percent black district to be the product of an unconstitutional racial gerrymander.

TABLE 3.8
Ratchet Effect in Southern Section 5 Congressional
Districts that Elected African Americans before 1992

	Percent Black			
	1973	*1983*	*1993*	*2003*
GA-5	44	65	62	56
TX-18	42	41	51	42
LA-2		45	61	64
MS-2		54*	63	63

*58% black by the time an African American won the seat.

Source: Black percentages for 1973, 1993, and 2003 from Michael Barone and Grant Ujifusa, *The Almanac of American Politics,* 1974, 1994, and 2004 (Washington, DC: National Journal, 1973, 1993, and 2003). The 1980s percentage is from Alan Ehrenhalt, ed., *Politics in America,* 1984 *and Politics in America: The 100th Congress* (Washington, DC: Congressional Quarterly Press, 1987).

In the challenge to the Texas plan drawn by Republicans in 2003, the plaintiffs who represented Democrats, African Americans, and Latinos sought to use the Supreme Court's positive statements about influence districts in *Ashcroft.* The plaintiffs contended unsuccessfully that districts in which either Latinos or blacks constituted a sizable minority and in which Democrats won election should be protected against the Republican gerrymander that removed Democrats from these districts.[73] Had the plaintiffs' position prevailed, then it might have become impossible to reduce minority concentrations in any district represented by a Democrat in which the minority population exceeded 25 percent. Acceptance of the plaintiffs' position might extend the nonretrogression approach to influence districts. Since Republicans struggle to win districts more than 30 percent black, interpreting the Voting Rights Act as protecting influence districts would limit the prospects for new plans that would increase Republican holdings.[74]

The impact of *Ashcroft* may be short-lived. When extending Section 5 of the VRA in 2006, Congress adopted language indicating that the Court's opinion was not in keeping with congressional intent. Consequently, courts are likely to return to the nonretrogression standard of *Beer. Beer's* ratcheting problem could produce over-concentration of minorities so that in a district more of the minority vote is "wasted," since it is not necessary to determine the outcome of the election.

Brunell's previously mentioned advocacy for one-party districts sees nothing wrong with ratcheting up minority concentrations. With African Americans giving 90 percent or more of their votes to Democratic candidates, the more heavily black the district, the larger the share of its residents who will be pleased with the election result. Brunell says of overwhelmingly black and overwhelmingly Democratic districts, "these districts are, in many ways, the districts that should be emulated around the country."[75] From this perspective the congressional plan used in Georgia in 1992 and 1994 with its three majority-black districts succeeded, since those three districts housed almost 62 percent of the state's African Americans, who sent three black members to Congress with overwhelming majorities. As noted above, by 2000 many black legislators would have opposed Brunell's proposal.[76]

Controversy

Arguments For

Section 5 of the VRA has been the most successful piece of civil rights legislation ever passed. It quickly eliminated barriers to black registration and voting[77] and has prevented cracking of minority concentrations in the course of redistricting.

Amending Section 2 in 1982 created a tool for requiring the replacement of multimember and at-large electors with single-member districts. Single-member systems are not designed to achieve proportional representation. Therefore in order to include representatives from minority groups it may be necessary to design districts likely to elect those kinds of legislators. Taking affirmative steps to create districts having a high concentration of minorities is appropriate.

In addition to the symbolic significance of descriptive representation, representatives from minority groups change the legislature. Minorities raise issues that white legislators ignore and thereby change the institution's agenda. Black members of Congress more often sponsor legislation and amendments with a racial emphasis than do whites who represent sizable minority populations.[78] Black members also differ from whites with large black constituencies in devoting more attention to racial concerns, giving racial matters greater emphasis in their newsletters, and include more pictures of blacks in their newsletters.

Scholars differ on the question of whether black legislators vote differently than white legislators who belong to the same party as the black legislator and have a large black population in their district. Carol Swain found little difference in the voting behavior of U.S. House black and white Democrats who have sizable African American constituencies.[79] On the other hand, Kenny Whitby argues that black Democrats are more responsive to black policy preferences than white members of Congress.[80]

Districts designed to elect minorities usually deliver. African Americans who live in districts that elect black legislators differ from blacks living in districts having white representatives. Blacks represented by an African American, as compared with those represented by whites, know more about their legislators' records and are more likely to recall the name of their legislator, to contact him or her, and to give the legislator high job approval.[81] At times when most black voters cast ballots for candidates who lose the presidency and their state's senatorial and gubernatorial elections, U.S. House elections are the only high-profile offices for which most African Americans back winners.[82] Federal pressure to create majority-black districts has had the effect of increasing the numbers of African Americans who have the experience of backing a winner, an experience that has positive consequences for the political system.

Arguments Against

The VRA stands as a unique alteration of traditional federalism. The preclearance provision of Section 5 infringes on state sovereignty by requiring all or parts of sixteen states to obtain the approval of the national government before implementing new districting plans. At times DOJ has forced states to take actions that the courts subsequently found to be unconstitutional.

Rewriting Section 2 of the Voting Rights Act to make it easier for minorities to achieve descriptive representation constituted a major shift from the traditional emphasis in American politics on individual rights to a notion of group rights. Replacing the need to prove an intent to discriminate with a results or effects test forces jurisdictions in which minorities do not have a share of seats proportionate to their share of the population to design majority-minority districts.[83] Expecting minorities to have a proportionate share of the seats is unrealistic, since representatives in American collegial bodies compete in single-member districts and not in multimember districts with electoral rules intended to produce proportional representation, as are used throughout continental Europe.

The careful separation of white and minority voters in the course of implementing Section 2 in the early 1990s hastened the partisan transformation of the South, a criticism if you are a Democrat but a positive result for Republicans. Bleaching surrounding districts to create the new majority-minority districts opened the way for a number of new Republicans in southern congressional delegations and state legislatures.

Republicans elected from bleached districts have little incentive to support initiatives favored by the newly elected African Americans, since the Republicans' districts have few minority voters and those who do live there infrequently vote for GOP candidates. Freshman Republicans elected from bleached districts had especially conservative voting records.[84] Consequently, southern legislatures may have become more conservative, as some minority legislators but even greater numbers of conservative Republicans replaced moderate Democrats.

Redistricting is the most political activity undertaken by a legislature. In addition to the partisan tensions that regularly accompany redistricting and the desperate struggles of some legislators to save their careers and the opportunistic efforts of others to secure more compatible districts, the early 1990s saw racial tensions fanned in the struggle to meet DOJ requirements and/or to avoid litigation. Months of conflict during which blacks accused their white colleagues of racism while white Democrats grew increasingly frustrated with their minority colleagues for collaborating with Republicans left residues of racial distrust that persisted and infected debates on policy issues that in the past had not had racial overtones.

Rebuttal

While a consensus exists that the racial gerrymanders cost Democrats congressional seats, a couple of dissenters claim that Republicans made no gains as a result of the new districts.[85] Kenneth Shotts dissents from the claim that increasing the numbers of Republicans in southern congressional delegations created an environment more hostile to minority policy preferences.[86] His research shows delegations to be more liberal following the racial gerrymanders of the 1990s.

Conclusions

The Voting Rights Act and subsequent court decisions have made equitable treatment of minorities second only to equal population as a consideration in districting politics. Creating equal population districts opened the way for the first African Americans to win legislative seats in the modern South. The ranks of minorities expanded once most of the South had to obtain federal approval before implementing new districting plans. The authority conferred under Section 5 of the VRA enabled DOJ to prevent gerrymanders designed to minimize black representation. In time these protections were extended to states that had concentrated language minorities.

Amending Section 2 of the Voting Rights Act extended the reach of federal law nationwide and initially allowed minorities to challenge hundreds of local arrangements where at-large or multimember districting thwarted minorities' political ambitions. DOJ used Section 2 to require that jurisdictions subject to Section 5 maximize the number of districts likely to elect minorities. Other states adopted similar approaches in order to head off litigation.

Ultimately, the Supreme Court found that a number of the racially gerrymandered districts in the early 1990s violated the Equal Protection Clause, since the major consideration in drawing these districts had been to separate blacks from whites. The districts drawn to replace those struck down by the courts had lesser concentrations of minorities yet, with one exception, continued to elect minority legislators.

The ability of minorities to win in some districts that were not majority-minority emboldened black state legislators to support reductions in the black percentages in districts. They embraced post-2000 plans that redistributed black voters in order to help white Democrats win adjoining districts. The success of the Democratic Party had become more significant than maximizing the number of black legislators, since when Republicans won legislative majorities, black political influence declined precipitously.

While the Supreme Court indicated a willingness to modify the nonretrogression standard for reviewing redistricting plans, Congress stepped in to undo that decision. Consequently, it seems likely that in the redistricting to follow the next census, DOJ may require jurisdictions to maximize their number of majority-minority districts and to require that minority concentrations not be reduced in those districts.

4

The Populations Are Equal and Minorities Have Not Been Discriminated Against. Now What?

THE TWO MOST IMPORTANT FACTORS that must be considered when drawing districts are the attainment of population equality among districts and the equitable treatment of minorities. The need for population equality is based on the Equal Protection Clause of the Constitution's Fourteenth Amendment. Concern about the treatment of minorities grows out of the Voting Rights Acts. These are legally enforceable. This chapter examines elements secondary to the first two elements, although states frequently stipulate that some of these factors be considered when drawing new maps. These factors include contiguity, compactness, respect for political boundaries, maintenance of communities of interest, and the protection of incumbents.

While it has proven possible to achieve equal populations among districts while simultaneously protecting the interests of minorities, as mapmakers consider additional factors it becomes impossible to achieve the whole range of ideals. As shown in some of the maps in the previous chapter, the effort to create minority districts frequently resulted in ungainly-looking districts. Districts that score poorly on measures of compactness have often split counties or other political units. Recall that historically counties were the basis for districts and rarely did congressional plans divide counties except in the largest urban areas. In this chapter, we will frequently note how various standards come into conflict.

Contiguity

Contiguity is the idea that a person could go from one end of the district to the other without leaving the district. With a few exceptions like the Upper Peninsula of Michigan and Virginia's Delmarva Peninsula, legislative districts have usually met the contiguity expectation. In 2001, twenty-seven states specifically required that congressional districts be contiguous.[1] Even when not set out as a consideration, other than instances where counties are divided by water, contiguity is generally honored. Louisiana's Saint Martin's Parish is the only major geographic unit of which we are aware that consists of two parts separated by another political unit (in this case, Iberia Parish projects between the two parts of Saint Martin). The contiguity requirement makes it inappropriate to create a predominantly black district by simply designating the heavily black areas in a series of cities as parts of a single district without linking them by a land corridor. To achieve at least a claim of contiguity, North Carolina's District 12 in 1993 extended across much of the Piedmont from Durham to Gastonia.

Districts such as North Carolina 12 stretched the concept of contiguity to the point that critics claim that it had been violated. North Carolina's Twelfth District, which appears in figure 3.2, seems to bisect the Sixth District. Portions of the Sixth District lie above and below the Twelfth, with components of each district united through touch-point contiguity. That is, at places these districts achieve contiguity in the way that diagonal black squares on a checker board are contiguous at a single point. At that same point, diagonal red squares are also contiguous at a single point. In the Four Corners region of the United States, New Mexico and Utah have touch-point contiguity, as do

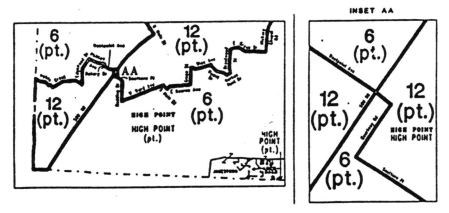

FIGURE 4.1.
Examples of touch-point contiguity in 1992 North Carolina congressional map.
Source: U.S. Bureau of the Census, 1993, GP-30.

Colorado and Arizona. Figure 4.1 shows two instances of touch-point conti-guity in North Carolina, as Districts 6 and 12 cross each other on diagonals.

A second practice that has led to questions about contiguity involves the use of water. Traditionally, water contiguity has been accepted as necessary to connect an island to the mainland or to link Michigan's Upper Peninsula to the rest of the state. Some recent plans used water to link parts of a district while avoiding including populations that differed from the majority of those within the district. For example, Virginia's Third District, which was drawn as a majority-black district in 1991, used the channel of the James River as a connector. In places the district was only as wide as the river and therefore avoided including anyone who lived on either bank, as it linked heavily black neighborhoods in Norfolk and Newport News with the black portions of Richmond and some rural counties upstream. The river was not simply some-thing that the district crossed—the district actually went down the waterway, leading some to refer to this as "duck contiguity."

Figure 4.2 shows examples of duck contiguity in the Maryland congres-sional plan used during the 2000s. Districts 1, 2, and 3 each have water

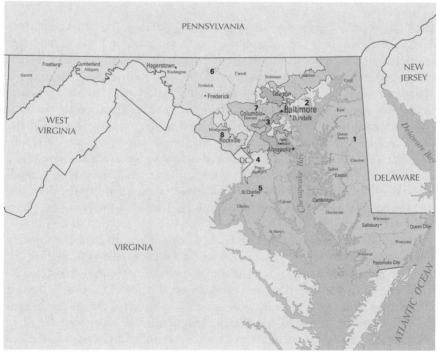

FIGURE 4.2.
Maryland congressional districts showing examples of duck contiguity.
Source: www.nationalatlas.gov.

contiguity as they connect across portions of the Chesapeake Bay waterways. The water contiguity in District 3 is minor as it reaches across Patapico Bay. The Second District does not come as close to having land contiguity as the Third District, while the First District extends clear across the Chesapeake Bay to link Republican voters between Annapolis and Baltimore with conservatives on the Eastern Shore.

A less controversial aspect of contiguity ties parts of a district together by crossing unpopulated territory. A narrow neck may link two parts of a district by going across the runway of an airport, a park, or an unpopulated portion of a military base. On maps these show up as narrow necks that connect two population concentrations. At times these may be desirable because they bring together communities of interest that have sprung up on either side of uninhabitable property. At other times, a neck or duck contiguity may be used to pack political partisans into a single district, thereby reducing their influence.

Compactness

The most compact geometric shape is a circle. But it would be impossible to have a state's legislative districts made up of a series of circles. A second-best geometric shape for compactness would be a square or a rectangle. Nineteen states required compact congressional districts following the 2000 Census.[2] Many people believe that having compact districts is desirable because it facilitates campaigning. A compact district may make it easier for voters to know which district they live in and, related to that, who represents them. In the noncompact districts shown in chapters 3 and 6, one could readily understand how voters could be confused as to who represented them. When a neighborhood is divided, voters may see signs for candidates along one side of the street on which they live and yet discover upon getting to the polls that they do not live in the district of the candidates whose advertising they have seen.

In *Shaw v. Reno*, Justice Sandra Day O'Connor emphasized her concern about the shape of North Carolina's Twelfth District. This long, skinny district, which stretched across 160 miles of the Carolina Piedmont, seemed on its face to violate the notions of compactness. Justice O'Connor observed, "We believe that reapportionment is one area in which appearances *do* matter." She went on to use highly charged language when she noted: "A reapportionment plan that includes in one district individuals who belong to the same race, but who are otherwise widely separated by geographical and political boundaries, and who may have little in common with one another but the color of their skin, bears an uncomfortable resemblance to political apartheid."

While a glance at North Carolina 12 gives a sense of a noncompact district, the assessment of compactness is not exclusively a matter of impression. Numerous measures of compactness exist.[3] From the multitude of measures of compactness, three became important considerations in the litigation that followed the *Shaw* case. For each of the measures a score of 1 would be assigned to a circular district. The smaller the value, that is as the value approaches 0, the less compact the district on any of the measures.

One of the measures of compactness, the dispersion score, first calculates the area encompassed in the smallest circle that completely surrounds a district. Then the area in the district is calculated. The dispersion score is the percent of the circle that is included in the district. A circular district would have the maximum score of 1, while a long narrow district would have a low score.

Other scores are based upon the perimeter of the district. In one popular measure, the perimeter of the district is calculated and then a circle having the circumference equal to the perimeter of the district is drawn. The perimeter score is the percentage of the area of the circle having the same perimeter as the district that is included in the district. Obviously, again, a circular district would have a score of 1. The smaller the value, the more contorted the perimeter of the district, since that yields a circle with a larger perimeter.

Other measures focus on the population and the extent to which the population of an area is included in the district. Since the plans challenged in the 1990s frequently excluded white populations as they sought to capture geographically far-flung minority populations, a measure that focuses on the share of the population in a geographic area in a district might also indicate the degree to which the district has been gerrymandered. One measure suggested putting a hypothetical rubber band around a district.[4] The population score is the percentage of the population in the area surrounded by the hypothetical rubber band that lives in the district. The rubber band measure would yield a high score for any regular geometric shape. However, a district in which portions have been cut away in order to avoid including certain populations would have a lower score.

There is no prohibition on drawing districts that score poorly on one or more of the compactness measures. However, in challenges to the districts drawn in the 1990s that raised questions of the significance accorded race, courts might consider evidence that the district scored poorly on a compactness measure as indicative that traditional districting principles had been subordinated to considerations of race. Compactness scores were also introduced in some of the litigation in the early part of the new century, but by that time, legislatures had ceased referencing race as a motivation for the maps that they created.

As table 4.1 shows, the district at the heart of the *Shaw* decision was among the least compact in the nation. North Carolina 12 ranked 433rd in terms of the dispersion score, 431st on the perimeter score, and 429th on the population score. Texas 29, a district drawn to create an Hispanic majority in Houston and invalidated in *Bush v. Vera*, had the lowest perimeter score in the nation, while the heavily black Eighteenth District, which split the city of Houston with the Twenty-Ninth, ranked 433rd. All but two of the eleven districts with the lowest perimeter scores faced legal challenges. Of the legal challenges only those to Illinois's "ear-muff district" and North Carolina 1 did not succeed, although the state redrew the latter to make it more compact. The other two districts among those with the worse perimeter scores, Texas 6 and 25, both abutted districts invalidated in *Bush v. Vera* and derived their strange shapes in large part because of the shapes given their majority-minority neighbors.

Texas 29 had such an irregular boundary that if a circle having the circumference equal to the district's perimeter were drawn, the Twenty-Ninth would fill less than 1 percent of the circle. A number of the other challenged districts would fill less than 2 percent of the circle by the district.

The other area measure, the dispersion score, in which a circle is fitted around a district, shows that some districts that scored relatively poorly would fill more than 10 percent of the circle. One exception in table 4.1 is North Carolina 12, which would fill less than 5 percent of a circle put around the district. A predominantly black district in south Florida scored as the least compact district based on the dispersion score. Although Florida 23 was the subject of a gerrymander suit, the court ruled that the challenge had come too late in the decade. Table 4.1 shows, however, that challenges succeeded against four of the eleven least compact districts on the dispersion scale.

The least compact district as calculated using the population score described above was Colorado 4. Neither this district nor the next five in terms of low population scores had to defend its plan in court. Only three districts with low scores on the population compactness measure drew a legal challenge. Of these three, Florida 23 escaped unscathed when the judge dismissed the suit.

On the population measure, even districts which ranked in the bottom fifteen in the nation included a quarter of the population in the area that would be captured if a hypothetical rubber band were to be placed around the district. Texas 18 and 29, which had some of the poorest scores in the perimeter measure, nonetheless contained approximately 40 percent of the population in the immediate vicinity of the district. The compactness measures are far

TABLE 4.1
The Least Compact Congressional Districts in 1993

District	Rank	Score
A. Perimeter Scores		
Texas 29*	435	0.008
Florida 3*	434	0.011
Texas 18*	433	0.011
Louisiana 4*	432	0.013
North Carolina 12*	431	0.014
Texas 30*	430	0.016
Texas 25	429	0.021
New York 12*	428	0.021
Texas 6	427	0.025
Illinois 4**	426	0.026
North Carolina 1**	425	0.028
Most compact: Wisconsin 5		0.718
B. Dispersion Scores		
Florida 23**	435	0.033
California 36	434	0.043
North Carolina 12*	433	0.045
Hawaii 2	432	0.052
New York 8	431	0.065
Florida 17	430	0.082
Florida 3*	429	0.111
New Jersey 13	428	0.115
New York 12*	427	0.122
Tennessee 4	426	0.124
Louisiana 4*	425	0.125
Most compact: Kentucky 6		0.641
C. Population Scores		
Colorado 4	435	0.18
Florida 20	434	0.21
Ohio 13	433	0.21
Texas 4	432	0.23
Arizona 6	431	0.24
Texas 14	430	0.25
Florida 23**	429	0.25
Florida 3*	428	0.26
North Carolina 12*	427	0.27
Texas 21	426	0.27
Most compact: Nebraska 2		0.99

*Successfully sued for being drawn predominantly on the basis of race.
**Unsuccessfully sued. The suit against Florida 23 was dismissed because it was filed so late in the decade. The court found for the state (defendant) in Illinois 4.

Source: Created by the author using figures in David C. Huckabee, *Congressional Districts: Objectively Evaluating Shapes*, CRS, Report for Congress 94-449 GOV, May 24, 1994.

from identical, although some districts like North Carolina 12 and Florida 3 score poorly on all of them.

The practice of splitting counties and carefully including some populations while excluding others, which was perfected as part of the racial gerrymanders of the 1990s, provided models for partisan gerrymandering in the next decade. Illinois's congressional plan has at least three districts (shown in figure 4.3) that rival the lack of compactness found in the affirmative action districts of the 1990s. The politically divided legislature adopted as its primary motive the protection of incumbents of both parties.[5] Democrat Lane Evans's Seventeenth District shed Republican counties while covering most of Illinois's Mississippi River border before pointing a finger eastward to pick up Democratic voters in Springfield and still farther east in Danville. The Fifteenth District extends along most of Illinois's eastern border, with a narrow hook pushing through parts of six counties almost to Kentucky. The Eleventh District looks like a misshapen "T"; it includes a notch out of Livingston County to allow incumbent Jerry Weller's proud parents to vote for their son. Each of these districts became more favorable to the incumbent, as the Seventeenth became 2 percentage points less Republican based on the 2000 presidential vote and the Fifteenth gained 2 percentage points of Republican support. The old Eleventh District had voted for Al Gore in 2000, but the new version of the district gave Bush a narrow plurality.

Tennessee, shown in figure 4.4, emerged with several elongated districts that extended across the state from south to north. As in Illinois, partisan advantage guided the mapmakers, as Democrats who controlled the legislature sought to reclaim a district from the GOP. The Third District swapped counties with the Fourth to make the former more Republican, while the Fourth District (which was open in 2002) elected a Democrat to replace the four-term Republican who ran unsuccessfully for the Senate. The Seventh District took on Republican areas from the Democratic Fourth and Sixth Districts and became 5 percentage points more Republican, based on the 2000 presidential vote. The Tennessee and Illinois maps suggest that in 2001 both partisan and bipartisan plans disregarded compactness in efforts to promote partisan outcomes. In the next chapter we will see that such efforts do not always succeed.

Voting rights attorney Laughlin McDonald criticizes the Supreme Court for invalidating strangely shaped districts only when they have a predominantly minority population. Although the plaintiffs' challenge to the Texas congressional plan adopted in the early 1990s included challenges to several predominantly white districts along with attacking three majority-minority districts, the Supreme Court limited its attention to the majority-minority districts.[6]

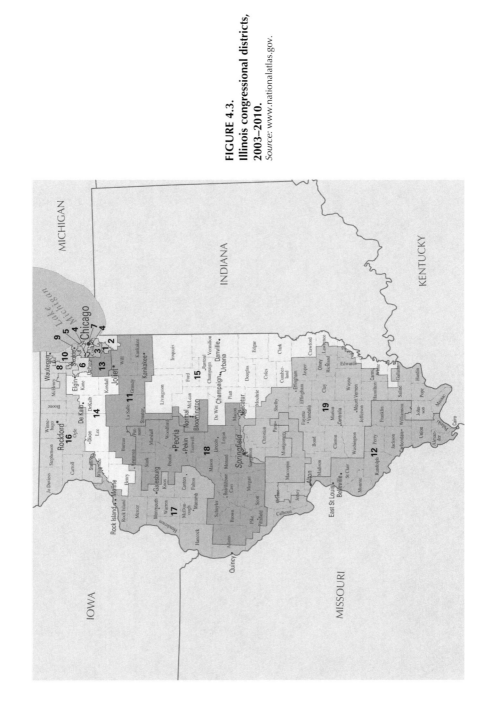

FIGURE 4.3.
Illinois congressional districts, 2003–2010.
Source: www.nationalatlas.gov.

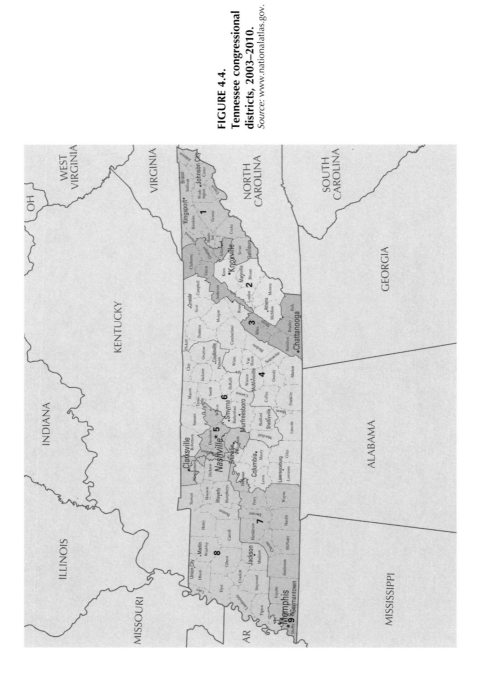

FIGURE 4.4.
Tennessee congressional districts, 2003–2010.
Source: www.nationalatlas.gov.

Respect for Political Boundaries

At the time of the post-2000 redistrictings, twenty-three states urged adherence to city and county boundaries.[7] When I have attended hearings conducted by legislative redistricting committees prior to the preparation of a new map, rural residents frequently asked that their county not be split between districts. These witnesses did not care too much about whether their county went into a predominantly Democratic or a heavily Republican district so long as it remained united. Three-quarters of the local officials surveyed by the Rose Institute preferred to see their communities kept intact.[8] The county high school serves as a unifying institution in many rural communities. Rural voters identify with the county high school's athletic teams or band and rally behind it as they compete against the high schools of other counties. People throughout the county go to the county seat not only for legal matters but also for shopping, and everyone reads the weekly county newspaper. With these forces in common, they do not want to see their county divided between congressional, Senate, or state house districts. Smaller cities and counties when split worry that no legislator will find them a sufficiently significant portion of the district to command attention.[9]

This concern of rural residents for maintaining the integrity of their county goes back to the traditional basis for legislative districting. Recall that prior to *Baker v. Carr*, except in the Northeast and the largest urban areas, many state legislators represented single counties. Frequently counties got one or more legislative seats and filled them in countywide elections. In the upper chamber of a legislature, the county boundaries were also important, with senatorial districts being composed of multiple counties in rural areas. Until *Wesberry v. Sanders*, few congressional districts split county boundaries. Those that did tended to be in America's largest cities.

In many states in the first rounds of redistricting following the *Baker* decision, every effort was made to avoid splitting counties. To avoid dividing counties, multiple legislators might be elected at-large from a county or from a district made up of multiple counties. Ultimately the demands for less and less population deviation among districts forced states to divide counties. States that needed to secure DOJ approval of their redistricting plans had to switch to single-member districts if a multimember district would submerge a minority concentration that could dominate a single-member district. Challenges brought pursuant to Section 2 of the Voting Rights Act, as described in the previous chapter, forced states and many local governments to subdivide multimember or at-large districts in order to create single-member districts in which the majority of the population belongs to a minority group.

Dividing counties in urban areas has now become widely accepted and is usually noncontroversial, since urban voters identify less with their county than do rural voters. Urban areas may actually enhance their position in the legislature by having multiple representatives. Cain notes that different legislators may represent different interests within the community.[10] A clear example would be the representatives of minority communities within a larger urban area.

Even with the demands for tiny population deviations, states with numerous counties can often draw congressional districts using counties as their primary building blocks. Iowa's constitution requires that counties not be split between congressional districts, and in 2001 the state honored that demand with a plan that limited the difference between most and least populous districts to 134 individuals.

The pressures in the 1990s to craft predominantly minority districts that could be achieved only by aggregating minority residents in distant communities resulted in more violations of county boundaries than at any time in the past. Table 4.2 shows the extent to which majority-black districts split counties in southern states subject to Section 5. In every instance, the frequency with which counties were split in order to form a majority-minority district exceeded the incidence of split counties in the remainder of the state. Moreover, the numbers of counties divided in order to create the majority-minority districts far exceeded the number of splits in the entire state in the previous decade. In Alabama, the newly designed 67 percent black Seventh District had fourteen counties, of which five were only partially in the district. Of Alabama's remaining fifty-three counties, only two were split between districts. The plan drawn for the 1980s split a total of just two counties. Thus to create the heavily black new district, five more counties were split than in the entire previous plan. None of Florida's three majority black districts contained all of a single county. Creation of the Third and Twenty-Third districts necessitated putting together black concentrations in multiple counties. The twenty-one counties split to create these three districts exceeded the fifteen splits in the 1980 plan. In the most extreme example, Louisiana's Fourth District (known as the "Zorro District" because it looked something like a Z) contained parts of twenty-eight of the state's sixty-four parishes. District 4 included only four entire parishes.

Before minimizing population differences became common, most states could largely avoid splitting counties. The narrowing of the population deviations demanded by courts has necessitated more county splits. Splitting counties reached new heights in the 1990s, when jurisdictions believed that they had an obligation to maximize the number of minority districts. In the new century, legislatures often violate county lines in order to pack members of a single party into a district.

TABLE 4.2
Counties Split for New Majority-Black Congressional Districts and Elsewhere in Southern Districts Drawn in the Early 1990s

	District No.	Splits in Black Districts	Splits in Other Districts*	1980 Splits
Alabama	7	5/14**	2/53***	2/67
Florida	3	14/14	8/46	15/67
		17		1/1
	23	7/7		
Georgia	2	12/35	6/102	3/159
	11	8/22		
Louisiana	4	24/28	4/36	7/64
North Carolina	1	19/28	15/62	4/100
	12	10/10		
South Carolina	6	11/16	2/30	1/46
Virginia****	3	11/18	11/123	6/141

*Counties split because they are shared with a majority-black district and a predominantly white district are not included in this column.
**Number of counties split / total number of counties in district.
***Number of counties split / total number of counties in state not included in majority-black districts.
****Includes independent cities and counties.

Source: Charles S. Bullock III and Richard E. Dunn, "The Demise of Racial Districting and the Future of Black Representation," *Emory Law Journal* 48 (Fall 1999): 1218.

Maintenance of Communities of Interest

Sixteen states adopted as one of their principles for congressional districting maintenance of communities of interest.[11] While redistricting committees are often encouraged to avoid splitting communities of interest, rarely are workable definitions provided to define what constitutes a community of interest. As we saw in chapter 3, if the community of interest is defined in racial or ethnic terms, then the Voting Rights Act may provide the basis for a challenge. One major case dealt with alternative communities of interest. Hasidic Jews in New York City went to court when the legislature split the one district from which they had been able to elect their preference in order to create a majority-black district.[12] The Supreme Court upheld the decision by the New York legislature to draw a heavily African American district even though that eliminated the prospects for the Hasidic Jewish community. The Court reasoned that the legislature appropriately gave precedence to black concerns, since the Voting Rights Act specifically addressed the interests of that community.

The challenges to the elongated, race-based districts of the 1990s raised questions about what constitutes a community of interests. Defendants in these cases argued that shared racial characteristics might suffice to define a community of interest even if the district stretched over hundreds of miles. In seeking to defend these districts, minority groups also pointed to shared socioeconomic characteristics, noting that the residents of these majority-minority districts tended to be less well educated and less affluent than the average for their state. These arguments proved unsuccessful when the record showed that the legislature had been primarily concerned with drawing a district in which a minority group would dominate. At the very end of the 1990s when North Carolina successfully defended a district that plaintiffs had claimed was race based, the successful defense rested not on characteristics shared by a community but on a finding that the legislature had been motivated chiefly by partisan rather than racial concerns.[13]

Protecting Incumbents

Especially when it comes to drawing the lines for state legislative districts and local legislative bodies, protecting incumbents often gets high priority because it is incumbents who create the new districts. Bruce Cain articulates the case for including the location of incumbents among the factors considered by a legislature: "It is hardly consistent with democratic theory to argue that a government whose legitimacy depends on duly elected representatives should permit their unnecessary and arbitrary removal."[14] While there is no obligation to protect incumbents, neither must a jurisdiction go out of its way to imperil them or to make their districts more competitive. Protecting incumbents cannot justify deviations from the equal population standards, nor would it withstand a challenge under the Voting Rights Act. One scholar estimates that the congressional plans drawn following the 2000 Census sought to protect 231 of the House incumbents.[15]

Plans prepared by legislatures in states where each party controls one chamber or where the governor does not belong to the same party as a majority of the legislators often produce plans that protect both parties' incumbents. On the other hand, when a single party controls the legislative process, it will likely protect its own incumbents but may seek to defeat opposing incumbents. For example, when Texas Republicans redrew their congressional map in 2003, they separated eleven of the seventeen Democratic incumbents from the bulk of their constituents; this resulted in the defeat of four of these incumbents and the retirement of a fifth, and a sixth incumbent changed parties and became a Republican.[16]

A 2004 Georgia case further defined the appropriate weight to be given incumbency. In remapping the state legislative districts, Georgia Democrats protected their own incumbents, while going out of their way to pair Republican incumbents—even though, prior to redistricting, Democrats' districts tended to be underpopulated while Republicans' districts were frequently overpopulated. Only one Democratic incumbent failed to have a district in which to run under the new plan, and she retired. On the other hand, eight of twenty-two incumbent Republican senators and thirty-six of seventy-three Republican representatives found themselves paired with another legislator.[17] Nine House districts forced two Republicans to compete for a single seat, while four multimember districts forced three Republicans to compete for two seats. The Republican senators who left the legislature because of the pairings took with them fifty-one years of seniority. The extent to which Democrats went to put multiple Republicans in the same district is shown in figure 1.3, which depicts House District 137; it wandered across parts of five southwest Georgia counties in order to put the only two Republicans in that corner of the state into a single district.

When the Democrats' plans came under review by a federal court, the unequal treatment of Democratic and Republican incumbents figured into the decision that invalidated the plans. The court rejected one of the Democrats' justifications for the plan, which was incumbency protection.[18] As the court noted, it protected only Democratic incumbents, and a plan that treated incumbents so differently depending on their partisanship did not provide an adequate justification for the population deviations in the plan.

As an aside, efforts to defeat Republican incumbents had major negative consequences for the Democratic Party. Democrats singled out Sonny Perdue for punishment, because while he had been the Democratic president pro tempore of the Senate—the highest office in that chamber—he switched allegiance and became a Republican. Irate Democrats immediately punished Perdue by taking away his office in the Capitol and relegating him to the back of the Legislative Office Building across the street. He also paid a price in terms of his committee assignments, as he lost seats on powerful committees and ended up on a set of distinctly second-rate ones. When it came time for redistricting, Democrats continued their revenge by transforming his district. Perdue, rather than seeking reelection in his drastically changed district, ran for governor and defeated the incumbent Democrat in 2002. A Republican member of Congress saw his district disappear when Democrats extended Jack Kingston's (R) First Congressional District more than halfway across the state and sent a finger into Colquitt County just far enough to pick up the home of Saxby Chambliss (R). Rather than face his fellow Republican, Chambliss ran for the U.S. Senate and defeated the incumbent Democrat Max Cleland.

While incumbency is almost always a factor in plans drawn by legislatures, it may be less significant when commissions carry out the task. In the states that have redistricting commissions and in Iowa, the entity responsible for drawing the districts may not consider where incumbents live. Four states that allow the legislature to redistrict prohibit it from considering where congressional incumbents live. In Iowa, almost half of the state legislators ended up paired with other legislators in the 2001 plan.[19]

Even in efforts to protect incumbents, it is unlikely that all can be given districts in which they feel comfortable. In both 1972 and 1982, the number of districts in which no incumbent competed increased substantially over the number in the previous election.[20] Undoubtedly some of these incumbents who retired could have won additional terms, but the uncertainty introduced by having to run in newly configured districts raised the costs of running to an unacceptable level.

Core Preservation

Related to the success of an incumbent following redistricting is whether the core constituency of the incumbent has been maintained intact in the incumbent's district. Removing core supporters from an incumbent's district may well condemn that legislator to defeat, as may a districting plan that divides the incumbent's strong supporters among multiple districts, forcing the incumbent to choose one district in which to run. In the redistricting carried out following the 2000 Census, ten states included in their principles to guide redistricting a statement calling for maintenance of district cores.

Of course, instances in which incumbents are paired (almost by definition) assure that at least one incumbent has been divorced from the core of the district he or she represented. When an area is losing population, this may be unavoidable. However, when a party sets out to disadvantage the opposition, separating an incumbent from the core of the district is an effective technique. When Texas carried out the mid-decade redistricting in 2003, one of the Republicans' chief objectives was the defeat of Martin Frost (D). In their successful attack on Frost, Republicans placed parts of his district in five new districts. Another target, Charles C. Stenholm (D) was paired with a Republican incumbent, Randy Neugebauer, with the new district consisting of 58 percent of Neugebauer's old district and 31 percent of Stenholm's old district. The Republican, having the core of his old district in the new one, easily defeated Stenholm 58 to 40 percent.[21]

Other Considerations

In addition to the factors discussed above, idiosyncratic considerations may prove extremely important to individual incumbents. Legislators may seek to block plans that remove from their districts the homes of relatives or, even more importantly, generous contributors. Access to potential contributors may also prompt incumbents to oppose removing facilities such as airports from their districts. Representatives John Lewis (D-GA) and Eddie Bernice Johnson (D-TX) have fought to retain international airports in their districts. The airlines, their suppliers, and those who have contracts to operate businesses in the airport provide campaign dollars.

Controversy

Arguments For

Counties provided the primary building blocks for legislative districts for most of the nation's history and in less populated areas people still identify with counties, so to the extent possible counties should be kept whole in districting plans. Even when the need to minimize population deviations makes it impossible to avoid splitting counties, mapmakers should strive to avoid districts that connect far-flung pieces of geography by means of touch points, waterways, or narrow necks since those designs make it difficult for voters to know what district they live in. When voters have trouble visualizing their districts, they may be less likely to know the name of their legislator. Moreover, needlessly far-flung districts make it difficult for candidates to campaign, and incumbents may rarely visit the more distant parts of their districts.

Districts should retain the core populations of incumbents since they have established relationships with their constituents. Moreover, the incumbents' experience benefits both their constituents and the legislature. The replacement of incumbents should come about as a result of voter dissatisfaction and not because of mapmakers' devices.

Arguments Against

The factors in this chapter cannot all simultaneously be achieved. Not only do they often conflict with one another, they are often at odds with the primary demands for population equality among districts and the avoidance of discriminatory practices. These secondary items are not legally enforceable, and to the extent that mapmakers try to honor them, it makes their jobs more difficult.

Communities of interest, especially in urban areas, do not coincide with county or city boundaries, so that giving precedence to traditional political boundaries may split communities of interest. Moreover, to unite communities that share interests may require drawing strange-looking districts in order to bring together people with similarities while avoiding those who lack the relevant characteristic and remain within the narrow population parameters permitted by courts.

The primary way to get major policy change requires replacing incumbents. Protecting incumbents denies the legislature the new blood needed to get policy innovations. Displacing incumbents by combining their districts or removing their cores is a standard part of redistricting in which the majority takes advantage of the minority. It has been this way for hundreds of years and will probably continue to be practiced in single-member district political systems.

Conclusions

The factors reviewed in this chapter have been lumped together as traditional districting principles. Three-fourths of the states included one or more of these in their guidelines for remapping congressional districts in 2001.[22] Arizona, Idaho, Minnesota, Nebraska, South Carolina, and Washington included all but one of the principles, although they varied in the item excluded from their checklist. A state's guidelines for redistricting can become important if the plan is subsequently challenged in court. The degree to which the jurisdiction honored the criteria it articulated can help in the state's defense and may become a factor in the court's decision. A state may be able to justify minor population deviations by noting that it adhered to traditional districting principles established prior to the session. On the other hand, if a jurisdiction fails to honor the principles laid out prior to the redistricting session, that may provide a basis for a court throwing out the plan.

To some extent the factors reviewed in this chapter are a "wish list," in the sense that it would be very difficult if not impossible to achieve all of these objectives simultaneously while also minimizing population differences and protecting the political interests of minorities. The greatest difficulty usually involves efforts to create majority-minority districts. Attaining that objective may prevent creation of more compact districts, result in disregarding political boundaries, and separate some incumbents from the core of their former districts. In the early 1990s, the concept of contiguity was stretched in the creation of some majority-minority districts, although it might have been possible to have created the desired districts without resorting to touch-point or water contiguity.

Respect for political boundaries must also give way to requirements that districts have equal populations. While Iowa has succeeded in maintaining whole counties when designing congressional districts, many states would find it impossible to avoid splitting counties when drawing congressional districts. No state could draw districts for its own legislature without dividing counties, and probably no state could apportion seats in its legislature without crossing some county lines. The requirements for equalizing populations among districts and not disadvantaging minorities by stacking them in multimember districts dictate the drawing of many single-member districts. If the minority population spreads across county lines, it may be necessary to ignore those lines when creating majority-minority districts.

Protecting incumbents becomes impossible when states lose congressional districts. It may also be impossible to maintain each incumbent's district even when the number of seats remains constant in areas of a state that have experienced substantial population loss or have failed to grow at anything approaching the rate of the rest of the state.

5

Partisan Gerrymandering: All's Fair in Love, War, and Redistricting

But for the federal judiciary to be ignorant of politics is dangerous. By failing to understand the way congressional elections work, or by choosing not to think much about it, federal judges have already created chaos over the difficult issue of how districts should be drawn.[1]

The gerrymander overcometh all. What demographics give, legislators can take away in the dead of the night.[2]

Even the most egregious partisan gerrymanders do not "lock-in" one party's control over the state.[3]

Partisan redistricting plans are not as successful as those who generate them expect, in part because the results are influenced by national political swings.[4]

PARTISAN CONSIDERATIONS DATE BACK AT LEAST as far as the term *gerrymander*, since the origin of the term was the effort of Massachusetts Governor Elbridge Gerry to promote the fortunes of his party at the expense of the Federalists. The governor would no doubt be pleased to see that his actions earned him a place in every introductory course in American politics. That the practice continues would not surprise him, and he might be impressed by the sophistication with which today's politicians carry out the activity for which he provided a name.

FIGURE 5.1.
The original gerrymander.
Source: Library of Congress, Rare Book and Special Collections Division.

Single-member districts are particularly well suited to partisan gerrymandering, although multimember districts with few seats as used in Ireland and
Japan can also be manipulated to advance partisan fortunes. And while gerrymandering goes back to the earliest days of the Republic, the current necessity
of adjusting district boundaries after each census has created unprecedented
opportunities to practice the art. While the decades during which districts
were infrequently redrawn caused many problems, as noted in chapter 2,

the inaction did prevent the current practice of the party that controls the redistricting process seeking to advance its goals at the expense of its opponents. The impetus to eliminate multimember districts—which were the most common format for choosing state legislators 40 years ago—generated by the Voting Rights Act extended the need to adjust district boundaries to many cities and counties that had previously chosen all of their commissioners and councilors at-large. These obligations, coupled with more sophisticated software, mean that the opportunities to gerrymander have never been greater than today.[5]

Successful Partisan Gerrymanders

Partisans devote so much attention to drawing districts that will benefit their party because they hope their handiwork will last for a decade. Usually districts are drawn only once a decade, so the individuals who craft the new map soon after the release of census figures can try to determine the partisan makeup of a legislative chamber for as many as five elections. As we will see later in this chapter, these efforts may prevail even in the face of substantial changes in partisan preferences in the electorate. Not surprisingly, however, there are other instances in which the clever machinations of a mapmaker come undone and can even backfire.

Because districting plans usually remain in place for a decade, parties invest resources in preparing for the process.[6] The surest way to be positioned to carry out a redistricting is to control all the relevant power positions immediately after the census. Party leaders recognize that if they can simultaneously win control of the governorship and both chambers of the legislature, the plan will at a minimum not hurt them and, more likely, provide advantages. Partisan gerrymanders of congressional districts are especially likely when the size of a state's delegation changes and partisan competition is heated.[7] If a state is losing congressional seats, the party in control can assess that loss against its opposition. If the state is gaining congressional seats, the party in control can usually design a plan that will give it a better-than-even chance of winning the new seat or seats. In states in which the size of the congressional delegation does not change, the majority party may nonetheless gain a seat or two by redrawing the districts. The sizes of state legislatures rarely change, so parties try to control the process in order to devise a more helpful plan.

A party that has little prospect of simultaneously winning the governorship and majorities in both chambers of the legislature may set as its goal in the election immediately preceding redistricting winning control of at least one of these levers of power. If the minority party can control a single chamber or win the governorship, it will be in position to block the most partisan ideas from the opposition and often be able to force a compromise plan. If compromise proves impossible, a party that controls only one of the locales in which the districting process plays out can veto legislative efforts, which will necessitate a court-drawn plan. Courts generally avoid taking sides in partisan debates, and therefore plans designed by judges are fairer to both parties than plans drawn when one party is wholly in control.

Responsiveness and Bias in the Legislature

The opportunity to reconfigure the political map of a jurisdiction has promoted widespread suspicions about the fairness of the outcome. Responsiveness and bias have become two widely accepted measures of plan equity.

Responsiveness

Responsiveness, also referred to as the "swing ratio," measures the degree to which the makeup of a legislative chamber will change when voter preferences change. Responsiveness and a higher swing ratio occur when a legislature has numerous competitive seats. Since the swing ratio is calculated as a party's percentage gain in seats divided by its percentage gain in votes, a high swing ratio indicates that a relatively small improvement in the party's share of the votes statewide translates into a larger pickup in seats. For example, an election in which Democrats increased their share of the vote statewide by 2 percentage points while adding 5 percentage points to their share of the legislative seats has a swing ratio of 2.5.

Most political scientists see advantages in designing districts to be competitive. Two arguments have been offered in favor of promoting partisan competition. First, districts with some prospect for partisan change will make a legislative body more responsive to shifting public preferences. Since legislators tend not to undergo dramatic changes in their preferences, achieving substantial new policy directions requires the replacement of one partisan majority with a majority from the opposing party.

Second, some have contended that competitive districts produce moderate as opposed to extreme legislators. The evidence for this second point is far from convincing. Indeed, the two reasons for having competitive districts are inconsistent. If competitive districts are desirable because they promote alteration in partisan control of the legislature and that in turn leads to different policy outputs, then it follows that when partisan control changes, newly elected legislators will have policy preferences quite different than those of their predecessors. Research finds that a change in partisanship results in the new legislator representing a different set of values and preferences within the district.[8] While swing districts may produce legislators more likely to engage in bipartisan efforts to resolve issues confronting the legislature, the overall record of legislators from marginal districts is quite similar to that of their fellow partisans and unlike the record of most members of the opposition party. Each year the *National Journal* ranks members of Congress from the most liberal to the most conservative. It is rare for any Democrat to be more conservative than the most liberal Republican. This is a recent phenomenon; during the 1940s, 1950s, or 1960s a number of Southern Democrats had more conservative voting records than the moderate Republicans who came from the Northeast and the West Coast.

If legislators use redistricting to eliminate competition, then a new plan may be less responsive to shifts in voter preferences. Legislators who win by comfortable margins have little reason to fear retribution at the polls. They can vote as party leaders or interest groups request, even if that means voting against constituency preferences. A more positive view of freedom from constituent demands holds that electorally secure members can behave as trustees and vote what they believe to be in the best interests of the nation or state. Yet a third perspective is that in one-party districts the only electoral fear for the incumbent involves a potential primary challenge. If the likely challenge would come from the party's true believers, that might prompt the incumbent to adopt extreme policy positions. Thus a Republican might increasingly vote for an extremely conservative social agenda, while a Democrat representing a one-party district might be tempted to support aggressive redistributive programs favored by the Left.

An extensive analysis of redistricting of state legislatures between 1968 and 1988 shows that in the first elections held under both partisan and bipartisan redistricting plans the swing ratios exceed those for elections not preceded by a new set of districts.[9] Consequently, redistricting results in greater responsiveness than doing nothing or allowing the silent gerrymander to persist.

Bias

A second measure used to assess the fairness of districting plans compares the degree to which a plan advantages one party over the other. The calculation of bias recognizes that single-member districts are not intended to and rarely do result in parties having shares of seats in the legislature equal to their share of the votes. While all electoral systems pay a bonus to the largest party, the dividends are especially great in single-member election systems.[10] Calculating bias tests the assumption that a fair system pays the same size dividend to Democrats when they win a given share of the vote as would go to Republicans if they polled that percentage of the vote. Thus if Democrats get 56 percent of the seats when winning 52 percent of the vote, then in a bias-free plan Republicans would also get 56 percent of the seats when winning 52 percent of the vote. Bias is measured as the deviation from the expectation that a plan will give each party the same seat bonus should it win a given majority of the vote.

Popular expectations consider a partisan redistricting plan much less likely to have little bias than will a bipartisan plan. As an example of bias, the 2001 GOP-drawn Michigan congressional plan would allow Republicans to win a majority of the fifteen seats with as little as 47 percent of the vote, while Democrats would need at least 58 percent of the vote to win a majority of the seats.[11]

Gelman and King's study of twenty years of redistricting of state legislatures finds that "the difference in seats between a Democratic- and Republican-controlled redistricting plan is, on average, a substantial 4 percent of seats."[12] A surprising finding coming out of this study is that while partisan plans favor their creators, partisan as well as bipartisan plans result in *fairer* (i.e., less biased) arrangements than if redistricting had not occurred. To explain this unexpected result, the authors note that "the largest effects of redistricting change an existing huge bias in favor of one party to small bias in favor of the other."[13]

Rarely do even partisan plans attempt to maximize a party's advantage. Factors other than maximizing partisan advantage, like equalizing populations and not discriminating against minorities, impose restraints on those who craft partisan plans.[14] In addition to the redistricting considerations introduced in previous chapters, party leaders may confront opposition within their own ranks. To maximize the number of seats that a party could hope to win will necessitate spreading the party's supporters strategically across districts. Incumbents who coast to victory would have to give up their excess supporters in order to convert districts that the party loses narrowly into districts that it can win. Often incumbents who objectively appear unbeatable may feel threatened and fight to maintain their comfortable margins. Even incumbents willing to compete in less secure districts for the good of the party may veto proposals that would deprive them of specific areas.

Responsiveness of Another Type

Responsiveness can take a meaning other than the degree to which changes in the electorate translate into shifts in the partisan control of seats. Those who study the consequences of redistricting have also explored whether legislators change their behavior following significant reconfigurations of their districts. If given a substantially different constituency, does the legislator vote differently on roll calls in order to represent the preferences of the median voter in the new district? Do legislators given electorally safe districts become less attentive to the concerns of their constituents?

An incumbent who loses in the "redistricting lottery" and gets a much less hospitable district confronts several options. Retirement may be especially attractive to older incumbents who do not want to expend the energy and raise the funds needed to introduce themselves to the constituents added to their districts.[15] A second option is to remain true to their principles and prepare to lose gracefully. A third possibility is to shift toward the position of the median voter in the new district. Research shows that incumbents who manage to win reelection in their altered districts change their roll call voting to come more into line with their new constituents.[16]

Legislators who win reelection with little if any opposition may devote less energy to district concerns and may ignore constituent policy preferences. Among the least partisanly competitive districts are most of those represented by African Americans. Swain speculates that the electoral security of these districts may result in incumbents being less responsive to constituents.[17] However, Claudine Gay shows that California legislators representing majority-minority districts where serious partisan challenges rarely occur are as responsive to their constituents' preferences as representatives of majority-white districts and react to changes in public opinion.[18]

Partisan Gerrymanders and the Courts . . . Part I

That a party in position to disadvantage its opponent in the course of redistricting would do so seemed so obvious that it contributed to the Supreme Court's refusal to consider a challenge to the malapportioned Illinois congressional delegation. Justice Felix Frankfurter dissuaded the Court from entering the "political thicket" because he saw redistricting as an entirely political issue.[19] When the Court finally acknowledged the justiciability of challenges to unequal apportionment plans, it based its opinion on equal treatment of different parts of the state. The Court did not object to plans that might have equally populated districts but discriminated against one of the political parties. Justice Sandra Day O'Connor, the only recent member of the Supreme Court to have served as a state legislator, consistently refused to overturn partisan gerrymanders. When politicians draw new district lines, partisanship will almost always be a factor. It may be muted under some circumstances but for political actors partisan considerations are never totally obliterated. As Justice Byron White acknowledged, "District lines are rarely neutral phenomena."[20]

In most states the legislature redraws congressional and state legislative districts. A norm in many states allows each chamber a largely unfettered hand in designing its own districts, which the opposite chamber then rubber-stamps.[21] Governors usually have a veto over districting plans, so that the key players are the state house, state senate, and governor. When one party controls the three participants in the redistricting process, the majority party can take advantage of the opposition and draw lines that enhance the majority's position.[22] On the other hand, if parties share control of the redistricting process, then while partisanship will no doubt influence the placement of some district lines, the ultimate plan will more likely provide a balance. Indeed, when each party controls part of the process, the resulting plan may seek to protect both parties' incumbents. Parties do not always exploit their upper hand, as demonstrated in California where in 2002 the Democrats who controlled the process nonetheless opted to protect incumbents of both parties (with the exception of one Democrat).

Despite a tendency for legislatures when redrawing districts to make them secure for one party or the other, a couple of states have taken an alternative stand. The Arizona constitution and the redistricting standards adopted in Washington call for the creation of partisanly competitive districts.[23]

While courts have not required that parties treat one another fairly, if a plan seeks fairness as its objective, courts may tolerate greater deviation from the "one person, one vote" standard. When Connecticut devised a plan designed to produce a legislature in which the partisan makeup would reflect partisan distribution in the electorate, the Supreme Court rejected a challenge that questioned the population deviations.[24]

California 1980s

Although dead for more than a quarter of a century, former Representative Philip Burton (D-CA) continues to be recognized as one of the most astute wielders of the redistricting pen. Burton took the lead in drawing the congressional plan for California following the 1980 Census. His plan, one of ten partisan gerrymanders that decade[25] and widely criticized for the way in which it separated Democrats and Republicans with the advantage going to his fellow Democrats, performed as its creator had anticipated. The last election under the previous plan had sent twenty-two Democrats and twenty-one Republicans to Congress. This balance in the congressional delegation paralleled the Senate representation, which had a Democrat and a Republican. Against this background of an evenly divided state, the Burton plan rewarded Democrats, with twenty-nine of the forty-five seats the new census gave California. At the end of the decade, the state still had a divided Senate delegation and a Republican governor in place of the Democrat who approved Burton's plan. George Bush won the state's electors with 51 percent of the vote in 1988. Nonetheless, at the end of the decade the Burton gerrymander had largely held its own, with Democrats still having a twenty-six to nineteen advantage.

Texas

A second example of the longevity of an effective gerrymander comes from Texas where another member of Congress, in this case Martin Frost (D), performed much as Burton had in California. Frost turned his attention to redistricting the Lone Star State following the 1990 Census, which gave Texas three new congressional seats. Republicans already controlled one Senate seat and had easily carried the state in the three presidential elections of the 1980s. Even in 1988, when Democrats nominated the state's senior senator, Lloyd Bentsen, for vice president, Democrats managed only 43 percent of the vote in the presidential election against another Texan, George Bush. With Republican fortunes rising in Texas, the GOP hoped to expand on their eight seats in the congressional delegation. Frost drove a stake through the heart of that ambition.

Frost's audacious plan sought to increase the minority presence in the delegation, while simultaneously protecting the seats of his fellow Anglo Democrats. His plan rewarded Mexican Americans and African Americans, two increasingly critical components of the Democratic coalition. He created a district in Dallas likely to elect an African American and anchored another district in the Rio Grande Valley which would almost certainly send a Hispanic to Congress. The third district, which became part of one of the most convoluted line-drawing exercises anywhere in the nation, separated Houston-area Latinos from blacks so as to maintain the Eighteenth District as one likely to elect an African American while creating a heavily Hispanic district just to the east. The growing number of Republican supporters were packed into a few districts where they would pile up overwhelming majorities.

The effectiveness of the Frost gerrymander got an immediate test. In 1992, the total vote received by Democratic congressional candidates came to just over 2.8 million, while Republicans attracted 2.6 million voters for their congressional candidates statewide. While the Democratic congressional vote in Texas only narrowly exceeded that for Republicans, Democrats extended their control over the delegation by winning twenty-one of thirty seats, or 70 percent of the seats. The only Republican gain came in a district where the

Democratic incumbent ran under a cloud and shortly after the election was indicted and convicted of bribery. The performance of Republican candidates running for Congress paled against that of their state legislative candidates, who won 42 percent of the state senate seats and 39 percent of the house seats in 1992 compared with 30 percent of the congressional delegation.

Two years later, Republicans running for Congress did even better, taking share of 57 percent of the vote statewide.[26] In this year, when Republicans captured a majority of the U.S. House for the first time in forty years, they experienced only modest gains in the Texas delegation, increasing their numbers from nine to eleven. Despite having won a majority of the votes, Republicans received less than 40 percent of the seats, being underrepresented by 20 percentage points. Frost had so successfully gerrymandered that winning 8.5 percentage points more of the vote netted Republicans 6.7 percentage points more seats, for a swing ratio of 0.79. In 1996, as table 5.1 shows, the Republican vote share came in at 54 percent and they held 20 of the 29 partisan offices in Texas elected statewide. Yet they came nowhere close to that share of the congressional seats, as they held only 43 percent of the Texas seats in Congress. For the remainder of the decade, the partisan makeup of the delegation remained fixed, although in each of those three elections, Republicans won a majority of the vote. In retaining a majority of the seats, Democrats frequently had a share of the seats 10 percentage points greater than their share of the statewide vote for Congress. As an indication of the pro-Democratic bias in Frost's plan, in 1992 51.6 percent of the vote won Democrats 70 percent of the seats. In 2000, the GOP almost matched the 1992 Democratic vote share, yet the Republicans' 50.8 percent of the vote got them just 43.3 percent of the seats.

While the Frost plan certainly played a major role in allowing Democrats to thwart the will of the majority of the statewide electorate, two other fac-

TABLE 5.1
Vote Share and Share of the Congressional Seats in Texas

Year	Democratic		Republican	
	Vote Share (%)	Share of Seats (%)	Vote Share (%)	Share of Seats (%)
1992	51.6	70.0	48.4	30.0
1994	43.1	63.3	56.9	36.7
1996	45.8	56.7	54.2	43.3
1998	46.1	56.7	53.9	43.3
2000	49.2	56.7	50.8	43.3
2002	45.1	53.1	54.9	46.9
2004	41.4	34.4	58.6	65.6

Created by the author

tors contributed. One is the well-known ability of incumbents to retain their positions even as the partisan preferences of the electorate change. And the other relates to the cheap seats argument discussed in chapter 2. The heavily black and Latino districts rarely involved competitive elections, and many of the residents in these districts had relatively less education and lower incomes. These conditions contributed to lower rates of turnout than in the more affluent districts that elected Republicans.

When it came time to redistrict following the 2000 Census, Texas failed to adopt a new plan. Republicans controlled the governorship and had a narrow majority in the senate. But the house, with a seventy-eight to seventy-two Democratic majority, refused to accept plans offered by Republicans. Ultimately a three-judge federal panel devised the new plan for the state's thirty-two districts. The presiding judge explained precisely how the court went about crafting the map. The court first placed the existing seven Hispanic and two black districts on the map. Next the judges drew in the two new districts gained through reapportionment and placed them in areas that had experienced the most rapid growth. "We then drew in the remaining districts throughout the state, emphasizing compactness, while observing the contiguity requirement. We struggled to follow local political boundaries that have historically defined communities—county and city lines."[27] The resulting map avoided pairing any incumbents as it relied heavily on the preexisting map, so that 78 percent of all Texans had the same member of Congress in the new districts as in the old ones. The court opinion concluded that "the plan is likely to produce a congressional delegation roughly proportional to the party voting breakdown across the state."[28] In the new plan, twenty-one of the thirty-two districts voted for George W. Bush in the 2000 election. In nineteen of these districts, Bush polled more than 60 percent of the vote, compared with the 59 percent he received statewide.

While the court expected its plan to reflect partisan voting preferences in the state, the power of incumbency overcame these efforts. In 2002, Democrats retained seventeen seats, the same number they had under the previous plan, while the Republicans added the two new seats to the thirteen they had previously held. Republicans won only 47 percent of the seats, even though they took 55 percent of the congressional vote statewide. Thus even though Republicans now controlled all twenty-nine of the state's partisan positions elected statewide, they could not yet win control of the congressional delegation. Their political gains registered for other offices led Republicans to expect far more than a gain of two seats. "A gain of five is our worst-case scenario," Representative Joe Barton (R) had predicted. "We could get to plus-ten but we would need to be creative."[29]

The unwillingness of the Democratically controlled state house to go along with the Republican plan did not help the Democrats when it came to the state legislature. Under Texas law, if the legislature fails to adopt a districting plan, then the Legislative Redistricting Board (the LRB, which consists of the lieutenant governor, house speaker, attorney general, comptroller, and land commissioner) will draw districts for the state house and senate. In 2002, the LRB had only one Democrat, House Speaker Pete Laney, which allowed Republicans to shape the state legislative chambers. The 2002 elections produced a house with an eighty-eight to sixty-two Republican majority. In the senate, Republicans emerged with nineteen of the thirty-one seats.

While states have usually drawn new districts only once in a decade unless ordered to make changes as a result of losing lawsuits, Texas Republicans saw a chance to right what they perceived to be a long-festering wrong. U.S. House Majority Leader Tom DeLay (R), who represented a suburban Houston district, pushed for a new plan. DeLay hoped that redrawing Texas would give Republicans in the U.S. House more breathing room, since after the 2002 election, they had only a 229 to 205 margin. Steve Bickerstaff provides a detailed account of the political machinations that went into the adoption of the new Texas congressional plan.[30]

The DeLay plan sought to put in play each of the seats filled by Anglo Democrats while protecting the seats of Republicans, Latinos, and African Americans. The plan enhanced the black concentration in a Houston district in order to facilitate the election of a second African American from that city. It also drew an additional district rooted in the Rio Grande Valley that extended into the Austin area. This heavily Hispanic district had the potential to send another Latino to Congress. Martin Frost, whose handiwork allowed Democrats to control the Texas delegation during the 1990s and traces of which had persisted through the 2002 election, attracted special attention from the Republican mapmakers, who set out to retire him. They dismantled his district and spread its parts among five districts in the Dallas–Fort Worth Metroplex, with 26.5 percent of the old district's population being the largest piece kept intact.

The new plan achieved much of what Republicans had hoped for. Frost lost his reelection bid (54 to 44 percent). As detailed in table 5.2, four other Anglo Democrats also either lost election or retired, while Ralph Hall, the most senior and conservative of the Democrats, successfully sought reelection as a Republican. Freshman Anglo Democrat Chris Bell lost the primary to an African American, who became the third black Texan in Congress. The effort to eliminate Austin liberal Lloyd Doggett failed, when he managed to defeat a Latina in the primary in the new majority-Hispanic district. Doggett's home and the largest number of his constituents remained in District 10, but in the new plan, that district became 63.5 percent Republican while his old district had been 60 percent Democratic. Chet Edwards narrowly held on to

TABLE 5.2

Consequences of Tom DeLay's Redistricting of Texas for Anglo Democratic Incumbents

2003 District	Democratic Incumbent	Terms Served	% of Old District Retained	% GOP	Outcome
1	Max Sandlin	4	40.1	63.0	Lost general 61% to 30%
2	Jim Turner	4	4.4	64.1	Retired
4	Ralph Hall	12	33.9	63.0	Reelected as Republican 68% to 30%
9	Nick Lampson	4	44.7	60.6	Lost general 56% to 43%
10	Lloyd Doggett	5	38.9	63.5	Reelected from Dist. 25 68% to 31%
11	Chet Edwards	7	35.2	64.0	Reelected 51% to 47%
17	Charles Stenholm	13	30.9	69.0	Lost general 58% to 40%
24	Martin Frost	13	20.4	64.3	Lost general 66% to 31%
25	Chris Bell	1	46.5	30.2	Lost primary 66% to 31%
29	Gene Green	6	80.6	35.8	Reelected 94% to 6%

Source: Plan Overlap Analysis prepared by Texas Legislative Council, October 9, 2003.

his district, which had cast 64 percent of its vote for President Bush. The other Anglo, Gene Green, continued to represent the heavily Hispanic Houston district. Of the four who lost general elections, all but Max Sandlin had to compete against a Republican incumbent in a district that favored the GOP.

The 2004 election, for the first time, resulted in Republicans having a larger share of the delegation seats (66 percent) than of the vote (59 percent). The swing ratio in 2004 was just over 5. While it is common for the party that receives most of the votes in a single-member district system to obtain a seat bonus, the payoff for Texas Republicans, even in 2004, remained smaller than Democrats had enjoyed for decades.

Unsuccessful Partisan Gerrymanders

Phil Burton, Martin Frost, and Tom DeLay all succeeded in crafting plans that paid handsome dividends to their parties. However, as the poet Robert Burns observed, "The best laid schemes o' mice and men gang aft a-gley." And so can redistricting plans in what have been labeled "dummymanders."[31] The term *dummymander* suggests that the creators misread the electoral tea leaves when drawing the district. In some instances, the districts may have accurately reflected partisan strength when drawn and the creators failed in their objectives because they did not anticipate new demographic trends. Suburbanization or the in-migration of a new ethnic group could transform a district that initially supported one party into one that elects candidates of the other party. An examination of seven partisan gerrymanders done in the 1970s concluded that in only one state did the effort succeed.[32]

Indiana 1980s

Indiana lost its eleventh congressional seat following the 1980 Census. The Republican-dominated legislature and governor devised what was considered at that time to be the most pro-Republican gerrymander in the nation.[33] Republicans who had held five of the eleven seats hoped to improve their standing with the new plan. The first test of the plan yielded inauspicious results for Republicans, who won a slight majority of the statewide congressional vote and, as table 5.3 shows, split the delegation holding on to their five seats. The GOP gerrymanderers had hoped for more than a fair plan; they had hoped that they could translate a majority of the vote into more than a majority of the seats.

In 1984, with Ronald Reagan amassing 62 percent of Indiana's vote, the GOP share of the state's congressional vote rose to 53 percent. Despite the

TABLE 5.3
The Republican Gerrymander in Indiana That Did Not Succeed

Year	Republican	
	Vote Share (%)	*Share of Seats (%)*
1982	50.8	50
1984	52.9	50
1986	49.0	40
1988	48.3	30
1990	45.1	20
1982–1990	49.2	38

increase, Republicans failed to make headway. Indiana's Republican secretary of state certified fellow partisan Richard McIntyre as the winner of the Eighth District by a margin of thirty-four votes. The Democratic candidate, Francis McClosky, appealed that decision. The Constitution makes each chamber of Congress the final arbiter of contested elections. The Democratic majority awarded McClosky the seat, finding that he had managed a four-vote majority.[34] (As a side note, the seating of McClosky was the triggering event for the radicalization of Newt Gingrich and his followers—which, a decade later, culminated in Republicans taking control of the House.)

In 1986, the Republican vote share slipped to 49 percent, but their share of House seats declined to four. They were lucky to hold on to that, since John Hiler won reelection by only 47 votes. In 1988, Republicans lost another seat, reducing them to three, and the final election held under the plan they had gerrymandered saw their numbers fall to only two of ten districts despite still winning almost half the vote statewide. The gerrymander failed to perform for Republicans because they had created too many marginal seats, seats that gradually moved toward the Democrats. Unlike in California and Texas, Republican greed in Indiana not only failed to give them a bonus of a sixth or even seventh seat, but made it impossible for them to retain a share of seats roughly approximating their support in the electorate.

Pennsylvania 2000s

A second story of redistricting gone bad again involves Republicans, this time in Pennsylvania. The Pennsylvania congressional delegation in 2001 had eleven Republicans and ten Democrats and, as table 5.4 shows, the parties evenly divided the popular vote. The Keystone State lost seats with the new reapportionment, as it has after every census beginning with 1930. The new

TABLE 5.4
Republican Vote Share and Share of the Congressional Seats in Pennsylvania*

Year	Vote Share (%)	Share of Seats (%)
2000	50.04	52.3
2002	60.3	63.2
2004	55.5	63.2
2006	45.3	42.1
2008	44.0	36.8

*Pennsylvania does not report results for candidates who have no opponent. In 2000, one Republican had no opponent and therefore the Republican vote share is reduced. In the other three election years, the total Democratic vote is reduced because of the absence of any challenger to the Democrat. In 2002, one Democrat had no opponent; in 2004 two Democrats had no opposition. In 2006, one Democrat drew no opponent.

Source: Prepared by author.

allotment gave the state nineteen seats. The Republican legislature set out to capitalize on the opportunity to draw the new districts and crafted a plan that they hoped would boost their share of the seats to thirteen or even fourteen.[35] Although the plan did not deliver as Republicans hoped, it elected a dozen Republicans and only seven Democrats when the GOP took 60.3 percent of the statewide congressional vote in 2002.

Two years later, Republicans got a substantial bonus in seats when they retained twelve seats even as their vote share slipped to 55.5 percent. In 2006, Democrats made major gains in Pennsylvania as they took control of the U.S. House. Democrats picked up four Pennsylvania seats, so the GOP share fell to 42.1 percent. This closely approximated the GOP component of the popular vote, which dropped 10 percentage points from 2004. The GOP's decline continued in 2008 as they lost another seat, so that their 44 percent of the vote yielded only 36.8 percent of the seats.[36] Thus the Republican gerrymander did not give them substantially more seats than their vote share except in 2004. Their efforts failed to sustain them when Democrats surged in 2006.

Although Republicans designed the Pennsylvania plan to favor their party, the elections in this decade suggest that the plan had little bias. In 2004 when Republicans got 55.5 percent of the vote it translated into 63.2 percent of the seats. Four years later, Democrats took about the same share of the vote and they got 63.2 percent of the seats. Thus the bonus going to the party that got a majority of the vote was almost identical.

Bipartisan Gerrymanders

An alternative, often favored by incumbents of both parties, produces districts that are secure for one party or the other and discourage competition between the parties. The same techniques that can be used to gerrymander a state to favor one party can also craft districts in which the minority party in a district has virtually no chance of success. Bipartisan gerrymanders are likely when neither party has complete control over the redistricting process. In a state in which the congressional delegation size remains unchanged, a new plan may simply bolster the prospects for incumbents of both parties. Incumbents happily swap out supporters of the opposition to a neighboring district in return for an increase in their own supporters coming from a district that elects a member of the opposite party. Most congressional districts (233) drawn to adjust for the 2000 Census were in bipartisan plans, up from 147 a decade earlier.[37]

California accounted for more than a fifth of these districts in bipartisan plans in 2002.[38] As one might anticipate with a bipartisan plan, members of both parties fared well. In 2002, thirty members of the California delegation won with two-thirds of the vote. Another nineteen members received 60 to 67 percent of the vote. Only four members, all of whom were Democrats, took less than 55 percent of the vote. All twenty Republicans had more than 60 percent of the vote, although this plan was crafted by a legislature dominated by Democrats. Table 5.5 compares the heavy distribution of very safe seats in 2002 with the two previous elections. Whether the comparison is with the 2000 presidential election or the previous midterm election, the number of seats won with more than 60 percent of the vote increased, while the number won with less than 55 percent of the vote dropped. Little partisan change occurred in California through the 2008 election, after which Democrats held a thirty-four to nineteen advantage.

Gerrymandering has generally been used in this volume and elsewhere to indicate one group taking unfair advantage of a weaker group. How can it be then that a bipartisan or sweetheart compromise meets the conditions so as to bear the label of gerrymander? Who is being disadvantaged if both parties join hands in support of a plan?

TABLE 5.5
Competitiveness in California Congressional Districts, 1998–2002

Winner's Vote (%)	1998	2000	2002
Less than 50	2	3	0
50–54	5	6	1
55–59	7	5	3
60–66	12	15	19
More than 67	26	23	30

Source: Created by author from results published in *The Almanac of American Politics*. Michael Barone and Grant Ujifusa, *The Almanac of American Politics, 2002,* and *The Almanac of American Politics, 2004.* (Washington, D.C.: National Journal, 2001 and 2003, respectively.)

Some would argue that the public is shortchanged when the parties conspire to create uncompetitive districts. At the heart of a bipartisan gerrymander, each party comes away with a set of districts in which it is almost guaranteed a victory. The minority party's voters in a district will be consigned to perpetual defeat and thus have no influence on the outcome. These voters may become discouraged and cease participating, although that seems unlikely since their votes while having no impact on the outcome of the congressional elections may still be important for statewide or local offices. Alternatively, Ronald Weber warns that the absence of competition in a congressional district may discourage participation by individuals of *both* parties whose votes could determine the outcome of statewide offices.[39]

Another possible disadvantage to designing uncompetitive districts is that incumbents, recognizing that they are invulnerable, may be unresponsive to the desires of their constituents. This seems unlikely on issues about which the constituents have serious concerns. While the incumbent may be safe from challenges from the opposite party, there remains the possibility of a primary challenge. Moreover, in a district made up disproportionately of members of one party, there may be little disagreement on policy preferences, so that unless the incumbent has personal reasons for opposing the constituency, it may be quite easy to vote with the constituency and satisfy its expectations.

District competitiveness may influence the distribution of federal funding for projects. With electoral security comes seniority and with seniority comes greater influence—so that a legislator from an uncompetitive district, all other things being equal, may be especially effective in securing pork barrel projects.[40] The politically powerful, who often come from secure districts, can be especially successful in embedding earmarks to fund projects and contracts in their districts. An alternative perspective, however, suggests that it is only the most electorally insecure incumbents who will go to the additional trouble of winning new projects for their districts.[41]

Half a century ago, Anthony Downs argued that in competitive districts, each party has an incentive to move toward the ideological center in order to appeal to the decisive swing voters who are undecided or Independents.[42] Each party's nominees might assume that they can count on the support from their fellow partisans and thus move toward the center so that the choices confronting the electorate in the general election differ relatively little. While that view is still articulated at times,[43] most research concludes that competitiveness does not prompt candidates to adopt moderate positions. Instead, Democrats in competitive districts tend to be mainstream Democrats and Republicans in these districts are well within the mainstream of their party. Consequently, when party control of a competitive district changes, the positions taken by the new member of Congress differ vastly from those of the predecessor.[44]

If a bipartisan gerrymander results in few competitive districts, a legislature is less likely to respond to changes in the electorate's preferences. As previously discussed, since changing legislative outputs usually requires changing the personnel, if few constituencies change partisan hands, then only if the legislature is almost evenly divided between the parties is there much prospect that an election will inject enough new blood to alter government policy. In a legislature having a high swing ratio, a small shift in public partisan preferences can substantially change party control of seats and usher in a cluster of new policies.

Competitiveness

At first blush, it appears that partisan gerrymanders may have contributed to a substantial reduction in competitive districts and thus fewer incumbent defeats. Table 5.6 charts the decline in the number of incumbent defeats over time. The table excludes years ending in "2" immediately following redistricting, when the newly configured districts may account for a number of defeats. The remaining four elections that are included for each decade present figures for periods when little if any redistricting occurred, since it excludes the first election year after the release of new census data. The trend shows a dramatic drop since the post-1940 Census, when 152 incumbents lost in the last four election years of that decade. During the next three decades, incumbent defeats stabilized at about 100 before plummeting to only 43 defeats in the 1980s. The 1990s show an increase largely attributable to the defeat of 34 Democrats in 1994, when Republicans claimed their first House majority in forty years. Had the incidence of defeats in 1994 been no greater than for the other three elections of the decade, then only 44 or 45 defeats would have occurred.

Early assessments of the post-2000 redistricting judged it to have reduced the number of competitive congressional districts to an all-time low.[45]

In 2002, political mapmakers, with few exceptions, went for maximum incumbent protection plans. Take Iowa [which is discussed later in this chapter], for example, where an independent redistricting commission drew the state's five districts county by county without taking politics into consideration. That process netted more competitive seats in Iowa than in California, Texas, and Illinois combined.[46]

In the three election cycles in the current decade, the electorate has rejected forty-seven incumbents. Despite assertions early in the decade that the post-2000 redistricting plans minimized the number of competitive districts, through the first three elections of the decade, more incumbents lost general elections than in the four elections held under the plans drawn in the 1980s. However, unless 2010 proves especially lethal to incumbents, the number of defeats in the current decade will be the second smallest in the seven decades included in table 5.6.

Not only do fewer incumbents now lose reelection battles, those who retain their seats tend to win by larger margins. The leading scholars of candidate recruitment have stated, "Competition in congressional elections . . . has all but disappeared."[47] Following the 2001–2002 redistricting, many observers judged fewer than one in ten congressional districts to be competitive. As long as incumbents or political parties dominate the redistricting process, competitiveness will likely suffer. Incumbents and parties much prefer largely predictable environments. Work by Bruce Cain and his collaborators shows that while the number of competitive districts had declined dramatically by 2002, much of the decline occurred between redistrictings rather than immediately after drawing new districts.[48]

The electoral success of House incumbents is, of course, not automatic. Incumbents spend extensive resources and much of their own time trying to persuade voters to return them to office. In these efforts incumbents have a number of advantages. As David Mayhew observed many years ago, "If a group of planners sat down and tried to design a pair of American national assemblies with the goal of serving members' electoral needs year in and year out, they would be hard pressed to improve on what exists."[49] Members of Congress return to their districts repeatedly, make numerous personal presentations, use the frank to fill constituents' mailboxes with newsletters,

TABLE 5.6
Defeats of U.S. House Incumbents

Year	Incumbent Defeats
1944–1950	152
1954–1960	100
1964–1970	107
1974–1980	103
1984–1990	43
1994–2000	68
2004–2008	47

Source: Harold W. Stanley and Richard G. Niemi, *Vital Statistics on American Politics, 2007–2008* (Washington, DC: Congressional Quarterly Press, 2008). Figures for 2008 added by the author.

assign staff to process casework, and issue press releases claiming credit for anything good that happens in the district.

During the late 1950s and the first half of the next decade, approximately 60 percent of House incumbents won reelection with more than 60 percent of the vote.[50] Since then the number of competitive districts has declined. Beginning with 1966, more than 60 percent of incumbents have won reelection with at least 60 percent of the vote, and frequently that figure has exceeded 70 percent. In 2004, more than 85 percent of House incumbents polled at least 60 percent of the vote.[51] Sam Hirsch, who has litigated numerous voting rights cases, concluded that the redistricting conducted after the 2000 Census "was the most incumbent-friendly in modern American history."[52] Bolstering that assertion, Hirsch points out that the forty-three incumbents who won reelection with less than 60 percent of the vote in 2002 was half the average number that had been reelected in similarly competitive contests in the *immediate aftermath* of the three previous post-redistricting elections. An editorial writer reviewing the weak 2002 challengers sneered, "The magnitude of incumbency's triumph in last week's elections for the House of Representatives was so dramatic that the term 'election'—with its implications of voter choice and real competition—seems almost too generous to describe what happened on Tuesday."[53]

While redistricting, particularly bipartisan gerrymandering, seems to offer an explanation for the greater security enjoyed by incumbents beginning in the mid-1960s, several political scientists writing in the 1970s who explored the impact of redistricting concluded that heightened incumbent security could not be attributed to the drawing of less competitive districts.[54] One study uncovered little evidence of partisan redistricting in the 1970s.[55]

While scholars writing in the 1970s found little evidence that redistricting produced greater electoral security, politicians overwhelmingly believe that the drawing of district lines has significant consequences. By large margins the potential candidates interviewed by Sandy Maisel and his collaborators saw district drawing as impacting partisan prospects.[56] And it is not just prospective candidates who believe redistricting to be consequential. The efforts made by each party to influence the drawing of district lines, support litigation to challenge what they perceive to be unfavorable lines, and recruit candidates in anticipation of redistricting sessions all indicate that they see the placement of district lines as having a great and lingering impact.

Bipartisan gerrymanders can make all or most incumbents more secure, but efforts to use new maps to dislodge incumbents have also succeeded. Key to plans that defeat incumbents is to separate incumbents from some of the constituents they have represented.[57] New voters added to a district have no relationship with the incumbent and so for them the situation is like an open-seat contest. A party in charge of redistricting that seeks to defeat an incumbent of the opposition party can add voters who do not identify with the incumbent's party to the district. The incumbent may lack sufficient time before the next election to cultivate support by traveling in the district, processing casework, and securing projects and, consequently, may be less well known among the voters recently added to the district.[58] Lacking time to develop ties in the new part of the district means that the incumbent lacks a personal vote (voters committed to him or her) and therefore must rely more heavily on votes generated through party loyalty.

The bleaching of districts surrounding the majority-black districts created in the early 1990s contributed to the election of Republicans from the whiter districts, as discussed in chapter 3. In addition, redistricting, by disrupting the relationships Southern Democratic incumbents had with their Republican-leaning constituents, opened the way for Republican gains in districts that did not become substantially whiter. Seth McKee has shown that in 1992 and 1994 and then a decade later following the Tom DeLay Texas gerrymander, voters added to districts of Democratic incumbents supported these legislators at substantially lower rates than did voters who had lived in the districts prior to the new maps.[59] In the 1990s the GOP benefited from the unpopularity of the Democratic Party, especially in the South.

Disrupting existing relationships between incumbents and voters, especially in a district that gives evidence from presidential or other statewide elections of tilting toward the opposition party, may enable the out party to recruit a stronger challenger to the incumbent. For example, the two Texas Democratic incumbents who lost to challengers in 2004 each faced an individual with at least ten years experience as an elected judge.[60] In 2000 and 2002, the incumbent Democrats had disposed of challengers who lacked office-holding experience.

Another perspective on the relationship between redistricting and incumbency advantage comes from Cox and Katz, who show that an altered district can prompt a weak incumbent to retire.[61] Thus the need to reestablish population equality among districts culls those who have lost touch with their constituents. Having an established calendar for redistricting also influences the behavior of the most promising potential candidates of the opposing party, who can wait to seek a congressional seat when it is most likely to be open or has an incumbent weakened as a result of having lost supporters from the old district.

In contrast with those who urge using redistricting to promote competitiveness, a recent book disagrees with those concerns and, instead, argues the virtues of uncompetitive districts. As mentioned in chapter 1, Brunell argues that more people would be satisfied with Congress, its policies, and their legislators if most voters lived in districts in which their party constituted an overwhelming majority.[62] High concentrations of supporters of one party also make the task of the representative easier, since cues from the constituency will overwhelmingly point in one direction.

Undoubtedly party considerations will stay in the forefront as redistricting using the 2010 Census gets under way. Those who lose in the legislature because their party is outnumbered will continue to attack these plans and will probably mention partisan considerations in their court pleadings. But to have any hope for success, the challengers will need to raise other concerns, such as allegations that the plan unfairly treats minorities or does not meet the most stringent requirements of "one person, one vote."

Partisan Gerrymanders and the Courts . . . Part II

Until 1962, the Supreme Court considered the whole issue of redistricting off-limits, as a political question. The Court waited another quarter-century before finding issues involving partisan gerrymanders justiciable. The same Indiana Republicans who produced the congressional plan described above set out to enhance their position within the state legislature, and those efforts ultimately came before the High Court.

Prior to 1986, a political party unfairly treated in the course of redistricting had no prospect of relief from the courts. In *Davis v. Bandemer*, the Supreme Court held out hope to disadvantaged political parties when it ruled that a party could use the Equal Protection Clause to challenge a plan.[63] The Indiana Democrats who sued in *Bandemer* did not get the new plan they sought, but the Court indicated what would be necessary for success. To win, a disadvantaged political party must prove both an intent to discriminate against it as well as an actual discriminatory effect. However a party's showing that its share of the seats in the legislature came up far short of its percentage of the popular vote does not suffice. Justice Byron White, writing for the Court, observed:

> An individual or a group of individuals who votes for a losing candidate is usually deemed to be adequately represented by the winning candidate and to have as much opportunity to influence that candidate as other voters in the district. We cannot presume in such a situation, without actual proof to the contrary, that the candidate elected will entirely ignore the interests of those voters. . . . To prevail, a party must demonstrate that it is unable to influence the political process which would include both evidence of continued frustration of the will

of a majority of the voters or effective denial to a minority of voters of a fair
chance to influence the political process.

Interestingly, the one member of the Court who had served in a state legislature, Sandra Day O'Connor, sided with the minority, who continued to
believe that courts should not hear challenges to partisan gerrymanders.

Three years after *Bandemer*, California Republicans challenged the Burton
Plan referenced earlier. The Republicans pointed out that in 1984 they had
polled a majority of the popular vote but had won only 40 percent of the
seats. In the next election they again got a smaller share of the seats than the
votes. They contended—as proved to be correct—that the Burton Plan had
consigned them to minority status in the congressional delegation for the
remainder of the decade. The trial court found that the plaintiffs had failed to
meet the second part, the effects test, of the *Bandemer* decision because they
failed to show that they had been shut out of the political process. The court
noted that while Republicans won a smaller share of the congressional seats
than of the vote, nothing prevented them from registering voters, organizing, voting, and campaigning.[64] As further evidence that Republicans had not
been excluded from California's political process, Republicans had elected
the governor and one of the senators in addition to having 40 percent of the
state's congressional seats.

In 2004, the Supreme Court encountered the question of partisan redistricting again. The case involved the Pennsylvania congressional redistricting described earlier in this chapter. As in every case since *Bandemer*, the
Court did not find the minority party sufficiently disadvantaged to warrant
judicial intervention. The plurality opinion of the Court in *Veith v. Jubelirer*,
subscribed to by four justices, recommended reversal of *Bandemer* since no
consensus has emerged as to what would have to be proved for a plaintiff to
prevail.[65] Another set of four justices believed that the plaintiffs had provided
sufficient evidence to win, but these four justices suggested three different
standards to support their conclusion. The swing justice, Arthur Kennedy,
did not find the evidence sufficient to throw out the Pennsylvania plan as an
unconstitutional partisan gerrymander. However, he separated himself from
the other four on the issue of reversing *Bandemer*. While Kennedy agreed that
a standard did not exist, he held out hope that at some point in the future a
standard would be devised and therefore voted to continue considering the
issue of a partisan gerrymander to be justiciable.

Justice Antonin Scalia, writing for the plurality, rejected the Fourteenth
Amendment as a basis for finding for plaintiffs, noting that the Equal Protection Clause "guarantees equal protection of the law to persons, not equal
representation in government to equivalently sized groups." The plurality
opinion cited one of the leading casebooks on voting rights for the proposi-

tion that, throughout its subsequent history, "*Bandemer* has served almost exclusively as an invitation to litigation without much prospect of redress."[66] Justice Scalia pointed out that those who had sought relief under *Bandemer* had achieved nothing except to rack up substantial legal fees.

The hesitancy of the Supreme Court majority to find the Pennsylvania gerrymander so extreme as to deny political influence to the Democrats proved accurate. As noted above, the 2006 elections showed that the system remained responsive, as Democrats gained four seats to take a majority of the delegation. The Democratic share of the seats won in the 2006 election slightly exceeded their share of the vote.

The Court's *Vieth* minority did not give up easily. When the *Larios* case from Georgia came before the High Court, it affirmed the district court opinion that the legislature had violated the Equal Protection Clause in favoring south Georgia and Atlanta at the expense of north Georgia and the suburbs. However, two justices signed an opinion stating their belief that the techniques used by Democrats in drawing the Georgia districts met the *Bandemer* thresholds.[67]

Reaction Gerrymandering

The twenty-first century witnessed a phenomenon in which states gerrymandered their congressional districts in an attempt to offset gerrymandering by the opposition party in another state. As recounted in the next chapter, Georgia Democrats manipulated the boundaries of their congressional districts in 2001 in an effort to pick up four seats. This triggered a reaction in Pennsylvania where, as noted earlier in this chapter, Republicans sought to offset the anticipated Democratic gains in Georgia. Michigan Republicans also drew new congressional districts, which they justified as countering what Democrats had done in Georgia.[68]

Attacking Partisan Gerrymanders through Different Means

With courts having proven unwilling to overturn partisan gerrymanders, political parties that have lost in the legislative arena have sought to eliminate plans that disadvantaged them by raising other issues. In *Larios*, Georgia Republicans succeeded in their challenge to what all sides acknowledged to be a partisan gerrymander by attacking it for regional population deviations.

A second ploy by the party that loses in the legislature is to challenge the racial equity of a plan. In several of the lawsuits brought challenging the racial gerrymanders of the 1990s, such as the plans that advantaged Demo-crats in Texas, Republican activists were among the plantiffs. Texas Republi-cans initially attacked the congressional plan as a partisan gerrymander and, when that failed, launched a second attack raising equal protection issues but in the context of having separated minority and white voters on the basis of race. In the next decade, Democrats challenged the DeLay Plan, citing as one of their allegations that it eliminated minority influence districts.

Interparty Conflict

As noted in chapter 3, courts have accepted partisanship to explain district lines that might trigger suspicions and be invalidated if based on racial con-siderations. Recall that the challenge to the last iteration of the prolonged 1990s challenge to North Carolina's Twelfth District hinged on whether race was the predominant factor. The state successfully argued that while race had received some consideration, the primary motivation was to carve out a safe Democratic district in the western half of the state.[69] The state explained that it had simply linked heavily Democratic precincts rather than focusing pri-marily on the racial composition of those precincts. Of course, since African Americans are the most loyal Democrats, an overwhelmingly Democratic district would also be a heavily black district.

Mapmakers learned quickly from *Cromartie v. Easley*, and when drawing districts to reflect population shifts of the 1990s, they focused on party. Their explanations and justifications pointed to partisan considerations, with race infrequently mentioned. This allowed the mapmakers, should they be ques-tioned, to explain that they were separating Democrats from Republicans.

Reducing Partisan Influence in Districting

While the legislature generally has the responsibility for redrawing congres-sional and state legislative districts, a few states have assigned this task to oth-ers. Frequently a shift in responsibility for redistricting comes about in the context of a reform effort designed to reduce the influence of partisanship. Where legislatures do not redraw boundaries, the power typically passes to a commission. In some instances the commission has sole responsibility, while in other states the commission becomes active only if the legislature fails to come up with a plan. While members of the commission may have less of a direct interest in the outcome than legislators do, not all commissions are buffered from partisan concerns and in some instances commissioners are active political players.

As noted earlier in the chapter, in Texas a nonlegislative body, which nonetheless consists of partisans, assumes the responsibility for drawing state legislative districts when the legislature fails to act. In contrast, in New Jersey an outsider chairs the Apportionment Commission, which consists of five Democrats and five Republicans. Invariably Democrats and Republicans have competing plans. The nonpartisan chair, who in the last three decennial rounds has been a Princeton political scientist, can try to work out a compromise. Ultimately, when attempts at compromise have failed, the chair has endorsed one of the plans, giving it the necessary sixth vote.[70]

The approach taken in Iowa is frequently pointed to as desirable because of the limited influence of party politics; however, the plan does not come from a commission. Instead, the Legislative Services Agency draws the map. In going about its task, the agency faces constraints not imposed in most states. When drawing congressional districts, it cannot divide counties, nor can it consider where the current incumbents live or the voting history of the counties. The agency simply tries to minimize the population variations among districts. Since Iowa has many counties with relatively small populations, it has been possible to design districts with relatively little population variation while meeting the other constraints. The legislature cannot change a plan submitted by the Legislative Services Agency but it can reject it, as the senate did in 2001. The Legislative Services Agency then submits a second and even a third plan if necessary for legislative consideration. The legislature cannot amend the first two plans, but should they both be rejected, legislators can seek to amend the third plan.

Iowa's 2002 plan contained evidence that the agency had honored the requirements of ignoring the homes of incumbents. The plan paired Republican incumbents Jim Leach and Jim Nussle in the same district. Both survived the 2002 election although it necessitated shifts in their constituencies. Leach ran in the Second District, much of which had been in the First District that he had previously represented. Leach won in the Second District in 2002 which contained five of the eight counties he had previously represented so that the citizens of Cedar Rapids and Iowa City continued to be his constituents. Nussle ran in the new First District, which contained nine of the counties from his old Second District and included Dubuque, Cedar Falls, and Waterloo. While the four incumbents who sought reelection succeeded, each of them had to introduce himself to a new set of constituents.

Table 5.7 shows that three of Iowa's four reelected incumbents saw their victory margins drop by 10 percentage points from 2000 to 2002. The reduced support for both Leach and Democrat Leonard Boswell put them in

TABLE 5.7
Impact of the 2002 Redistricting on Iowa Congressional Incumbents

	Vote Percentages	
Incumbent	2000	2002
Jim Nussle (R)	55	57
Jim Leach (R)	62	52
Leonard Boswell (D)	63	53
Tom Latham (R)	69	55

Source: Michael Barone with Richard E. Cohen, *The Almanac of American Politics, 2004* (Washington, DC: National Journal, 2003).

the marginal category. Incumbents who draw less than 55 percent of the vote often become targets in the next election, as eager challengers and national party organizations mark these incumbents as vulnerable. Even Tom Latham, who had no opposition in 1998 and had managed 61 percent of the vote in his first election in 1994, fell to 55 percent of the vote in 2002. Only Nussle did better in 2002 than in the previous election, as his 57 percent of the vote marked his strongest performance ever. The new plan from the Legislative Services Agency did shake things up in Iowa, even though all the incumbents survived. Heightened competitiveness in most of the incumbents' districts did not happen in other states.

Iowa's congressional districts remained competitive through 2008. The winners in fourteen of the twenty elections held between 2002 and 2008 received less than 60 percent of the vote. In 2006 no Iowa candidate got as much as 60 percent of the vote. The Second and Third districts have not cast as much as 60 percent of the vote for a candidate this decade. Leach narrowly lost his reelection bid in 2006, the year that also saw a Democrat elected in the First District.

Arizona's Independent Redistricting Commission, which unlike most commissions consists of citizens rather than politicians, has two members of each party and they choose an Independent as the fifth member. In 2002 the commission produced six relatively compact districts along with a strangely shaped Second District that runs from the western suburbs of Phoenix to the California border, then north to Utah. The strangest feature of the district is the thread that extends through the Grand Canyon to pick up the Hopi reservation in Navajo County. Because of the rivalry between Hopis and Navajos, it made sense to separate the two tribal reservations, leaving the Navajo in the First District. The previous plan had also separated the two tribes, although with a less bizarre design than in the 2002 plan.

Even with the operation of an independent commission and the need to fit in two new districts, Arizona's ultimate plan initially proved very incumbent friendly. The five incumbents who sought reelection, as shown in table 5.8, all won easily. Three of the incumbents increased their vote shares, while only Ed Pastor (D), who had the largest victory margin in 2000, saw his vote share slip. One of the new districts located in the southwest corner of the state elected Arizona's second Hispanic, with a comfortable 59 percent of the vote. Only the other new district, the vast First, which extended almost the entire length of the eastern border, proved competitive, with Republican Rick Renzi squeezing out a 3 percentage point victory even as he outspent his opponent by a 2.5:1 margin.

Although the Arizona constitution calls for the creation of competitive districts, the 2002 election saw only the newly created First District hotly contested. However, a longer-term assessment suggests that the Arizona commission, like Iowa's Legislative Services Agency, fostered more competition than most legislatures that carried out redistricting. Over the next three elections, three of the districts changed hands, as Democrats picked up the Fifth and Eighth districts in 2006 and added the First District in 2008 when Renzi retired. In 2008, winners in six districts took less than 60 percent of the vote, and three districts had winners with less than 55 percent of the vote.

TABLE 5.8
Electoral Results of the Arizona Congressional
Redistricting Done by an Independent Commission

		Vote Share	
Dist.	Member	2000	2002
1	Rick Renzi (R)	new	49*
2	Trent Franks (R)	66**	60
3	John Shadegg (R)	64	66
4	Ed Pastor (D)	69	67
5	J. D. Hayworth (R)	61	61
6	Jeff Flake (R)	54	66
7	Raul Grijalva (D)	new	59
8	Jim Kolbe (R)	60	63

*Renzi won 49% to 46%.
**2000 vote for retired Rep. Bob Stump (R).

Source: Election returns from Michael Barone with Richard E. Cohen, *The Almanac of American Politics,* 2004 (Washington, DC: National Journal, 2003).

The examples from Arizona and Iowa fit within a broader pattern. A study of redistricting plans from the early 1990s and 2000s concluded that plans fashioned by a court or a commission produced a larger share of competitive districts than when a legislature designed them.[71]

Controversy

Arguments For

With districting the most political activity, one must expect that a defenseless minority party will get the short end of the stick. Since members of both parties will exploit any advantage they have, to try to curb partisan gerrymanders is to swim against the tide. Partisan gerrymanders are indeed the political thicket that prudent judges will avoid. Sandra Day O'Connor, the only recent judge to have served as a legislator, understood the inherently political nature of redistricting and wisely refused to join her colleagues who wanted to undo plans that advantaged one party.

Attempts to design plans that produce legislative bodies in which the parties have seat shares that approximate their percentage of the popular vote are unlikely to succeed over the course of a decade due to the absence of a proportional representation electoral system. Even efforts to treat both parties fairly can fail due to unforeseen circumstances such as shifts in voter loyalties.

Since citizens have much more positive attitudes about the government and their legislator when represented by the candidate they supported, Brunell urges legislators to prepare maps that minimize competition so that the winning party has an overwhelming majority. A set of one-party districts will maximize the share of the electorate that had the opportunity to see its preferred candidate in office.[72] Plans that dampen competition will promote long tenure by incumbents, and as legislators gain seniority they typically enhance their ability to shape policies preferred by their constituents.

Arguments Against

The majority party may come up with plans that succeed in keeping its opponents permanently consigned to minority status. In the worst-case scenario, a party that consistently attracts the bulk of the popular vote statewide cannot win a legislative majority because of the unfairness of the maps. Designing maps that produce an unresponsive legislature thwarts electoral majorities from achieving their policy preferences. If the districting arrangement consistently prevents a majority of the electorate from securing control of the legislature, public cynicism will grow.

Allowing mapmakers to arrange voters so as to minimize the number of competitive districts results in most legislators not having to appeal to swing voters. Legislators who need appeal only to their own partisans tend not to be politically moderate. An absence of moderates may make compromises in the legislature difficult under circumstances of divided partisan control in the legislature, or when the chief executive and the legislative majority belong to different parties.

Conclusions

Efforts by one political party to take advantage of the other gave us the term *gerrymander*. Today, just as two hundred years ago, redistricting involves raw politics. It is not surprising, therefore, that when a party has the power to do so, it takes advantage of the opposition. Underpopulating or overpopulating districts, the distribution of minorities, and strange configurations have often had at base a desire to give one party a larger share of the seats than its proportion of the votes.

Some clever politicians have managed to devise districting plans that helped their parties for at least a decade. In other instances, however, the intended beneficiary ends up losing seats as a result of trying to spread its supporters too thinly.

The losing party after a redistricting session that produces a partisan plan will call the result a gerrymander and express righteous indignation at the failure of the majority to acknowledge basic fairness. While the possibility has existed that the aggrieved party may be able to secure relief from the courts, the hope has proven as elusive as the pot of gold at the end of the rainbow. A party that loses the redistricting battle must demonstrate that the plan discriminates against racial or ethnic minorities or that it treats different geographical areas within the state unequally in order to get a plan thrown out. Simply questioning the partisan fairness of the plan has never succeeded.

Plans not intended to disadvantage either party may come from independent commissions or legislatures when neither party has complete control. While these plans may be fairer from a partisan perspective, if they result in districts packed with one set of partisans, they will not promote competition.

6

Gerrymandering Georgia: A Case Study

The interesting case of Georgia particularly deserves a separate study in its own right, given the dramatic realized and potential Republican gains there as a result of racial redistricting.[1]

The state is not the same state it was. It's not the same state that it was in 1965 or in 1975, or even in 1980 or 1990. We have changed. We've come a great distance. I think in—it's not just in Georgia, but in the American South, I think people are preparing to lay down the burden of race.[2]

Over the past forty years the dominate forces behind Georgia redistricting have shifted from malapportionment and rural dominance in the 1960s and 1970s to fair racial representation in the 1980s and 1990s to most recently partisan gerrymandering.[3]

WHEN IT COMES TO REAPPORTIONMENT AND REDISTRICTING, Georgia has traveled a long and difficult road. The Empire State of the South has repeatedly had to defend its maps in federal court since the 1960s. Each decade the Department of Justice has found at least one Georgia plan lacking in terms of racial fairness. Two factors account for Georgia's difficulties: malapportionment that advantaged rural communities and a history of racial discrimination.

"One Person, One Vote" in Georgia

When the U.S. Supreme Court launched the Redistricting Revolution in 1962, three practices made Georgia susceptible to judicial demands that districts have equal populations. As the measures of malapportionment in table 2.1 show, Georgia legislative districts had some of the nation's largest population deviations. Additionally, the county unit system gave rural voters an extraordinary influence in statewide elections.

The End of the County Unit System

The 1917 Neill Primary Act used the Electoral College as a rough model for weighting votes in Democratic primaries for statewide and some congressional offices.[4] Candidates for governor and other offices subject to this legislation got unit votes for each county they carried. The 8 most populous counties had six votes each, the next 30 largest four votes each, and the remaining 121 two votes each.[5] A statewide candidate could secure the Democratic nomination with as little as 12.5 percent of the popular vote by winning the 103 smallest counties with their total of 206 unit votes. The Talmadge machine relied on this malapportionment, and in 1946 Gene Talmadge won the gubernatorial primary even though James Carmichael won a plurality of the popular vote. During the life of the county unit system, Republicans were not a factor in statewide or congressional contests; the Democratic nominee invariably won the general election.

In the wake of the *Baker v. Carr* decision,[6] Fulton county resident James Sanders sued the state Democratic Party, arguing that the primary system which gave Fulton County only 1.5 percent of the unit votes despite having almost 15 percent of the voters in the state violated "one person, one vote." A three-judge federal panel found that the six-four-two scheme violated the new "one person, one vote" standard, but would have allowed the practice to continue if the disparity in the unit votes of counties did not exceed the difference in the weight of the votes of states in the Electoral College. The Supreme Court found the analogy to the Electoral College inappropriate and banned the county unit system.[7]

State Senate

A separate suit challenging the apportionment of the state legislature produced a court order to distribute seats in one chamber on the basis of population.[8] The senate consisted of fifty-four members, all but two of whom represented three-county districts. The counties took turns electing senators, so that even the smallest county in the state elected a senator every third term. To ensure that small counties had their turn to select a senator, only voters in the county in line to elect a senator voted in that election. This arrangement prevented senators from earning seniority, making that chamber much weaker than the house. For that reason and because redistricting the house would require changing the state constitution, senate districts were redrawn prior to the 1962 elections. Atlanta's Fulton County went from one senator to seven, while Savannah and Macon each got multiple senators. Where senate districts previously had three counties, some grew substantially. The Fourteenth District, which elected a peanut warehouser named Jimmy Carter, expanded from three counties to seven.[9]

Congressional Districts

Having felled the county unit system and the malapportioned senate, Atlanta-based plaintiffs turned their attention to the congressional districts. As discussed in chapter 2, District 5 had 823,680 people, more than twice the state's ideal district population of 394,312. Seven of the ten districts were underpopulated by anywhere from 3.65 to 30.98 percent. The Supreme Court threw out the congressional district maps for violating Article I of the Constitution.[10]

State House

Beginning with the 1868 constitution, the 8 most populous counties had three members; the 30 next-most-populous counties received two representatives each; and the remaining 121 counties each had one representative. Because of population differences, one vote in tiny Echols County carried 133 times the weight of a Fulton County vote, and the representatives of about a quarter of the population could control the General Assembly (as shown in table 2.1). Urban and high-growth counties were disadvantaged.[11] After the Supreme Court ruled in an Alabama case that both chambers of the state legislature must be based on population, Georgia held a special election in 1965 to fill the newly configured 205 house seats.

As occurred with the redrawing of the senate three years earlier, the new house districts resulted in a more diverse legislature. Giving urban areas a share of seats proportional to their population opened the way for both African Americans and Republicans to crash a previously all-white, Democratic affair. The redistricted senate welcomed its first black member in decades and three Republicans in 1963. In the house seven African Americans and twenty-three Republicans took the oath of office following the 1965 special election.

"One Person, One Vote" in the Twenty-First Century

From the deluge of court challenges to districting plans evolved the notion that state legislative plans should limit population deviations to a range of 5 percent above or below the ideal. Many jurisdictions treated the +/–5 percent deviation as a safe harbor. These bounds held inequities in representation and voting to what seemed to be legally acceptable limits. A compelling state interest in having compact districts, following county and city boundaries, maintaining continuity of representation, or not splitting existing precincts can justify deviations in state legislative districts.

The Department of Justice, Voting Rights, and Redistricting

Because it used a literacy test and fewer than half of its adults voted in the 1964 presidential election, Georgia was one of the states with long traditions of discriminating against potential black voters made subject to Section 5 of the Voting Rights Act of 1965. Section 5 requires that Georgia submit redistricting plans for federal approval prior to implementation. The state can either submit the plans to the U.S. attorney general or it can seek a declaratory judgment that a plan is not discriminatory from the district court of the District of Columbia.

The Department of Justice (DOJ) was slow in developing standards for implementing Section 5.[12] The expectations concerning redistricting were fleshed out as Georgia sought to comply when redrawing its districts. In 1970, Andy Young won the Democratic nomination in the Fifth Congressional District, which contained the City of Atlanta and some of its suburbs. Young managed 43 percent of the vote in his effort to unseat a two-term Republican. As the legislature went about reconfiguring the district to meet equal population requirements in 1971, it carefully excluded Young's home from the new Fifth District. It also excluded the home of Atlanta vice-mayor Maynard Jackson. Jackson, like Young an African American, might be a formidable candidate for the Democratic nomination. DOJ refused to accept this plan—the only congressional plan DOJ vetoed in the 1970s—until it was reconfigured to include the homes of these two possible candidates and the black percentage of the population increased from 38.3 to 44.2. In 1972 Young joined Houston's Barbara Jordan as the first southern black members of Congress in the twentieth century. In 1973 Jackson became Atlanta's first African American mayor.

Georgia also had to redo its maps for the General Assembly, and this necessitated a different map more favorable to African Americans put in place for the 1974 election. That year saw African Americans increase their seats in

TABLE 6.1
Numbers of Majority-Black Districts and Black Legislators

	House	Senate	Congress
Plans used 1974–1980	24	2	0
Blacks elected 1974	19	2	1
Plans used 1982–1990	29	9	1
Blacks elected 1990	27	8	1
General Assembly Committee plans 1991	35	10	2
LBC Task Force plans 1991	42	13	3
MAXBLACK plans 1991	51	15	3
Plans used 1992–1994	41	13	3
Blacks elected 1992	31	9	3
Plans used 1996–2000	37	11	1
Plans used 2002	38	13	2
Blacks elected 2002	39	10	4
Plans used 2006–2009	41	13	2
Blacks elected 2006	44	12	4

Sources: Robert A. Holmes, "Reapportionment Strategies in the 1990s: A Case of Georgia," in *Race and Redistricting in the 1990s,* ed. Bernard Grofman (New York: Agathon Press, 1998), 191–228; data from redistricting plans provided by the Georgia Legislative Reapportionment Office.

the house from fourteen to nineteen. The senate continued to have two black members.

By 1980, the Fifth District, which had been 44 percent black when it initially elected Young, had a 50.3 percent black majority. However, like many districts that contain urban cores, the Fifth District was underpopulated. Pursuant to the nonretrogression rule, DOJ would not sign off on a plan that reduced the black percentage. At a minimum, the new plan would have to add roughly equal numbers of whites and blacks as it went about achieving population equality. The Legislative Black Caucus (LBC) had as its goal a 65 percent African American Fifth District. It was widely accepted in the early 1980s that districts needed to be almost two-thirds black for African Americans to be able to elect their preferences.[13] One LBC senator proposed a plan to make the Fifth District 73 percent black, and in the house one plan had the district at 74 percent black. LBC efforts gained no traction in the house, which minimally increased the black percentage.

The senate took a very different approach and increased the black concentration to 69 percent of the population. A couple of factors motivated this increase. Republican Paul Coverdell, who was elected to the U.S. Senate in 1992, knew that boosting the black percentage in the Fifth District would reduce the black percentage in the neighboring Fourth District. Coverdell hoped that a whiter Fourth District would elect a Republican. However, the coalition of Republicans and African Americans working for a blacker Fifth

District came up far short of a majority in the senate, so the plan had to attract white Democrats. Key to securing those needed votes was senate leader Tom Allgood, whose district in Augusta might have been given a large black majority which would have endangered his reelection. He supported the effort of his African American colleague Julian Bond to boost the black concentration in the Fifth District, in return for less pressure to increase the black percentage in the Augusta senate district.[14]

The conference committee endorsed a 57 percent black district (54 percent black among those of voting age),[15] which DOJ rejected in light of the alternatives with higher black concentrations. Arguing that it was not guilty of retrogression, the state sought vindication from the district court of the District of Columbia. The week-long trial focused not on the adequacy of the black concentration or on retrogression or its absence. Instead, the verdict hinged on the motivation behind the districting decisions. The state contended that it divided the Fourth and Fifth districts on a north-south axis that largely followed the line between Fulton and DeKalb counties. Following the move toward equal population districts, these two counties had each dominated its own congressional district. The state's explanation that it sought to maintain a black population in excess of 20 percent in the Fourth District in order thwart the possibility of Republicans winning that district proved unconvincing.

DOJ noted that because the black population was expanding into south DeKalb,[16] using the county boundary to separate the congressional districts divided a single African American community. DOJ attorneys latched on to testimony provided by then Lieutenant Governor Zell Miller, who urged the maintenance of a mountain district. Miller, who comes from a mountain county just below the North Carolina line, explained that people in his part of the state had unique interests and needed a member of Congress to represent those interests. DOJ argued that African Americans in Atlanta also constituted a distinct community that should be contained in a single district with a member of Congress to shepherd their interests.

In ruling against the state, the three-judge panel emphasized what it saw as racism underlying the districting decision. The court noted that because the plan was not guilty of retrogression, there was no discriminatory effect. The court, however, concluded that the state failed to prove an absence of a discriminatory purpose and under *Georgia v. United States* the submitting authority must prove its plan does not discriminate.[17] The court pointed to the statement by Joe Mack Wilson, who chaired the house redistricting committee, "The Justice Department is trying to make us draw nigger districts and I don't want to draw nigger districts."[18] Wilson told black representative Al Scott, "If you blacks want anything . . . higher than this 57 percent [black district], you better be prepared to get it from the Justice Department or the courts." Another legislator quoted Wilson as saying, "I'm not going to draw a honky Republican district and I'm not going to draw a nigger district if I can help it."[19] The court asserted in its findings of fact that "Joe Mack Wilson is a racist."

After the Supreme Court refused to review the *Busbee* decision, the legislature adopted a new plan that boosted the black percentage in the Fifth District to 65.02 percent and 59.6 percent black among registrants, whereupon DOJ signed off. The litigation and subsequent special session needed to raise the black percentage in the Fifth District resulted in a court order that delayed the election cycle for the Fourth and Fifth districts. The November 2 election chose 433 members of the House but was primary day in the two Atlanta-area districts. These two districts held their general elections on November 30 and returned white, Democratic incumbents in each district.

In 1986 John Lewis, an African American, won the district. As Coverdell had hoped, in 1984 a Republican won the Fourth District where the black population had been reduced to 13 percent.

DOJ also objected to plans for the state house and senate. The LBC came up with a plan that had forty-three majority-black house districts, although the caucus set its goal as thirty-six majority-black house seats and twelve in the senate. The plans adopted by the General Assembly had twenty-nine house and eight senate districts with black majorities. As with the congressional plan, Africans Americans and Republicans worked together on the state legislative plans. DOJ required only minor adjustments, and the 1982 elections saw modest gains with the number of black senators increasing from two to four while the house contingent stagnated at twenty-one.

The 1990s

By the time of the next census, DOJ had substantially changed its standards for assessing districting plans. From the time of the initial enactment of the Voting Rights Act (VRA) in 1965, the legislation's chief function had been to prevent implementation of *new* discriminatory laws in states having historically low minority participation. While the VRA succeeded in preventing new acts of bias, as when DOJ blocked Georgia's 1971 and 1981 redistricting plans, Section 5 was not designed to root out discriminatory practices in place prior to 1964. To deal with existing electoral systems, Congress rewrote Section 2 when renewing the Voting Rights Act in 1982 so that plaintiffs challenging an existing electoral system need not prove intent to discriminate. Plaintiffs could prevail by showing that the plan had a discriminatory effect or result.

Congress

Georgia legislators approached the post-1990 redistricting committed to creating a second majority-black congressional district. Doubling the number of majority-black districts would prevent charges of retrogression, and legislators anticipated that unlike in the two previous decades their plan would have no difficulty securing approval from DOJ. Shortly before the special session to draw plans for Congress and the state legislative chambers, I met with the Legislative Black Caucus (LBC). At that time, the LBC's primary objective was a second district likely to elect an African American. Caucus member Eugene Walker, who chaired the senate redistricting committee, told his colleagues that to draw a second district with a black majority would require linking the African American populations in three different urban areas, since black concentrations in a single urban area were sufficient for only one district, John Lewis's Atlanta district. The plan adopted by the special session of the General Assembly drew a new 60.6 percent black district by linking the black population in south DeKalb (some of the same area at the heart of the 1982 *Busbee* litigation) with black concentrations in Augusta and Macon, using part of the old cotton-growing Black Belt to tie the three urban areas together. The plan split the three urban counties along racial lines in order to bump up the black population in the new Eleventh District.

Republicans developed their own redistricting operation rather than work with the state's Legislative Reapportionment Office. The LBC had hoped to have a third redistricting program through the American Civil Liberties Union office in Atlanta. When the ACLU did not get its operation up and running, Republicans offered access to their system to LBC members.

There is disagreement over who gets credit for having come up with the initial design, but before the expiration of the sixty-day period given DOJ to review the plan with two black districts, someone in the black-Republican coalition discovered a way to draw three majority-black districts. Former state representative Bart Ladd (R) claims that he gave the plan with three black districts to Cynthia McKinney.[20]

Ladd's account, which may include a few dramatic embellishments, is that he figured out how to link black concentrations in each of two sets of three urban areas together to develop both a second and a third majority-black district. Ladd, a Delta pilot, then flew to Washington, where he presented his map to DOJ. He had not drawn a complete map showing the location of all eleven districts but only the feasibility of the three majority-black districts. DOJ was intrigued but told Ladd that he would need to demonstrate how to draw the eight majority-white districts and stay within acceptable population tolerances. Ladd returned to Atlanta where he and others at the Republican redistricting office worked like college students pulling all-nighters before a big exam and completed the task. The three-district plan developed on the Republican computer had to be transmitted to the state's reapportionment office. At this time, data and materials rather than being transmitted electronically were physically taken on floppy disks. File names were limited to eight characters or letters; the name given the three-district plan was "MAXBLACK," which became the name for this proposal and was at times more generally applied to other efforts to maximize the number of majority-black seats.[21]

The coalition of some LBC members and Republicans came nowhere close to a majority in either chamber of the Georgia legislature. To force the MAXBLACK plans on the state would require help from DOJ. The careerists at DOJ had long supported increasing the numbers of black officials, as indicated by their demands when reviewing Georgia redistricting plans from earlier decades.[22] In the early 1990s, the objectives of the careerists found support among the top tier of appointed officials. Republicans named by President George H. W. Bush to run the Justice Department saw how promoting black interests could also advance the GOP, as acknowledged in the testimony of Assistant Attorney General for Civil Rights John Dunne (quoted in chapter 3).[23]

DOJ's rejection of the state's two-majority-black-district plan came in the midst of a growing split within the LBC. The chair of the LBC, Michael Thurmond, and the chair of the senate redistricting committee, Eugene Walker, favored plans with two black districts. A group led by Cynthia McKinney, and civil rights activist Tyrone Brooks, both of whom are from Atlanta, and two Albany representatives met with DOJ officials to lobby for the three-district plan. When the representatives of the General Assembly, which included the chairs of the two chambers' redistricting committees, Rep. Bob Hanner, a white, and Sen. Eugene Walker, a black, met with the DOJ preclearance staff, they were attacked. According to Hanner, at a four-hour meeting with DOJ representatives,

> The Department of Justice was snapping at Gene Walker. A black Department of Justice attorney came down hard on Gene. He also came down hard on Mike Thurmond and the Legislative Black Caucus when they went to defend the second plan. People at the Department of Justice may not have realized then that Cynthia [McKinney] was running for Congress. Therefore Justice came down harder on Gene since they knew he was running for Congress.[24]

The rejection letter from the assistant attorney general identified problems with the congressional plan. While the state had from the outset been committed to creating a second majority-black district, John Dunne's letter puts this in a negative light. "A concern was raised with regard to the principle

underlying the congressional redistricting, namely that the Georgia legislative leadership was predisposed to limit black voting potential to two black
majority districts."[25] While Dunne did not demand the creation of a third
majority-black district, he criticized the state's plan because it "did not make
a good faith attempt to recognize the concentrations of black voters in the
Southwest [part of Georgia] and has not yet been able to adequately explain
the departure from its own stated criteria in what appears to be resulting in
minimization."

A second concern focused on the way in which the more than 60 percent
black Eleventh District had been drawn. DOJ, wanting a still higher black concentration, questioned the decision not to split Baldwin County. "This majority black district not only limits the black percentage of the district but also
ignores the community of interest which black residents of Baldwin County
share with those in the surrounding counties."[26] The issue here differed from
the objection registered a decade earlier, where the black population spread
out from Fulton into DeKalb county. Baldwin County's black concentration
was miles from other black concentrations in neighboring counties.

The legislature immediately responded to DOJ's objections and increased
the black concentration in District 2 from 39.4 to 49.1 percent by pulling
into the district the black population on the south side of Columbus. Blacks
constituted 45 percent of the voting age population and 43 percent of the
registered voters in the newly configured district. But since the new map still
had not produced a third majority-black district, DOJ issued a second letter
denying preclearance on March 20, 1992.

DOJ infuriated legislative leaders by the way it conveyed its evaluation of
the second plan. Rather than contacting legislative leaders or the state attorney general's office, which had transmitted the plan to DOJ, Justice sent the
rejection letter to leaders of the Legislative Black Caucus. The state's legal office and its legislative leaders were frantically trying to get a copy of the rejection letter even as a member of the LBC read it at a news conference.

In the second letter, Dunne pointed to a plan adopted by the state senate
but rejected by the house. The senate plan had attached the black population
of Savannah to the Eleventh Congressional District. DOJ favored this alternative and chided the state because "this configuration was abandoned and no
legitimate reason has been suggested to explain the exclusion of the second
largest concentration of blacks in the state from a majority black congressional black district."[27]

Dunne next turned his attention to southwest Georgia. "In southwest
Georgia a review of the proposed remedial plan indicates a similar concern.
Although the submitted plan has increased the black percentage in the 2nd

Congressional District, it continues the exclusion of large black population concentrations in areas such as Meriwether, Houston and Bibb counties from this district." An interesting element here is the inclusion of these three counties, none of which is in the southwest corner of the state. Bibb and Houston are in Middle Georgia. A decade later portions of these counties were at the heart of a new Middle Georgia district. The emphasis of this second critique was not the development of geographically coherent districts but rather the creation of a third district having a black majority.

Since the rejection of the first plan had not prompted Georgia to meet DOJ objectives, this second letter explicitly outlined what it would take to secure preclearance. Quoting the Dunne letter:

> Several alternative redistricting approaches which created a southwest district with a majority black voting age population by including additional black communities such as the City of Macon and which did not diminish the effectiveness of the minority electorate in the 11th by including Chatham, were suggested to the legislature during the redistricting process. Despite the existence of the alternatives, however, the state refused to recognize potential black voting strength in the state and has failed to explain adequately the choices made during this round of Congressional redistricting.

DOJ demanded that Macon's black population be swapped from the Eleventh to the Second District and that Savannah's African Americans be appended to the Eleventh District. Making this swap would produce a third majority-black district, and all of the major concentrations of African Americans would now live in a majority-black district. The three districts managed to corral 61.6 percent of Georgia's black population.

Many white Democrats felt that they had done enough. They had doubled the number of majority-black districts and had created a third district with a heavy black concentration—what would be considered to be a black-influence district under the *Ashcroft v. Georgia* decision of 2003.[28] The legislature faced a time crunch, since it received the second rejection letter with only days remaining before its forty-day session ended.

After heated debate, the speaker took the extraordinary step of casting the deciding vote for the plan that created three black districts. In addition to Lewis's 62 percent black Fifth District, the Eleventh District (shown in figure 6.1) which now went from the Atlanta suburbs to Augusta and then ran along the Savannah River to pick up approximately 60,000 citizens of the city made famous in *Midnight in the Garden of Good and Evil*,[29] was 64 percent black. The other black district, the Second in southwest Georgia, achieved a 57 percent black population by including the black neighborhoods of Albany, Columbus, and Macon. To draw this final district, technicians in the Legislative

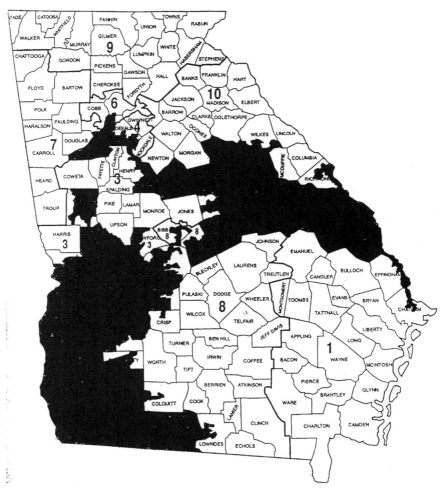

FIGURE 6.1.
Georgia's congressional district plan adopted in 1992 (majority-black districts shown in black).
Source: Prepared by the Carl Vinson Institute of Government, the University of Georgia, July 1992.

Reapportionment Office went around the edges of the district, precinct by precinct. Majority-black precincts ended up in District 2, while those with white majorities went into a neighboring district. In creating these districts, the legislators and their technicians focused almost exclusively on race in order to boost black populations as high as possible to satisfy DOJ demands. DOJ approved this third iteration.

The 1992 elections sent three African Americans to Congress. The Democratic field in the Eleventh District included three black legislators active in the redistricting process, along with a white and a black newcomer.[30] Cynthia McKinney, the LBC member urging DOJ to demand a three-black district plan, led the primary with 31 percent of the vote. The remainder of the black vote split, allowing the one white candidate, George DeLoach, to finish second with 25 percent of the vote. McKinney easily won the runoff with 56 percent of the vote and coasted to victory in the general election with 73 percent of the vote.

Despite having a 57 percent black population, the bulk of the electorate in the Second District remained white. The Democratic primary attracted a large field of black challengers, including state legislators from Albany and Columbus, a community leader from Macon, and two minor candidates. Incumbent Charles Hatcher, like his predecessors who represented this southwest Georgia district, had served on the Agriculture Committee. In the course of promoting peanut production and other farming interests he devoted less attention to his bank balance, and this omission placed him in the midst of the major scandal of 1992. The U.S. House operated a bank into which representatives deposited their paychecks.[31] The bank covered overdrafts at no charge until the receipt of the legislator's next paycheck. Rep. Hatcher had the second highest number of overdrafts at the House bank. In addition to the 819 overdrafts, he had recently divorced his wife and married a young member of his staff.

Even with these problems, Hatcher led the large primary field with 40 percent of the vote. His runoff opponent, attorney Sanford Bishop, had fourteen years' service in the Georgia house and most recently a term in the senate. In the runoff, Bishop retired the incumbent by taking 53 percent of the vote.

While African Americans picked up two additional Georgia congressional districts, their partners in designing the MAXBLACK plan did even better. In 1991 Republicans held only one Georgia congressional district and had never held more than two in the post-Goldwater era of modern Republicanism. With the black population gathered into three districts, Republicans doubled their high point by winning four seats in 1992. Each of these gains came in a district with a substantially reduced black population (as shown in table 6.2). Jack Kingston won the First District, which lost 50,000 Savannah African Americans to the McKinney district, making the First nine percentage points whiter. Mac Collins won the Third District, after Macon's black population went into Bishop's district. John Linder, who had lost with 48 percent of the vote in 1990, inched his vote share up to take the Fourth District by a margin of 2,600 votes. His district became substantially whiter when the black precincts in south DeKalb became the northern terminus of McKinney's district.

TABLE 6.2
Changes in the Racial Makeup of Georgia
Congressional Districts Following the 1992 Redistricting

District	% Black	1991 Incumbent	% Black	1996 Incumbent
1	32	White Democrat	23	Republican
2	37	White Democrat	57	Black Democrat
3	35	White Democrat	18	Republican
4	25	White Democrat	12	Republican
5	67	Black Democrat	62	Black Democrat
6	20	Republican	6	Republican
7	9	White Democrat	13	Republican
8	36	White Democrat	21	Republican
9	5	White Democrat	4	Republican
10	23	White Democrat	18	Republican
11		new district in 1993	64	Black Democrat

Source: Prepared by author.

In 1994, Republicans won three more congressional seats, two of which became whiter in the course of redistricting. A few months after the GOP became the majority within the Georgia delegation, they picked up an eighth seat when Nathan Deal, who represented the Ninth District, changed parties. While the bleaching of neighboring districts to obtain the African Americans needed to create three majority-black districts cannot account for all of the Republican success, the racial gerrymanders certainly helped. Georgia's congressional delegation, which had only one African American and one Republican and eight white Democrats prior to redistricting, was transformed into a delegation that by April of 1995 had three African Americans, eight Republicans, and no white Democrats.

State Legislature

As with the congressional districts, a minority of the LBC pushed for MAX-BLACK in the General Assembly, which meant fifteen majority-black senate districts and fifty-one majority-black house districts. As table 6.1 shows, these objectives exceeded the proposal from the LBC task force, which sought thirteen majority-black senate districts and forty-two majority-black house districts. The plans approved by the legislature had even fewer predominantly black districts, with ten in the senate and thirty-five in the house.

DOJ objected to plans for both legislative chambers in the same letters in which it rejected the congressional plans. It took two more efforts before DOJ signed off on the thirteen-majority-black-district senate plan and three more plans to get to forty-one African American house districts. Tyrone Brooks, one of the most fervent advocates for the MAXBLACK approach, exulted, "We got 98 percent of what we were fighting for."[32] With the new plans in place, one additional African American senator and four more representatives won in 1992. The new plans included the first rural districts to send African Americans to the house.

In a reprise of the congressional experience, Republicans made out better than African Americans in the General Assembly. Republicans increased their ranks in the senate from eleven to fifteen, and in the house their numbers rose from thirty-five to fifty-two, one of the largest gains by Republicans in any legislative chamber in the nation in 1992—generally a bad year for the GOP and the last time Georgia voted Democratic for president.

A Mid-Decade Adjustment

After the Supreme Court ruled that racial gerrymanders were justiciable in *Shaw v. Reno*, George DeLoach, loser of the 1992 runoff to Rep. McKinney, filed a challenge to the Eleventh Congressional District. The plaintiffs emphasized the elements that seemed relevant from Justice Sandra Day O'Connor's *Shaw v. Reno* opinion.[33] They pointed out that the district running from the Atlanta city limits into Savannah was longer than North Carolina's Twelfth District, criticized in *Shaw*. They also noted how the district had carefully skirted around white populations in order to maximize the black percentage.

In the Georgia case, the Court elaborated on the concerns articulated in *Shaw*. In *Miller v. Johnson*, the Supreme Court clarified that it was not the shape of the districts per se that mattered but the degree to which race dominated the motivations of those who created the districts.[34] When, as in the creation of the Second and Eleventh Districts, the legislature elevates race above traditional districting principles such as compactness, continuity, respect for communities, and adherence to the political boundaries of cities and counties, the plan violates the Equal Protection Clause of the federal Constitution.

The trial court judges and the majority of the Supreme Court found much to criticize in the way that DOJ had dealt with Georgia. The two line attorneys who oversaw the Georgia submissions had so little recall of the events when testifying that the Court found their "professed amnesia less than credible." The Court also criticized the cozy relationship between ACLU attorney Kathy Wilde and DOJ. "It is obvious from a review of materials that Ms. Wilde's relationship with the DOJ Voting Section was informal and familiar; the dynamics of that of peers working together not of an advocate submitting proposals to higher authorities." The opinion continued, "Succinctly put, the considerable influence of ACLU advocacy on the voting rights decisions of the United States Attorney General is an embarrassment."

Interestingly, while the Democrats later accused the Justice Department of George W. Bush of playing politics, his father's DOJ also weighed political considerations. However, the decision to require the maximization of majority-black congressional districts in Georgia and elsewhere did not evoke criticism from national Democrats, since to do so might jeopardize their relationships with black leaders and the African American vote critical to the success of the Democratic Party.

Invalidation of the plan that DOJ had demanded prompted a special session of the General Assembly. The senate favored a plan with only one majority-black district. The house tried to devise a plan that would retain three majority-black districts.[35] By 1995, growth in the ranks of Republican and black house members made it possible for a coalition of these strange bedfellows to constitute a majority. To prevent that, Speaker Tom Murphy (D) knew that he must support a plan that would retain the support of the black Democrats, who had adopted the stance, "Three seats, no retreat."[36] Indeed, if black Democrats became alienated, they might support a challenger to Murphy when it came time to renew his tenure as speaker in 1997. Ultimately, the house and senate failed to resolve their differences on the congressional plan, although they did redraw portions of the state house and state senate in order to head off threatened challenges to those plans.

When the legislature failed to take corrective action, the trial court came up with a plan. The judges used as their benchmark the last constitutional plan, the one adopted in 1982. Like the 1982 plan, the judges' map had a single majority-black district. Since it is assumed that federal judges will not discriminate against minorities, the court's 1995 plan did not require DOJ approval.

The court plan looked more like traditional Georgia maps. The plan demanded by DOJ had divided numerous counties and was characterized by twists and turns with fingers reaching out to pick up black neighborhoods. In contrast with the 1992 plan that split a dozen counties to create the Eleventh District and another eight counties to get a black majority in the Second District, its replacement split only six counties, all in the Atlanta metropolitan area (as shown in figure 6.2). Fulton County had to be split because its population exceeded what would be tolerated under a "one person, one vote" standard. The plan split three of Fulton's neighbors, whose large populations made it difficult, if not altogether impossible, to keep them whole while com-

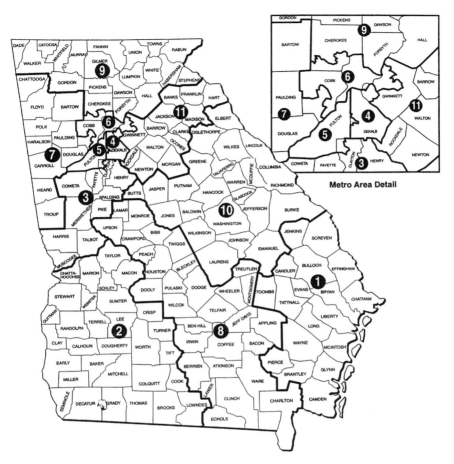

FIGURE 6.2.
Court-drawn congressional district plan of 1995.
Source: Prepared by the Carl Vinson Institute of Government, the University of Georgia, January 1996.

bining them with smaller counties and still be within the population limits. The benchmark plan adopted in 1982 had divided only three counties; thus the 1995 plan was a major step back toward the benchmark in terms of county unity.

The failure to have more than one majority-black district prompted yet another suit. In *Abrams v. Johnson*, the U.S. attorney general and the ACLU argued that the new plan should have at least two if not three majority-black districts.[37] Both the trial court and the Supreme Court rejected that logic. The Supreme Court supported the decision by the district court to use the 1982 plan as the benchmark. Having rejected the two-district plans as unacceptable, DOJ could not now demand their adoption. Nor could the plan that had been ruled unconstitutional be a benchmark against which to assess retrogression. The Supreme Court accepted the district court finding that Georgia's African American population was not sufficiently compact to permit the drawing of a second majority-black district.

The *Abrams* decision addressed the preconditions from *Thornburg* and accepted the finding by the district court of sufficient white crossover voting so that racial polarization did not prevent adoption of the plan. The court had the advantage of the results of the 1996 election. While DOJ had argued that the black-preferred candidate could not win in the new Fourth District, a district that according to 1990 Census figures had a 33 percent black voting age population, Cynthia McKinney won handily.

Elections during the remainder of the decade demonstrated the adequacy of the districts drawn by the district court. McKinney and Sanford Bishop in the Second District, where the black population dropped from 57 to 39 percent, continued to win reelection with little difficulty. Both Bishop and McKinney attracted 30 percent of the white vote and that, in combination with more than 90 percent support from the black community, sufficed to win these majority-white districts.[38]

The General Assembly redrew portions of the house and senate plans following the invalidation of the congressional plans in *Miller v. Johnson*. An attorney had threatened suit challenging five senate and twelve house districts, claiming that like McKinney's congressional district, considerations of race had received priority over traditional districting principles. While the General Assembly could never agree on new congressional plans, self-interest prompted the legislators to modify their own plans so as to stave off further litigation. These new plans reduced black concentrations in the districts held by several party and committee leaders.[39] Despite eliminating some majority-black districts, the plans used from 1996 to 2001 had eleven majority-black senate districts and thirty-seven majority-black house districts. Despite reducing the number of majority-black districts, the new plans elected two more black senators, bringing their number to eleven, and the number of black representatives increased to thirty-three.

The 2001 Democratic Gerrymander

During the 1990s, Georgia experienced some of the most rapid population growth in the nation. In percentage terms, Georgia grew more rapidly than any other state east of the Mississippi, as its population increased by more than 26 percent. This dramatic population explosion netted two additional members of Congress. Embarking on the new century with thirteen members of Congress gave Georgia its largest congressional delegation ever.

While Georgia had grown dramatically during the decade, the growth was not evenly distributed across the state. North Georgia continued to boom, while South Georgia attracted relatively few new residents. Central cities experienced slow growth or no growth, while subdivisions sprouted up farther and farther from the urban core, so that four-lane highways sheathed in fast-food restaurants, strip malls, and car dealerships crisscrossed what had been rural in 1990.

One response to the population shifts would have increased districts in areas that experienced the most growth. This would have been especially easy when eliminating population deviations for the state house and senate, since the populations for districts in these legislative bodies are much smaller than for Congress. In each state legislative chamber at least one district had twice the population acceptable under "one person, one vote."

Despite Republican gains in the legislative and executive branches during the 1990s, Democrats still controlled the governorship and both chambers of the General Assembly in 2001. Since the growth areas tended to be Republican and the less dynamic areas tended to be Democratic, simply rewarding growth with additional legislative seats was unacceptable to Democratic leaders. Recent election returns compounded the challenge for Democrats. Beginning in 1996, Republicans had attracted more votes than Democrats in state legislative contests. If one added up all the votes cast for Democratic candidates running for the state senate in 1996 and all the votes for Republicans running for the state senate, 52 percent of the ballots went to Republicans. Republicans repeated the feat of outpolling Democrats in 1998 and 2000 (as shown in table 6.3). Republicans also took small majorities of the votes for house members beginning in 1996, although as with the senate, they never came close to winning a proportionate share of the seats. Democrats confronted the challenge

TABLE 6.3
**Percentages of the Votes and Seats Won by
the Republican Party in Georgia's General Assembly, 1996–2000**

	Senate		House	
	Votes	Seats	Votes	Seats
1996	52	39	51	41
1998	51	39	53	43
2000	55	43	52	42

Calculated by the author.

of taking a minority of the vote and spinning it into a majority while adjusting for population differences and in doing so minimizing the redistribution to high-growth areas. In an earlier time, the Democrats might have had to yield to the demographic patterns and allow Republicans a shot at winning majorities. That scenario, however, harkens back to a time when voters chose their representatives. With the techniques now available to aid those drawing district lines and the willingness of courts to look the other way, we live in an era when it is the representatives who choose their constituents.

Critical to Democratic efforts to retain control of the state legislature and their desire to reclaim a majority in the congressional delegation was the availability of computer-assisted geographic information systems (GIS). The GIS software merged political and demographic data with a mapping capability.

The maps drawn in the early 1990s that were ultimately invalidated in *Miller v. Johnson* had provided the testing grounds for the maps produced in the next decade. During the 1990s, Georgia's Legislative Reapportionment Office split counties and used narrow land bridges to unite distant populations that shared a racial characteristic. In 2001, rather than uniting populations of the same race, the technicians brought together distant populations that shared a partisan tie.

Since the early 1970s, Georgia has maintained a professional Reapportionment Office. The former director of this office, Linda Meggers, began working on redistricting as a graduate student in 1971 and spent a career there. Her technical experience earned her a national reputation among those who work with the census to adjust populations after each new decade. During much of a decade, Meggers operated with a skeletal staff and provided assistance to local governments that needed to redraw the boundaries for county commissions and city council districts. As the time for the new census drew near, Meggers increased her staff in preparation for cleaning up the population figures provided by the Census Bureau and for gathering and merging political data with the census materials. In previous years, the Reapportionment Office had worked closely with the Democratic leadership in developing plans. This all changed in 2001 when the Reapportionment Office was largely bypassed, especially in the development of the blatantly partisan senate plans.

Another difference was that previous governors took a hands-off approach to redistricting. After all, it was legislators' political futures that the new maps affected, and so the chief executive left it up to them. Governor Roy Barnes (D), a very savvy politician, recognized the potential for a Republican takeover of one or both legislative chambers. He had no interest in becoming the first Georgia governor to have to learn how to lead a divided government. To help with the redistricting, Barnes brought in an outside consultant, who drew maps with little input from the reapportionment office. Individual

Democratic legislators got to see the proposal for their district but nothing else. Those who objected were warned that if they did not accept this plan they would be even more dissatisfied with the next iteration.

Spinning a majority of seats out of a minority of support was not easy for Democrats, since election results suggested that if they had not already become the minority party, they soon would sink to that level. They turned to several strategies to stretch their thin resources. First, they made more efficient use of their party's core constituency. Toward this end, districts that had been packed with African Americans in the 1990s had some of their minority population redistributed. By reducing the black concentrations in majority-black districts, the state risked running afoul of Section 5 of the Voting Rights Act. In reviewing districting plans in the past, the Department of Justice and courts had refused to permit reducing minority concentrations. When retrogression (the reduction of minority concentration) occurred, DOJ rejected plans.

In an effort to secure DOJ approval, the state developed evidence showing it could reduce minority concentrations without endangering the ability of minorities to elect their preferred candidates. For decades, an assumption guiding redistricting had been that black candidates could win only in overwhelmingly black districts. This belief guided DOJ when it demanded a 65 percent African American Fifth District in 1982. Columbia University political scientist David Epstein analyzed the electoral patterns for Georgia legislators from the 1990s.[40] He estimated that in a district in which blacks constituted at least 45 percent of the adult population, their preferred candidate had a fifty-fifty chance of winning. As the black concentration rose, the probability that blacks could elect their preferred candidate increased. Members of the Legislative Black Caucus found Epstein's analysis convincing and joined in support of plans that reduced black concentrations. African Americans removed from the majority-black districts could then be redistributed to help white Democrats win nearby districts. LBC members recognized that if Democrats lost their majorities in the General Assembly, black legislators would lose the committee chairs they held and have much less influence in shaping legislation. The post–2000 Census redistricting plan for the state senate reduced the black voting age population (BVAP) in majority-black districts by an average of more than 10 points. Three districts that had been more than 60 percent BVAP emerged in the new plan less than 51 percent BVAP.

More generally, Winburn shows that safe Democratic senate districts became about 10 percentage points less Democratic in the course of redistricting, yet still retained very secure margins in 2002.[41] Safe Democratic house districts became 7.6 percentage points more Republican but still voted almost three to one Democratic in 2002.

Democrats efficiently used their loyalists removed from secure districts. Eleven competitive house districts in the previous plan emerged in the new plan voting 53 percent Democratic in 2002, a gain of more than 11 percentage points over the old districts. In the senate, six districts that had voted more than 60 percent Republican before redistricting became competitive, as Democrats took 48.4 percent of the vote in 2002.

Going back to the county unit days, Georgia had multimember districts in the house until the 1992 plan. A review of various alternatives as they set out to redraw the lower chamber in 2001 convinced Democrats that no plan utilizing only single-member districts would give them a majority. As a second strategy, Democrats pushed through a plan with twenty-three multimember districts. Fifteen of these elected two legislators each, while six districts elected three and two districts sent four representatives to the house. Most of the multimember districts were in the Atlanta metro area, as Democrats attached smaller Republican populations to predominantly Democratic districts, allowing Democrats to win all of the seats in the larger district, as illustrated in chapter 1.

A third Democratic strategy weakened the GOP by pairing some of its members. That this was done to reduce the experience of the opposition party becomes obvious, since often adjacent to a district that included two Republicans would be a GOP-leaning district that included no incumbent. Since Georgia law requires that legislators live in a district a year before being elected, Republicans paired with colleagues could not move to a nearby district that had no incumbent. Pairing resulted in Republicans losing four senators and fourteen representatives.[42]

To accomplish the pairing, creating multimember districts and reallocation of Democratic loyalists, the new plans split numerous counties. Even counties small enough to fit within a single district did not escape the Democrats' redistricting software. More than a third of the small counties were split between house districts, and almost half of the counties that could have been maintained intact in a senate district were divided.[43]

As a fourth strategy Democrats wasted as many Republican votes as possible by overpopulating Republican districts while stretching their limited Democratic votes by underpopulating Democratic districts. If a mapmaker sought to draw equally populated districts, the result would approximate a normal curve, with a few outliers being underpopulated or overpopulated by 4.5 percent or more. As figure 6.3 shows, the distribution of senate districts was anything but a normal curve and instead had a "U" shape, with very few districts coming close to the ideal population and many districts at least 4 percent above or below the ideal. Eighteen districts were overpopulated by at least 4.25 percent and Republicans won sixteen of these, including ten

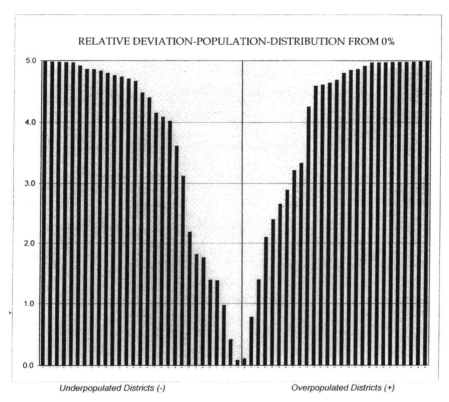

RELATIVE DEVIATION-POPULATION-DISTRIBUTION FROM 0%

Underpopulated Districts (-)   *Overpopulated Districts (+)*

This chart indicates the population deviations as positive differences to illustrate the deviation from 0.0%.
Deviations to the left of the chart represent underpopulated districts, to the right overpopulated districts.

1. Range of Deviation:	from:	-4.989	to:	4.995	range:	9.984
2. District Populations:	from:	138,894	to:	153,489	range:	14,595
3. Ratio of Max to Min::			1.11	*The most populous district divided by the least populous.*		
4. Average Deviation:			3.78	*The average of the absolute value of all deviation percentages.*		
5. Standard deviation:			4.11	*The dispersion of the deviations about the mean as a %.*		

FIGURE 6.3.
Senate districts distributed on the basis of population. Deviations from –5% to +5% (each bar represents one district).
Source: Plaintiff's demonstrative exhibits *Larios v. Cox*, 300 F. Supp. 2d 1320 (N.D. Ga. 2004).

overpopulated by 4.9 percent or more.[44] In 2002 Democrats won seventeen of nineteen senate districts underpopulated by 4 percent or more. Similar patterns characterized the house plans.

Looking at a few of the new districts will help us understand the consequences of the Democrats' machinations. Senate plans had long, narrow

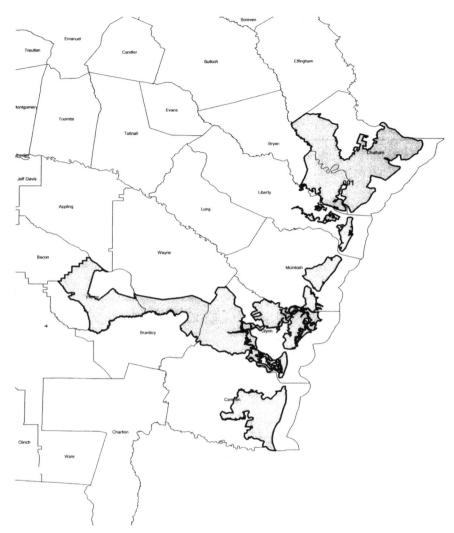

FIGURE 6.4.
Senate District 1 as adopted in 2002.
Source: Plaintiff's demonstrative exhibits *Larios v. Cox,* 300 F. Supp. 2d 1320 (N.D. Ga. 2004).

districts that lumped together patches of Republicans. As shown in figure 6.4, District 1, represented by the minority leader in the senate, which had contained most of Chatham and a little bit of Bryan, now extended the entire length of the Georgia coast while also reaching north of Savannah into Effingham County, with another arm extended inland toward the southern part of the district to include chunks of Brantley and Pierce counties. In several of the counties, the First District contained only barrier islands. As it went through Liberty County it managed to pick up absolutely none of the population.

A second extraordinary bit of mapping transformed the district of minority caucus chair Bill Stephens. In the old map, his district contained all of four counties and most of Cherokee County. These counties were stacked up from north metro Atlanta to the North Carolina border. In the new configuration (shown in figure 6.5), Cherokee, one of the state's fastest-growing counties, which could have constituted a senate district by itself as its population came within 3 percent of the ideal for a senate district, was split three ways. Stephens's new district still ran to the North Carolina border, but rather than stopping there, it tiptoed along the state line all the way to South Carolina. It took a narrow path across two of the counties along the state line before ballooning in Georgia's northeast corner to include all of Rabun and parts of two other counties. At one point, the district narrowed to only 740 feet, at which point it consisted of part of a lake.[45] The district defied any conventional notion of compactness or community of interest. Cherokee County voters focus on things such as sprawl and how to navigate traffic as they head toward

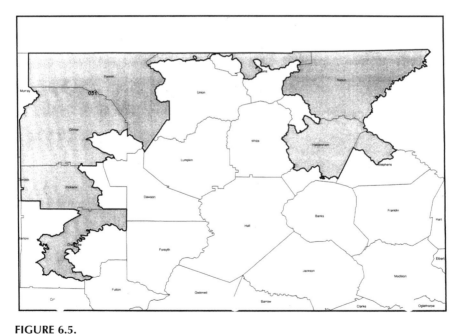

FIGURE 6.5.
Senate District 51 as adopted in 2002.
Source: Plaintiff's demonstrative exhibits *Larios v. Cox,* 300 F. Supp. 2d 1320 (N.D. Ga. 2004).

Atlanta and their jobs. These concerns are completely alien to the mountain folk who live in Rabun, where there are no interstate highways and traffic congestion comes only during the preschool sale at Walmart. Shortly after the release of the map, an *Atlanta Journal Constitution* reporter set out to go from one end of the district to the other. It took him almost eight hours and he drove 199 miles.[46]

Shortly after adoption of the maps, I spoke to the Rotary Club in Rabun County on the subject of redistricting. When I opened the floor for questions, the first person to speak was the local state representative, who pleaded, "Tell these people here that I had nothing to do with those Senate maps!" It was obvious that Representative Ralph Twiggs had heard frequent criticism from his constituents over the senate maps, which denied them a meaningful voice in the senate by attaching them to the far more populous, distant metropolitan Atlanta end of the district.[47]

A third remarkable senate district, District 24, appears in figure 6.6. The map adopted in 1996 gave the Twenty-Fourth five entire counties between Richmond County and Clarke County. When redrawn in 2001, the district had all of only one county—Glascock, which with a population of 2,557 was

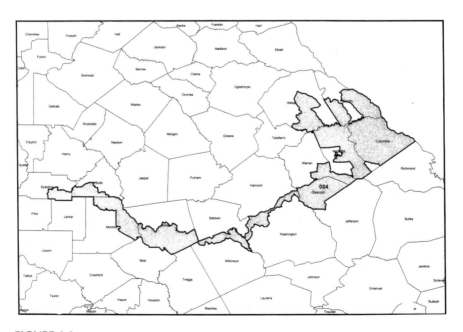

FIGURE 6.6.
Senate District 24 as adopted in 2002.
Source: Plaintiff's demonstrative exhibits *Larios v. Cox*, 300 F. Supp. 2d 1320 (N.D. Ga. 2004).

the state's third smallest—and included parts of ten other counties. The new Twenty-Fourth, one of the least compact districts, formed a narrow crescent more than halfway across the middle of the state.

Democrats manipulated a fourth district in an attempt to save the senate's most marginal Democrat. Carol Jackson had narrowly escaped defeat in both 1998 and 2000. In an effort to ease her reelection battles, her mountain district, which had been composed of eight entire counties in the northeast corner of the state, now contained all of her home county (White) and Union and then parts of seven other counties. Critical to making this a safer district was its extension into Gainesville to pick up the only majority-black precinct in this part of the state. Extending Jackson's district into Gainesville resulted in dividing Hall County, which could easily be a single senate district, into four districts. The Republican who had represented Hall before redistricting found himself spread across parts of eight counties.

Georgia Democrats feared that the Bush administration Justice Department would refuse to preclear the plans which so discriminated against Republicans. Therefore Georgia did not submit the plans to DOJ but instead took them to the district court of the District of Columbia. In the hearing the Justice Department served as the defendant, and although it found no fault with the congressional or state house plans, it urged the court to reject three senate districts that had their voting age populations reduced to being barely majority-black. The court agreed with DOJ that these districts no longer allowed blacks to elect their preferred candidates and ordered Georgia to increase these districts' black percentages. Georgia did as ordered but appealed to the Supreme Court, which reversed the lower court, embracing Georgia's argument for lower black majorities.

As noted in chapter 3, the Supreme Court ruled in *Georgia v. Ashcroft* that a state could either have a limited number of districts with large black majorities or have fewer heavily black districts coupled with a number of districts in which black support could determine the outcome, although it would be unlikely that an African American would win.[48] The Supreme Court pointed to the testimony of U.S. Representative John Lewis that "giving real power to black voters comes from the kind of redistricting efforts the State of Georgia has made."[49] Even the expert retained by DOJ to discredit Georgia's plan acknowledged that African Americans would likely win these districts despite the reductions in black population concentrations.

With the concurrence of the entire LBC except for one senator and one representative, the General Assembly made little effort to increase the number of predominantly black districts, adding only one in the house and two in the senate. The LBC expected to increase its ranks by two senators and from four to seven representatives.[50] While the number of African American representatives rose to thirty-nine, that constituted an increase of only three. The senate LBC contingent declined by one following the defeat of a member surrounded by rumors of corruption. After his defeat he was convicted in federal court and is currently serving time.

Court Plan: Republicans Prevail

The *Ashcroft* decision became moot in light of another case. Republicans challenged the legislative districts and in *Larios v. Cox* they prevailed.[51] The Court based its decision on the magnitude of the population variations. Governor Barnes and his allies had assumed that since population deviations in their plans stayed within +/–5 percent of the ideal, they could withstand any legal challenges. While courts might have looked the other way had only a few districts nudged up toward +/–5 percent deviations, as noted earlier and shown in figure 6.6, many Georgia districts pushed the limits.

When challenged to justify the extraordinary number of districts pushing the outer edge of the +/–5 percent deviations, the Court rejected the state's explanation that it underpopulated districts in order to protect the representation of South Georgia and Atlanta. The Court referred back to *Reynolds v. Sims*, the Alabama redistricting case from forty years earlier, to remind Georgia that giving greater weight to voters in some parts of the state than others violated the Equal Protection Clause.[52] Nor did the Court accept Georgia's second justification that it designed the plan to protect incumbents since, as the court pointed out, only Democratic incumbents benefited while many Republican incumbents were paired.

When the legislature failed to redraw the state, the Court hired redistricting expert Nathaniel Persily to devise new maps. The new maps held population deviations to +/–1 percent. The Court directed the law professor to pay no attention to where incumbents lived. The Persily maps paired a remarkably large number of incumbents so that they unintentionally shared one feature with the Democratic maps that they were to replace. Persily paired sixty-six house incumbents, with four house districts actually having three incumbents each. Ironically, one of the incumbents who was placed with two of her colleagues had chaired the house Legislative and Congressional Reapportionment Committee, which refused to devise a new map following the *Larios* decision. The new senate map placed twenty-three of its fifty-six incumbents in districts with colleagues.

Many incumbents were paired while nearby districts had open seats. The Court responded favorably to requests from both Democrats and Republicans and made minor adjustments to unpair incumbents when that could be easily accomplished; the maps used in 2004 had only four incumbent pairings in the senate and eight in the house.

Under the Court's nonpartisan plan Republicans did much better, particularly in the house, increasing their numbers from seventy-five to ninety-five, thus marking the first time in more than thirteen decades that the house had a Republican majority. In the Senate the new districts enabled Republicans to consolidate their majority by increasing their numbers from thirty to thirty-four.

The plans drawn by the Court retained thirteen majority-black senate districts while adding three majority-black house districts, to increase that number to forty-one. By 2006 the Senate had a record twelve black senators and forty-four African Americans served in the house (this included the first two African American Republicans).

Congressional Plan Revisited

With both chambers and the governorship in Republican hands, the GOP turned its attention to the congressional plan Democrats had adopted. The Democratic maps had, like those for the General Assembly, sought to maximize their party's advantage. When the maps were drawn, Republicans held an eight to three advantage. Democrats needed only six seats to reclaim a majority in the U.S. House. Governor Barnes, who at this time was being mentioned as a possible Democratic presidential contender, set out to eliminate much of the Democratic deficit. The plan, if it worked as intended, would result in Georgia sending seven Democrats and six Republicans to Congress. The nomination of weak candidates thwarted Democratic ambitions as they won five seats in 2002; two years later they added a sixth seat.

Much like the legislative plans, the congressional map included strangely configured districts, but in this instance the contorted design sought to unite geographically separated Democrats. The strangest-looking district was the Thirteenth, nicknamed the "dead cat on the expressway" district because its far-flung features resembled an animal flattened by heavy traffic. The most marginal district, the Eleventh, resembled something of a combination fish-hook and cross of Lorraine as Democrats sought to pull fellow partisans out of urban areas in Bartow, Coweta, and Troup counties while uniting them with black populations in Cobb, Douglas, and Muscogee. Republicans constantly criticized the map for its irregular shape and failure to respect county lines. While the court-drawn map of 1995 had split only six counties, the new map divided thirty-four counties.

In crafting a new plan, Republicans had as their primary political objective bolstering Phil Gingrey, who, against the odds, had managed to win the Eleventh District. However, the movement of blacks from Atlanta into Douglas and Cobb counties made his prospects for long tenure poor. The new plan bolstered Gingrey's prospects by giving him a district in which George W. Bush had polled 71 percent of the vote in 2004, compared with 51 percent in his old district. Gingrey easily secured reelection in 2006 and 2008.

A second objective was to dislodge one, or perhaps both, of the white Democratic members of Congress. In designing the new districts, Republicans operated under a self-imposed constraint. In light of their repeated criticisms of the convoluted shapes of the districts drawn by Democrats, they pledged that their new maps would honor Georgia's traditional principles and respect county boundaries to the extent possible. Keeping this pledge should also result in more compact districts.

The new plan did not increase Republican holdings in the congressional delegation. Although competing in more compact, more Republican districts, the two white Democrats, John Barrow and Jim Marshall, won reelection by the narrowest margins of any Democratic House incumbents in the nation in 2006. Barrow, who early in the evening feared he had lost, escaped defeat by 864 votes, while his neighbor to the west, won by 1,752 votes. Although the white voters added to these congressional districts strongly supported the Republican challengers, the short-term upsurge in Democratic support in 2006 allowed the incumbents to hold on.[53] Had Republicans given greater priority to displacing the Democratic incumbents and split a few more counties or drawn less compact districts, they could have claimed two more seats. Obviously, Georgia Republicans did not approach redistricting with the same partisan vengeance that guided their Texas cousins two years earlier in the redistricting described in chapter 5.

Republicans took care not to reduce African American percentages in the four districts represented by black members of Congress so as to avoid a charge of retrogression. They even increased the black percentage in Sanford Bishop's district from 44.5 to 47.5.

The Republican plan eliminated almost half of the county splits in the Democratic plan that it replaced. Table 6.4 presents three measures of compactness for the Democratic Plan of 2001 and the Republican replacement. Since convoluted districts have longer perimeters, the two plans can be compared on that dimension; for the entire state the new plan reduced total perimeters by more than 3,100 miles, or by more than one-third. The new version of Gingrey's District 11 had a perimeter less than one-third its predecessor, while District 13 saw its perimeter shrink by more than 50 percent.

TABLE 6.4
Measures of Compactness for Georgia Congressional Districts, 2001 and 2005

District	2001 Democratic Plan			2005 Republican Plan		
	Perimeter in Miles	Perimeter Score	Dispersion Score	Perimeter in Miles	Perimeter Score	Dispersion Score
1	1,106.76	0.12	0.39	763.77	0.26	0.49
2	697.12	0.26	0.44	692.98	0.29	0.46
3	949.72	0.15	0.46	495.02	0.21	0.54
4	112.97	0.25	0.42	135.93	0.23	0.45
5	188.24	0.09	0.26	108.48	0.26	0.49
6	211.99	0.12	0.36	173.88	0.29	0.46
7	480.31	0.07	0.33	227.78	0.24	0.58
8	1,054.98	0.04	0.37	713.98	0.18	0.28
9	872.07	0.12	0.34	371.31	0.40	0.38
10	487.17	0.20	0.28	614.32	0.20	0.32
11	1,167.02	0.03	0.20	306.40	0.36	0.55
12	770.70	0.11	0.17	738.29	0.20	0.42
13	596.30	0.03	0.19	246.75	0.12	0.39
Sum	8,695.35	N/A	N/A	5,588.89	N/A	N/A
Min.	N/A	0.03	0.17	N/A	0.12	0.28
Max.	N/A	0.26	0.46	N/A	0.40	0.58
Mean	N/A	0.12	0.32	N/A	0.25	0.45
Std. Dev.	N/A	0.08	0.10	N/A	0.07	0.09

Source: Bryan Tyson, the Republican staffer most involved in his party's redistricting efforts in 2001 and 2005.

The second measure, which looks at the ratio of the area of the district compared to the area of a circle with the same perimeter as the district, showed only the Fourth District to be slightly less compact. District 13 continued to have a low compactness score of 0.12, which is four times the value for the previous version of the district. District 11 had also filled only 3 percent of the area of a circle having the same perimeter as the district in the Democratic plan. Under the Republican plan, it filled more than a third of a circle with a similar perimeter. Dramatic improvements occurred in most districts on this dimension.

The final measure compares the ratio of the area of the district to that of the minimum circle which could be drawn that completely encapsulated the district. Again, the higher the value the more compact the district. Only District 8 failed to show an improvement. District 11, which had been the third least compact on this measure in the Democratic plan, emerged as the second *most* compact in the Republican plan. This measure also showed Districts 12 and 13 having values twice as high under the Republican as compared with the Democratic plan.

Conclusions

The history of redistricting in Georgia can be viewed through multiple lenses. It could be described as a prolonged assault on white Democrats. A second perspective would focus on changes in the expectations of African American legislators.

As long as the county unit system and the distribution of legislators skewed in favor of rural counties remained undisturbed, white Democrats held all the cards. Only with the onset of the Redistricting Revolution did the first African Americans enter the General Assembly. The requirement for "one person, one vote" also made Republicans more than occasional visitors.

Much of the subsequent change came as a result of DOJ demands. After each census beginning with 1970, DOJ rejected Georgia's senate plans and until 2001 also rejected the state's plans for congressional and state house districts. DOJ used the preclearance provision of the Voting Rights Act to demand the creation of greater numbers of majority-black districts and frequently forced Georgia to increase black concentrations in the majority-black districts it had drawn.

As long as white Democrats filled most legislative seats, the two disadvantaged groups joined forces against a common enemy. Beginning in the early 1980s and lasting into the 1990s the black Democrat–Republican coalition, a coalition that included many of the legislature's most liberal and most conservative legislators, worked to take seats from white Democrats. Since the biracial, bipartisan, ideologically diverse coalition had so few seats in the General Assembly, it would have made little progress but for DOJ's veto, which provided the leverage to force white Democrats to create additional districts with black majorities. White Democrats preferred to maintain districts with black concentrations sufficient to elect a Democrat but too few to elect an African American. Once DOJ required the adoption of plans that cordoned off the most loyal Democrats, Republicans could often win the bleached neighboring districts.

Republicans got more out of these joint efforts than did African Americans. The greatest disparity came following the 1992 redistricting. In that year's election, Republicans picked up three seats in Congress, four in the senate, and seventeen in the state house compared with African American gains of two congressional, one senate, and four state house seats. In the 1982 neither partner made gains in the state house, and each added two senate seats. Republicans won the Fourth Congressional District in 1984, two years before John Lewis won the Fifth District.

Although Republicans wanted to renew the partnership, the Legislative Black Caucus cast its lot with white Democrats in 2001. That round also marked the first time that the bulk of the LBC endorsed the state's proposal. In 1981, only one LBC member backed the legislature's congressional plan, and for this she was labeled an "Aunt Jane"—the female equivalent of an Uncle Tom. She was one of two blacks on the house redistricting committee.[54] Ten years later the LBC split; most members supported the advances offered by the Democratic leadership, but a minority joined the GOP in demanding the MAXBLACK option.[55] In 2001, all but two LBC members signed on with the Democratic leadership's plan.

Part of the explanation for the changing relationship between the LBC and Democratic leadership is that the latter became more sensitive to black concerns. That learning curve occurred as African Americans increasingly entered the chamber leadership. In 1981, blacks had little formal power in either chamber, although Senator Julian Bond did find allies for his effort to create a heavily black congressional district. In 1991, African Americans chaired and held three other seats on the eighteen-member Senate Reapportionment Committee. Eugene Walker also served as senate majority whip. The LBC was less well positioned in the house, having just two of twenty-five seats on its Legislative and Congressional Reapportionment Committee, although one of its members had just wrapped up a term as gubernatorial floor leader. Those who had entered the legislature's leadership ranks embraced the stand of their party; those who responded to Atlanta's Concerned Black Clergy and the ACLU and supported the MAXBLACK demands had often clashed with the Democratic Party leadership and held no major posts granted by the party.[56]

At the onset on the new century, blacks served as majority leader and assistant administration floor leader in the senate and chaired the Senate Reapportionment Committee. In the house, African Americans chaired the Democratic Caucus and served as secretary of the house redistricting committee. African Americans also filled three of the six seats on the conference committee that hammered out differences between the two chambers. From these positions, the LBC could have vetoed the plans.[57] Former representative Holmes writes of the LBC, "It played an integral role in determining the number and size of multimember districts as well as the minimum black population percentage in Democratic preference vote. . . . Overall, the GLBC had its most successful redistricting session in the history of the legislature."[58] From 1991 to 2001, LBC strategy shifted from MAXBLACK to maximizing Democratic seats.

Redistricting in Georgia also traces the changing expectations about what constitutes a district winnable by African American candidates. In 1982 the LBC, DOJ, and many judges believed that a district must be at least 65 percent black, since so few whites would support a black candidate regardless of his or her qualifications. A decade later Cynthia McKinney and her allies urged DOJ to push the black percentages as high as possible but accepted 57 percent as a majority-black district in southwest Georgia. By 2001, the LBC embraced plans lowering black percentages to a bare majority of the adult population. In the early 1990s some African American incumbents objected to reducing the black percentages in their districts, fearing it could endanger their reelections.[59] This became less of a concern as a sizable minority of whites demonstrated a willingness to vote for African American candidates.

Another consideration behind the shift in LBC tactics, allies, and demands came from their members' advances in the legislature. By the beginning of the new century, senior LBC members had become committee chairs and chamber leaders. All of that would disappear if Republicans achieved majorities, a likely prospect in light of recent electoral and demographic trends. For the first time, the LBC ceased trying to maximize the number of seats likely to elect blacks and agreed to see black concentrations reduced in order to bolster Democratic prospects in neighboring districts. When DOJ sought to prevent reductions in black concentrations in three senate districts, the LBC fought its longtime ally. LBC member Robert Brown, vice chair of the Senate Redistricting Committee, testified in favor of reducing black concentrations in senate districts. "There are other examples of that around the state that I think suggest that there has been some change from that rigid, if there's an African American on the ticket, there's an automatic no vote for whites. So, I think that's changed significantly."[60]

The reunion of the Democratic Party came too late. The 2001 Democratic gerrymander slowed GOP growth in the house but failed to prevent GOP senate gains. Packing Republicans into districts at rates pushing the upper limits of what was thought to be the acceptable maximum while underpopulating Democratic districts by like amounts proved fatal. When the courts threw out the plans for the General Assembly it evoked the adage that "pigs get fat while hogs get slaughtered."

After the redistrictings of the mid-2000s, white Democrats who filled almost every office in Georgia in 1960 saw their ranks in legislative chambers at their lowest ebb. Republicans had achieved majority status, while black Democrats outnumbered white Democrats by four to two in the congressional delegation, twelve to ten in the senate, and forty-one to thirty-four in the state house.

While redistricting gets much of the credit for the transformation of Georgia legislative establishments, two other factors have come into play. The white population of the South, including that in Georgia, has undergone a secular realignment.[61] Redistricting has, at times, provided a catalyst to the partisan changes already under way. The second factor, of course, is the application of the Voting Rights Act by DOJ.

7

Looking to the Future

One man's gerrymander can easily be another man's nice set of districts.[1]

One party's gerrymander, of course, is the other party's priceless master-piece.[2]

THE CENSUS BUREAU BEGAN PREPARATIONS to enumerate the population of the United States well before 2010. Although a new census occurs only once a decade, the Census Bureau regularly updates population estimates for states, and consequently, by mid-decade it had developed projections of which states will gain representation in the next reapportionment and which states will give up seats in the House. At the state and local level, governments also prepare for the census, with the goal of a full count in order to maximize their representation in Congress and access to public funding as outlined in chapter 1.

No one studies the census figures or projections of likely gains and losses of House seats more closely than Kimball Brace, who heads Election Data Services. Since the mid-1970s, Brace has drawn new districts in more than half the states, and he creates widely used post-election maps. With each annual release of census estimates, Brace works up projections concerning what the next census will likely mean for reapportionment.

Projections for 2010 and Beyond[3]

In December of each year the Census Bureau releases estimates of state populations made at the midpoint of the year. Table 7.1 includes the results of three projections for states that will gain or lose seats based on the estimates as of July 2009. These estimates predict a continuation of the trends discussed earlier in this book. The Midwest and Northeast supply the seats that shift southward and westward.

The first column contains the long-term projection based on population changes from 2000 through the middle of 2009. Projections in the second column rely on midrange projections of population changes from 2004 to 2009. The third column shows projections based on the changes in the most recent

TABLE 7.1
Projections for Changes in the Apportionment of
U.S. House Seats following the 2010 Census

	Time Period Used to Make the Projection				
	2000– 2009	2004– 2009	2008– 2009	Projected Seats as of 2013	Most or Fewest Seats Since
States gaining seats					
Arizona	2	2	1	9–10	ever
Florida	1	1	1	26	ever
Georgia	1	1	1	14	ever
Nevada	1	1	1	4	ever
South Carolina	1	1	1	7	1932
Texas	3	4	4	35–36	ever
Utah	1	1	1	4	ever
Washington	1	1	1	10	ever
States losing seats					
California	1			52–53	1992–ever
Illinois	1	1	1	18	1872
Iowa	1	1	1	4	1862
Louisiana	1	1	1	6	1902
Massachusetts	1	1	1	9	1792
Michigan	1	1	1	14	1932
Minnesota	1	1	1	7	1902
New Jersey	1	1	1	12	1932
New York	1	1	1	28	1822
Ohio	2	2	2	16	1832
Pennsylvania	1	1	1	18	1812

Source: Compiled by author from Election Data Services press release, December 23, 2009.

year for which census estimates have been released. Since the rate of population change can vary from year to year, the projections have minor variations. However, there is much consistency in the identity of the likely winners and losers from the 2010 Census. All three projections show Texas the biggest gainer, expected to add three or four seats. Arizona is projected to pick up one or two more seats. While the projections earlier in the decade had Florida adding two seats, its growth has slowed, and by 2009 the Sunshine State was expected to gain a single seat. Georgia, Nevada, South Carolina, Utah, and Washington score an additional seat on all three projections. Projections based on Census Bureau estimates released prior to 2009 often showed Oregon and North Carolina earning additional seats, but the most recent figures have them coming up short. New seats would boost Texas to thirty-five or thirty-six members of Congress, while Florida would have twenty-six representatives. Six or seven seats will go to the states of the Old Confederacy. Four western states will add a total of four or five seats.

A number of the projected winners for the 2010 Census have a history of adding seats. With a gain in 2010, Georgia will have added seats in each of the last three censuses, and Nevada will have gained seats in three of the last four. Arizona has grown following each of the last six censuses, and Florida has expanded the size of its delegation following every census beginning with 1900. Texas, expected to be the biggest winner, has seen its congressional delegation grow following every census except for 1850 and 1940.

Of the states projected as winners, all except South Carolina would achieve a level of representation in Congress that they have never previously enjoyed. With seven seats, South Carolina will have regained the seat it lost in 1932. To find a time in which South Carolina had more than seven seats one would have to go back to the 1830s, when it had nine members in Congress.

The projections also show little variation in states from which the seats will come, with Ohio losing two representatives. All three projections show Illinois, Iowa, Louisiana, Massachusetts, Michigan, Minnesota, New Jersey, New York, and Pennsylvania each losing a seat. The mid-length projection even has California slated to lose a seat, which would be the first reduction ever in the Golden State's congressional delegation. Following every census California has gained representation. If these projections come to pass, the Northeast will drop four seats, while the Midwest will see its delegations reduced by six. Population flight following devastation caused by Hurricane Katrina will cost Louisiana a seat, its second loss in the last three censuses.

Anticipated losers include a number of states that will continue to see their influence decline. Massachusetts has lost seats following two of the last four censuses, and New Jersey has experienced a loss following three of the last four censuses. Michigan seats have declined following each of the last four censuses. The string of continuous declines in seats is even longer for Ohio, for which 2010 will be the fifth consecutive loss, while New York is projected to experience its seventh consecutive loss and in Pennsylvania it will be the ninth decade with a loss. Illinois has emerged with fewer seats following every census beginning with 1930, with one exception.

States projected to lose seats would drop to their lowest levels in decades. Except for the possibility that California might lose a seat, all of the other states would drop to their fewest members of Congress since the massive reapportionment in 1932. Five states' projected losses would result in their smallest delegations in at least a century and a half. Not since adding five seats in 1812 has Pennsylvania had as few as the eighteen seats anticipated for 2012. Should Massachusetts fall to nine seats, that would be the fewest number of seats since the initial allocation of eight seats by the Constitution in 1789. Following the first census, Massachusetts grew to fourteen seats.

If the projections based on shifts from 2004 through 2009 come to pass, then each of the nation's ten most populous states in 2000 will undergo a change in the size of its congressional representation. Texas, Florida, and Georgia will grow, while California, New York, Illinois, Pennsylvania, Ohio, Michigan, and New Jersey will contract. The net gains for the South will increase its dominance in the Electoral College, where it already has the largest number of votes. In the 2012 presidential election the South will choose 159 to 160 electors, or about 59 percent of the votes needed to become president. While the 2008 presidential election saw Barack Obama winning three southern states, the region remains far more Republican than other parts of the nation.

The fullness and accuracy of the count will determine the allocation of seats for those being distributed right around 435. On the assumption that the House will not become larger, the critical effort for a state on the bubble is to make sure that it finishes in line for seat number 435 or lower, since if its population entitles it to seat 436 or 437, that means that it fails to get a seat.[4] Table 7.2 shows the estimates for which states would be in line to get the last five seats allocated through reapportionment, based on the Census Bureau estimates of population changes from 2000 to 2009, along with the next five states which would just miss an additional seat. If reapportionment were conducted based on the population estimates as of 2009, California would narrowly retain all its current seats. The other seats among the last five to be allocated would provide additional representatives to South Carolina, Arizona, and Washington. Missouri's ability to hold onto its ninth seat would be by a margin of fewer than 5,300, while Washington would secure a tenth seat by a margin of less than 10,000 people.

According to projections based on population change from 2000 to 2009, Texas would come up about 10,000 people short of acquiring a thirty-sixth seat.

TABLE 7.2
Estimates Based on Population Change from 2000–2009 of which States Would Receive the Last Five House Seats and which Would Narrowly Miss Getting a Seat

Seat Number	State
Last five seats	
431	South Carolina (7th)
432	Arizona (10th)
433	Washington (6th)
434	Missouri (9th)
435	California (53rd)
Next five seats	
436	Texas (36th)
437	Florida (27th)
438	Minnesota (8th)
439	Oregon (6th)
440	North Carolina (14th)

Source: Election Data Services press release, "New Population Estimates Show Slight Changes for 2008 Congressional Apportionment, but Point to Changes for 2010," December 23, 2009, using the "long term" projection in Table K.

Florida would miss adding another seat by a slightly larger margin. Oregon, which had anticipated gaining a sixth seat in projections made earlier in the decade, is now shown coming up short by almost 25,000 people. Some earlier projections had shown North Carolina taking a fourteenth seat, but a slowdown in its growth rate leaves it short 60,000 people. Of the five states that narrowly miss having additional seats all but Minnesota would be making gains. Minnesota comes within about 12,000 people of retaining its eighth seat.

Table 7.2 provides projections based on population shifts for nine years. Election Data Services has provided a number of other projections for the last five states to be included and the first five to be excluded in the upcoming reapportionment based on population trends for different lengths of time.[5] The margins separating the last five winners from the next five states that are losers are very small, which means that population shifts from the time that these estimates were made in mid-2009 to the actual census in April of 2010 could result in a different ordering than is presented in table 7.2. Another factor that could produce change would be differences in the success of states' efforts to get a full count. Yet a third factor would be the distribution of military personnel. Recall that following the 2000 Census, North Carolina edged out Utah for the 435th seat based on the inclusion of North Carolinians serving in the military abroad.

Table 7.3 reports the regional distribution of seats from the 1940s until the current decade, while the last column shows the projected number of seats each region will have after the 2010 Census. The Midwest share of seats, which has shrunk with each decade, will have lost 43 seats after the next census from its base of 148 in the 1940s. This constitutes a decline of 29 percent. The Northeast is projected to have lost 42 of the 133 seats that it held in the 1940s, a decline of almost one-third. These regions were the two most populous in the 1940s and the 1960s. The South has grown by almost a third in its House representation since the 1940s to become the nation's most populous region. The projections for the 2010s show the South with at least 30 more congressional seats than any other region. The West will have more than doubled its House representation since the 1940s. Half of the West's seats come from California. While the growth in California has been especially dramatic, the rest of the region almost doubled its representation, going from 26 seats in the 1940s to 49 or 50 after the next census.

The reallocation of seats across regions has political implications. The South has become the nation's most Republican region. Some of the new allocations for this region will probably send Republicans to Congress and, if recent presidential voting patterns maintain, will add Electoral College votes to Republican nominees. The Northeast, once a Republican stronghold, has become the nation's most Democratic area, with Democrats now holding all congressional seats in New England and as of 2010 all but 2 from New York.[6] Loss of seats by this region will likely reduce the number of Democrats in Congress and result in Democratic presidential nominees having slightly fewer electors that they can count on. Illinois, Michigan, and Minnesota have usually voted for Democrats in recent presidential elections and in 2008 were joined by Ohio and Iowa. As of 2010, each of these five states had a Democratic

TABLE 7.3
Continuing Shift in Regional Seats Projected through the 2010 Reapportionment

Region	1940s	1960s	1980s	1990s	2000s	2010s
Midwest	148	138	126	117	111	105
Northeast	133	122	108	100	95	91
South	105	106	116	125	131	137–138
West	49	69	85	93	98	102–103

The Midwestern states are Illinois, Indiana, Iowa, Kansas, Kentucky, Michigan, Minnesota, Missouri, Nebraska, North Dakota, Ohio, Oklahoma, South Dakota, and Wisconsin. The Northeastern states are Connecticut, Delaware, Maine, Maryland, Massachusetts, New Hampshire, New Jersey, New York, Pennsylvania, Rhode Island, Vermont, and West Virginia. The South consists of Alabama, Arkansas, Florida, Georgia, Louisiana, Mississippi, North Carolina, South Carolina, Tennessee, Texas, and Virginia. States in the West are Alaska, Arizona, California, Colorado, Hawaii, Idaho, Montana, Nevada, New Mexico, Oregon, Utah, Washington, and Wyoming.

Source: Created by the author.

majority in its congressional delegation, and all but Minnesota had a Democratic governor. While Democrats have faired well recently in these states, the voters have frequently favored Republicans across a wide range of offices and have shifted between the parties in presidential elections. However, if the vote patterns in 2012 parallel those from 2008, reapportionment would reduce the Electoral College vote for the Democratic nominee in the Midwest.

The political consequences of shifts in the West are more difficult to anticipate. Republicans have usually done well in Arizona and Nevada, but Nevada voted for Barack Obama in 2008 and Democrats hold most of these states' congressional seats in 2010. Utah has been among the most Republican states, and the GOP will likely benefit from the growth in its delegation. Washington has the strongest Democratic tradition among the four western states in line to gain seats and has voted for the Democratic presidential nominee consistently beginning with 1988. However, in earlier years, it had often been in the Republican column. In 2010, Democrats held both of Washington's Senate seats, the governorship, and six of the nine congressional seats.

All other things being equal, the reapportionment following the 2010 Census should help Republicans, although in some of the states making gains, like Texas, growth is largely attributable to a larger minority population that, in time, may elect more Democrats.

Some projections go beyond 2010. Following the 2005 Census Bureau estimates, Kimball Brace worked up projections for 2030 based on population changes for the first five years of the new millennium.[7] Based on population shifts during the first five years of the century, projections for 2030 showed Florida adding nine seats, Texas eight, Arizona five, and Nevada and North Carolina growing by two seats each over their 2000 apportionment. Georgia, Oregon, Utah, Virginia, and Washington would have one more seat following the 2030 Census than they had in 2005. The losing states continue to be those that have experienced less growth than the nation as a whole in the past. New York would suffer the greatest loss, giving up six of its twenty-nine seats while Pennsylvania and Ohio would drop by four each, Illinois by three, and Massachusetts and Michigan by two each. Projected to lose one seat from their 2005 holdings are Alabama, Connecticut, Indiana, Iowa, Kentucky, Louisiana, Missouri, Nebraska, New Jersey, Rhode Island, West Virginia, and Wisconsin. Of course, projections being made decades into the future, while interesting to contemplate, may be far from what actually transpires.

The Preparation

Long before the census forms go into the mail, the Census Bureau launches an extensive effort to identify where people live and verify mailing addresses. In recognition that as many as a third of the forms sent out will not be returned and that many Americans do not have a street address, the bureau hires tens of thousands of part-time workers who will fan out to complete the enumeration through personal contact.

The Census Bureau is not the only entity that prepares well before the numbers are collected. The awarding of seats following the census will occur late in December of 2010, and the Census Bureau will release the figures needed to carry out the actual drawing of districts. The requirement that districts have equal numbers of people can be met using the census data showing the number of individuals and adults by race and ethnicity in each census block. In most jurisdictions population figures do not fully meet the needs of those who will draw the lines. In jurisdictions where political parties participate in designing new districts, they will want to know the partisan consequences of alternative districting plans. To that end, the parties need to merge the census population figures with information on voting histories. In order to be positioned to draw the new districts in time for the next round of elections, parties begin gathering electoral data at the precinct level well in advance of the release of the census figures. Some states do the job in-house, while other states hire firms like Election Data Services.

In many states, parties, especially a party that controls neither legislative chamber nor the governorship, have their own redistricting operations. This requires the acquisition of the software and the technical expertise needed to design districts that will favor a particular party.

Another component to a political party's redistricting strategy is retention of legal talent. Law firms exist that have established relations with one party or the other, and these law firms developed expertise during previous redistricting cycles in the course of defending partisan plans. These experienced litigators stand ready to spring into action to seek an injunction to prevent the implementation of a plan that would harm their party. Jurisdictions in which districting plans must receive federal approval subject to Section 5 of the Voting Rights Act need lawyers who can help with the submission process if they choose the administrative route or to file suit in the district court of the District of Columbia if they opt for the judicial approach.

In the past, many of these efforts got funding from the parties themselves. However, the McCain-Feingold campaign finance law restricts the use of soft money for redistricting purposes. The limitations on the funding that parties can direct toward designing new districts is forcing changes in the funding for the 2010 round. Democrats got a jump on Republicans in getting support from friendly 527 groups. These groups take their name from a provision of the tax code that allows them to raise unlimited amounts of money from generous contributors. Thus the 527s, to some extent, have replaced parties as recipients of unrestricted contributions from wealthy individuals. On the Democratic side, redistricting assistance will likely come from the Foundation for the Future and the Democratic Redistricting Trust. Making America's Promise Secure, a conservative group headed by former senator Trent Lott and former house speaker Newt Gingrich, will support efforts to craft Republican districts. The Republican National Committee has the services of Tom Hofeller, who has been instrumental in Republican efforts across the nation in each of the three previous rounds of redistricting.

In anticipation of the actions taken by legislatures beginning in 2011, the parties and their support groups will get involved in elections for state legislators and governors in 2010. Democrats admit that they did not devote enough attention to creating favorable environments at the state level a decade ago.[8] In preparation for 2010, Democrats vow not to allow Republicans to steal a march on them as the GOP did with spectacular success in Texas in 2002, which resulted in the new plan and dramatic gains outlined in chapter 5.[9]

The Count

As noted above, the projections based on Census Bureau estimates made in the middle of 2009 indicate a number of states competing for the last few seats to be apportioned. The definition of who shall be counted could determine which states get one of those final seats. Everyone living in the United States, whether that individual be a citizen or not, is counted, along with those who are serving the nation abroad.

To encourage participation, the Census Bureau will spend $340 million on advertising, two to three times what it spent a decade earlier.[10] The Bureau will disseminate its message about the importance of participating in the census in twenty-eight languages and, in addition to television advertising, will utilize Facebook, MySpace, Twitter, YouTube, and comic books. The Census Bureau has also sponsored a NASCAR race car and turned to well-known public figures to publicize the importance of participating in the enumeration.

As in the past, getting an accurate count of the homeless and those not legally in the country will prove challenging. Although the Census Bureau promises not to report the name or address of noncitizens to the Immigration and Naturalization Service, many who are illegally in the country prefer to avoid contact with any public official. Some immigrants may hesitate to return census forms because of suspicions about government queries derived from negative experiences in their home country.[11]

Efforts to secure a full count have received widespread but not universal support in the Latino community. The National Association of Latino Elected

Officials has endorsed the effort and created a poster for display in churches during the 2009 Christmas season. The poster, which featured pictures of Mary and Joseph, pointed out that Jesus was born when his parents went to Bethlehem to participate in a Roman census.[12]

A leading dissenter, Miguel Rivera, the chair of the National Coalition of Latino Clergy and Christian Leaders, has urged nonparticipation as a way to bring pressure for comprehensive immigration reform. He has written:

> Do *not* step out of the shadows to be counted, only to be forced later to turn back to the same shadows again. If all undocumented immigrants need to be counted, then move forward with comprehensive immigration reform, so that all duly counted will benefit equitably as well. . . . Before enumeration, let's move forward with legalization.[13]

In addition to the difficulty in tracking down those who fear that being identified may result in deportation, the 2010 count may encounter resistance from a new source. Some conservative groups that distrust government data-gathering efforts have counseled their followers not to return census forms. This behavior, if widespread, will increase the cost of the census, contribute to an undercount, and cost states and localities funding under a variety of federal programs keyed to population.

Senator David Vitter (R-LA) sought unsuccessfully to change the criteria for inclusion in the census. The Vitter Amendment, which the Senate rejected on a near party-line vote, would have excluded noncitizens residing in the United States. Had Congress adopted the amendment, California would have lost five seats, Illinois and New York would have each lost an additional seat, and Texas would have added only one rather than three or four in 2011.[14] With noncitizens excluded, Iowa, Louisiana, Michigan, and Pennsylvania would retain seats likely to go to other states, while Montana would reclaim a second seat lost in 1992. Counting only citizens would also have resulted in the redistribution of seats within states, especially in lower chambers, unless the noncitizens were found throughout the state. Large cities with greater numbers of noncitizens might have lost seats to the suburbs or rural areas.

Rules for the Next Redistricting

In contrast with the unsuccessful Vitter Amendment that would have cost cities legislative seats, the Census Bureau will provide information from the 2010 Census that could be an advantage for cities. In the past, the census assigned prison populations to the locales in which the prisons were located, many of which are in rural areas. The 2010 count will indicate where prisoners came

from, and most lived in cities. States will have the option of assigning prisoners to the jurisdiction where they are incarcerated or to the jurisdiction from
which they came. States in which Democrats do redistricting will be more
likely to allocate prisoners to their preincarceration home, and since prisoners are disproportionately minorities that decision will increase populations
in heavily minority, urban areas that tend to elect Democrats and reduce the
population in rural areas where Republicans are more likely to do well. Assigning prisoners to their former homes will also result in urban areas getting
more federal dollars from programs that allocate funds based on population.

As jurisdictions adjust their boundaries to reflect population shifts during the first decade of the twenty-first century, they will continue to need to
achieve near absolute population equality in congressional districts. Congressional districts will have tiny deviations or perhaps even the smallest deviations possible, except for situations like Iowa where the state can offer a compelling rationale for small differences in district populations (i.e., no plan can
split a county). As a result of the *Larios v. Cox* decision, state legislators may
face new pressures to minimize population deviations when drawing their
own districts. States may encounter greater demands to justify population
deviations even when the range is within +/–5 percent.

The extension of Section 5 of the Voting Rights Act in 2006 for another
quarter-century means that covered jurisdictions will need to secure federal
approval of their districting plans through 2031. The rules under which DOJ
conducts Section 5 reviews in 2011 may be more like twenty years ago than
in the 2000s. In addition to extending Section 5 for another quarter-century,
Congress overturned Supreme Court interpretations that the civil rights
community believed limited the scope of that key provision. Specifically, the
Supreme Court had ruled that DOJ could reject only those plans that left
minorities worse off and therefore had to preclear plans that maintained the
status quo even if an intent to discriminate motivated their adoption. In the
next round of redistricting, evidence of intentional discrimination will suffice
to sustain a denial in a Section 5 jurisdiction.[15]

Will DOJ reinstate the early 1990s practice of rejecting plans that fail to
maximize majority-minority districts? Or will DOJ be sufficiently chastened
by the *Shaw*-type decisions, as Persily suggests, and not interpret plans that
fail to maximize as evidence of an intent to discriminate? With evidence that
a sizable minority of whites will often vote for minority candidates,[16] will DOJ
approve plans like those adopted in 2001 that set lower thresholds for African
American concentrations when it appeared likely that a biracial or multiracial
coalition would likely elect a minority candidate?

A second change Congress made when extending Section 5 in 2006 reversed the Supreme Court's decision in *Georgia v. Ashcroft*.[17] The Court had

ruled that a jurisdiction could satisfy Section 5 in either of two ways. One was the traditional nonretrogression approach of not reducing minority concentrations in heavily minority districts. Alternatively, the Court had approved a Georgia senate plan that reduced African American concentrations, and contained a mixture of districts in which the minority population was so heavily concentrated that it almost ensured that their preferred candidate would win, along with influence districts with lower percentages of minorities. In influence districts the minority population had little prospect of controlling the outcome, but their numbers would suffice to ensure that the winner would be responsive to the minority population's policy desires.

Reversing *Ashcroft* reduces the likelihood of plans with numerous districts in which minorities constitute between 25 and 50 percent of the adult population. DOJ's emphasis in 2011 may again be to maximize the number of districts in which minority populations dominate. Columbia University law professor Nathaniel Persily suggests that DOJ may accept districts in which the minority group is less than a majority of the population if minorities constitute the bulk of the Democratic primary electorate and the Democratic nominee invariably wins the general election.[18] Now that Latinos have become the nation's largest minority group, they might be the primary beneficiaries from such an effort. In recent years, Republicans have had their greatest successes in districts having few minorities. Therefore should DOJ and private plaintiffs push jurisdictions to maximize their majority-minority districts, Republicans will likely win neighboring, heavily white seats. White Democrats would likely lose, since they have done best in districts that have a sizable black minority but one too small to elect an African American. It is precisely that kind of district that the Supreme Court approved in *Georgia v. Ashcroft*.

The next round of mapmaking may see a concerted effort to design new districts in which Latinos have an opportunity to control the outcome. As the nation's largest minority group, Hispanic leaders hope to emerge with more seats in Congress and state legislatures in 2013. Representative Linda Sanchez (D-CA) would like to see three more Latinos sent to Congress from Los Angeles, and in Texas Latinos may seek creation of favorable districts in the Dallas–Fort Worth Metroplex, Houston, and the Rio Grande Valley.[19] Increasing the numbers of Latino districts may not only threaten Anglo ambitions as it did in earlier decades but put African Americans and Latinos on a collision course. Eight of the thirty-nine members of the Congressional Black Caucus, including Ways and Means Chair Charlie Rangel (D-NY), have more Latino than black constituents.[20] Increased participation rates among Latinos could enable members of their community to take over these districts, with their prospects improved when open seats come available.

As a consequence of the 2006 Voting Rights Act, the conditions under which DOJ reviews plans submitted pursuant to Section 5 could be similar to its approach in 1991. That would mean that DOJ could require that jurisdictions devise plans to maximize the number of seats that minority candidates would likely win. This would result in increased concentrations of minority voters. By reversing *Ashcroft*, Section 5 could continue to ratchet up minority concentrations in districts over time. This might well mean that larger numbers of minority votes would be wasted, in the sense that districts would become so heavily minority that the probability that the minority population could not control the outcome would approach zero.[21] Rigid implementation of the nonretrogression standard could result in districts, especially in state legislatures, exceeding 80 percent minority. Obviously if multiple districts having that level of minority concentration were adjacent to one another, an alternative plan might create one or more additional districts in which the minority population would have a good chance of selecting its preference.

Even if DOJ stands willing to accept districts in which minorities constitute less than a majority if it appears that a biracial or multiracial coalition could elect the minority-preferred candidate, jurisdictions seemingly have no obligation to draw such districts. The 2009 decision of the Supreme Court in *Bartlett v. Strickland* held that jurisdictions *must* consider race when doing redistricting only if a single minority group could constitute a majority of a district's adult population.[22] If a district containing a majority of a single ethnic group cannot be drawn, then a court cannot impose a district that might allow the minority to elect its preference if doing so would contravene state laws.

The Supreme Court has interpreted the first prong of the *Gingles* test (as described in chapter 3) to require that a group constitute a majority of the adult population in an alternative district before a challenge to a plan could succeed under Section 2 of the Voting Rights Act. Although jurisdictions have no obligation to draw districts in which multiple minority groups when added together constitute a majority of the voting age population, all but 25 congressional districts experienced an increase in their percentage of minorities between 2000 and 2008.[23] In 205 districts, including most of the Sun Belt, minorities make up at least 30 percent of the population. Even if the minority populations are too diverse and too scattered to be aggregated into districts dominated by a single group, their growing presence suggests a challenge for GOP mapmakers. Since most minority group voters have preferred Democratic candidates in recent elections, Republicans attempting to create districts secure for the GOP for the next decade must factor in projections for the growth of these various groups along with expected participation rates.

Where Republicans are in charge of drawing new lines, they may pack the disparate minorities into one or more districts where the groups can compete to see whether one of their own can win the legislative seat or an Anglo will be left to represent the diverse interests.

While it is appropriate for a jurisdiction to consider the location of minority concentrations, those drawing the districts should consider other factors such as compactness, contiguity, traditional political boundaries, and the location of incumbents. When defending a plan in court, it helps if jurisdictions can demonstrate that they acted in accord with the factors and followed the procedures that they identified as guides for redistricting. Considering factors in addition to where minorities live leaves a jurisdiction better positioned to withstand a *Shaw*-type challenge.

Another way in which to defeat a *Shaw* challenge is to emphasize partisan considerations in the legislative record when explaining the placement of district lines. Justifying the placement of lines in terms of partisan advantage remains legitimate in the eyes of judges. The Supreme Court has shown little interest in untangling what it acknowledges to be a strong correlation between race and partisanship and appears willing to accept state claims that they gave precedence to partisan over racial considerations. The Court has yet to articulate standards under which challenges to partisan gerrymanders can succeed, a task that four justices consider to be impossible.

If partisans can take advantage of the opposition when drawing new districts they will almost certainly do so. As noted above, Democrats and Republicans began preparing to protect their interests well before the census. Governors elected in 2008 and 2009 will still be in office when it comes time to redistrict. The 2010 elections, however, will play an even greater role in determining who will draw the next decade's districts. A total of thirty-seven states choose governors in 2010, and these states also choose some if not all of their legislators. While some of the governors selected in 2010 will be incumbents, many states will select a new chief executive, and these contests will often be heated. The popularity of President Obama and his policies at the time of the 2010 elections may influence the outcome in the gubernatorial and state legislative contests.

In addition to the redistricting done by political entities, some states have transferred redistricting responsibilities to independent commissions, as described in chapter 1. In thirteen states a commission draws state legislative districts. Two of these commissions consist of elected officials who, if one party holds most of the slots, may come up with a partisan plan. In five other states, a commission assumes responsibility if the legislature fails to act. In some of these states the commission consists of political figures and, as occurred in Texas in 2002, the plan may favor one party. In five states a commission designs congressional districts, and the Iowa Legislative Services Agency proposes congressional plans that the legislature can reject.

Keeping in mind that the players undoubtedly will change in a number of states, if the redistricting were to be done under the same political circumstances as existed early in 2010 (i.e., the state has a Democratic governor and Democrats control both chambers of the legislature), Democrats would control the process in thirteen states likely to have a total of 107 congressional seats following the 2010 Census. The largest of these states are New York with 28 seats, Illinois with 18 seats, North Carolina with 13 seats, Massachusetts with 9 seats, and Maryland with 8 seats. Republicans control six states having more than one congressional district. These six states are likely to have a total of 92 seats, with 35 or 36 of them in Texas, 26 in Florida, and 14 in Georgia. In five states having more than 1 congressional seat, an independent commission will be charged with drawing the new districts, with the largest delegations being New Jersey (likely to have 12 seats), Arizona (projected to have 9 or 10 seats), and Washington (with 10 seats). This leaves eighteen states in which neither party controls all of the positions involved in redistricting. These states account for 191 seats, with California having 52 or 53, Michigan 14, Pennsylvania 18, Ohio 16, and Virginia 11 seats.[24]

The 2010 elections may eliminate divided party control, with one party consolidating its power. Despite losses in 2009 and 2010 described in the next paragraph, Democrats will probably win the California governorship and may be favored to replace Republican chief executives in Connecticut, and Minnesota, allowing Democrats to draw districts in these states. Republicans may have the inside track to replace retiring Democratic governors in Oklahoma and Tennessee and could eliminate divided party control.[25] On the other hand, some of the states in which a single party would be able to dictate the terms of redistricting today may have divided control by the time the task is to be done.

With 1998 and 2002 standing out as notable exceptions, the party that controls the White House almost always loses ground in the next midterm election. If that pattern reemerges in 2010, and 2009 results point in that direction, it will impact partisan legislative control. New Jersey and Virginia elections in 2009 witnessed a Republican rebound from the 2006 Democratic gains and additional advances in 2008 helped by President Obama's coattails. The GOP ended a dozen years or more of control of the governorship in these states. Virginia Republicans swept all three statewide offices and made gains in the state house. The Virginia senate, where Democrats hold a 21 to 19 edge, does not come up for reelection until 2011. The 2010 victory of Republican Scott Brown to fill the remainder of Ted Kennedy's term in deep-blue Massachusetts is an even more dire omen for Democrats as they approach the midterm. Nationwide, if the Democratic tide ebbs in 2010, Republicans will emerge poised either to draw the districts in an increased number of states or to thwart a Democratic gerrymander.

The next redistricting will occur under a condition not previously experienced. In each of the four rounds of redistricting carried out after the 1969 *Allen* case expanded the scope of Section 5, a Republican attorney general led the Department of Justice. In 2011, a Democratic Justice Department will administer Section 5. Will that make any difference? Democrats charged that President George W. Bush's Justice Department succumbed to partisan considerations in some of its decisions. Specifically, DOJ approved the Tom DeLay-inspired redrawing of the Texas congressional districts even though the careerists in the department responsible for reviewing the plan had urged its rejection.[26] Some Republicans now fear that the Obama Justice Department will approve plans drawn by Democrats but reject those from Republicans.[27]

On the other hand, it was a Republican Justice Department that required the creation of numerous majority-minority districts following the 1990 Census, which added a dozen African Americans to the South's congressional delegation and saw Latino ranks in Congress grow by seven. Moreover, the mid-decade redistricting plan approved by the Bush DOJ created the opportunity for Texas to send a third African American to Congress. Although unsuccessful, the Texas plan also sought to promote the election of two additional Latinos.[28] While white Democrats suffered as a result of the bleaching of some districts in order to concentrate minorities in others, it would be surprising should a Democratic administration oppose those efforts—efforts made more likely as a result of the 2006 Voting Rights Act.

Based on the experience of previous decades, federal judges and the experts hired to assist them will ultimately draw some states' plans. In some states in which the parties share political control, neither side will blink, which will necessitate a court's stepping in to provide new districts in time for the 2012 elections. In some other states, the losing party will go to court, and if it succeeds federal judges may have to craft new maps even if those drawn in the political process are used for 2012. In the last decade, courts drew congressional maps in ten states.

Most of the media attention devoted to redistricting will focus on partisan battles and implications for minorities, yet other intense struggles will take place largely out of public view. Individual legislators, especially those who represent areas where the population has grown slowly or declined, will play a high-stakes game of musical chairs. Lynn Westmoreland (R-GA), who heads the National Republican Congressional Committee redistricting effort, recalls, "I have seen grown people cry when they find that their own career can be over because other politicians are looking out for their own interests."[29] While some legislative activities fail to attract full attendance, no one willingly misses a session at which district lines are under consideration lest they be dealt an inhospitable district or, worse, no district at all.

In states in which the legislature draws congressional districts, the fate of members of Congress rests in the hands of those who covet the opportunity to go to Washington. In states gaining seats or where retirements have been announced, some of that ambition can be fulfilled by the placement of open seats. But in other states a sitting member of Congress may be sacrificed, especially if the member of Congress does not belong to the party that controls the state legislature. Congressional incumbents may be most vulnerable in states that have imposed term limits on legislators, since those about to leave the legislature may see in redistricting an alternative to forced retirement from politics.

Conclusions

While a number of questions surround the upcoming redistricting and others will doubtless come up as legislatures, commissions, and courts carry out the process of adjusting for population shifts, one thing remains certain: The process, at least when conducted by a legislative body, will involve politics. Governor Elbridge Gerry used his position to promote his party; in 2011, scores of politicians will follow suit, and they have the advantage of sophisticated software and seasoned experts to assist them. Computer software will enable those responsible for drawing districts to honor the traditional districting principles, but partisan greed or, as in Georgia in 2001, desperation may induce mapmakers to push the envelope, as they go about placing widely dispersed partisan pockets into a single district.

Notes

Chapter 1

1. Robert G. Dixon Jr., "Fair Criteria and Procedures for Establishing Legislative Districts," in *Representation and Redistricting Issues*, ed. Bernard Grofman, Arend Lijphart, Robert B. McKay, and Howard Scarrow (Lexington, MA: Lexington Books, 1982), 7.

2. Quoted in Richard L. Engstrom and John K. Wildgen, "Pruning Thorns from the Thicket: An Empirical Test of the Existence of Racial Gerrymandering," *Legislative Studies Quarterly* 2 (November 1977): 466–67.

3. *Veith v. Jubelirer*, 541 U.S. 267 (2004).

4. The South is defined as the eleven states that seceded: Alabama, Arkansas, Florida, Georgia, Louisiana, Mississippi, North Carolina, South Carolina, Tennessee, Texas, and Virginia.

5. Garrison Nelson, "The Matched Lives of U.S. House Leaders: An Exploration" (paper presented at the annual meeting of the American Political Science Association, New York, August 31–September 3, 1978).

6. What Nelson means by having one leader come from within five counties of another is that by indicating the home counties of congressional leaders on a map and then counting the counties from the home of one leader to that of another, one would cross no more than five counties.

7. For a review of the different districting techniques used following the 2000 census, see Michael P. McDonald, "A Comparative Analysis of Redistricting Institutions in the United States, 2001–2002," *State Politics and Policy Quarterly* 4 (Winter 2004): 378. McDonald notes slight variations in the responsibility of the legislatures among the states, and the number of states reported here reflects all instances in which the state legislature had some hand in the districting process. McDonald's excellent review

of the variation in redistricting processes provides much of the information in this section. Figures as to how many state legislatures now have redistricting responsibilities differ from the counts reported by McDonald for 2000.

8. *Growe v. Emison*, 507 U.S. 25 (1993).

9. Karen Foerstel, "National Parties Mobilize for Battle over Lines," *Congressional Quarterly Weekly* 59 (March 10, 2001): 554.

10. Gregory L. Giroux, "The Hidden Election: Day of the Mapmaker," *Congressional Quarterly Weekly* 58 (February 19, 2000): 346.

11. For a particularly insightful account of this process, see Steve Bickerstaff, *Lines in the Sand* (Austin: University of Texas Press, 2007).

12. Peverill Squire, "Results of Partisan Redistricting in Seven U.S. States during the 1970s," *Legislative Studies Quarterly* 10 (May 1985): 259–66.

13. Gary W. Cox and Jonathan N. Katz, *Elbridge Gerry's Salamander* (Cambridge, UK: Cambridge University Press, 2002): 102.

14. David T. Canon, *Race, Redistricting, and Representation* (Chicago: University of Chicago Press, 1999).

15. Several single-state studies appear in Charles E. Menifield and Stephen D. Shaffer, eds., *Politics in the New South: Representation of African Americans in Southern State Legislatures* (Albany: State University of New York Press, 2005). In that volume Janine A. Parry and William Miller ("African Americans in the Arkansas General Assembly: 1972–1999") find that because of small numbers blacks have had little influence in shaping legislation. Although also relatively small in number, blacks have had greater success in Tennessee. See Sharon D. Wright, "The Tennessee Black Caucus of State Legislators," *Journal of Black Studies* 31 (September 2000). Willie M. Leggette in "The South Carolina Legislative Black Caucus, 1970 to 1988," *Journal of Black Studies* 30 (July 2000), reports that blacks had little influence in the South Carolina legislature more than a generation ago; more recently, Republicans have dominated both chambers. Also see Kerry L. Haynie, *African American Legislators in the American States* (New York: Columbia University Press, 2001).

16. Rufus P. Browning, Dale Rogers Marshall, and David H. Tabb, *Protest Is Not Enough: The Struggle of Blacks and Hispanics for Equality in Urban Politics* (Berkeley: University of California, 1985).

17. James W. Button, *Blacks and Social Change* (Princeton, NJ: Princeton University Press, 1989).

18. Frank R. Parker, *Black Votes Count: Political Empowerment in Mississippi after 1965* (Chapel Hill: University of North Carolina Press, 1990), 52.

19. Georgia law requires that a legislator live in the district represented for at least a year before the election. The timing of the new maps prevented either Republican from moving to an adjacent open seat.

20. For a description of various proportional representation systems, see David M. Farrell, *Electoral Systems: A Comparative Introduction* (New York: Palgrave, 2001), chapters 4 to 6.

21. Matthew 13:12.

22. Andrew Gelman and Gary King, "A Unified Method of Evaluating Electoral Systems and Redistricting Plans," *American Journal of Political Science* 38 (May 1994): 514–54.

23. The program, Judge-it, is available at gking.harvard.edu/judgeit/.

24. Thomas L. Brunell, *Redistricting and Representation: Why Competitive Elections Are Bad for America* (New York: Routledge, 2008).

25. "Judge Calls Counting Missionaries Unfair," *New York Times*, March 29, 2001, A12.

26. Peter Bragdon, "Simple Question, Tough Answer: Whom Should Census Count?" *Congressional Quarterly Weekly Report* 47 (August 12, 1989): 2146.

27. Mark Monmonier, *Bushmanders and Bullwinkles* (Chicago: University of Chicago Press, 2001), 135.

28. Rhonda Cook, "Georgia Looking to Right Wrongs with 2000 Census," *Atlanta Journal Constitution*, January 30, 2000, C9.

29. "The Knock on the Door," *Economist*, June 13, 2009, 34.

30. For a clear and detailed explanation of how this could work, see Monmonier, *Bushmanders*, 122–23.

31. Monmonier, *Bushmanders*, 127.

32. *Department of Commerce v. U.S. House of Representatives*, 525 U.S. 316 (1999).

33. Representative Carolyn B. Maloney (D-NY) quoted in David Baumann, "Still No Consensus on the Census," *National Journal* 31 (April 10, 1999): 957.

34. "The Knock on the Door," 34.

Chapter 2

1. Chief Justice Earl Warren in *Reynolds v. Sims*, 377 U.S. 533 (1964).

2. Since 1912 Illinois had elected twenty-five members from districts and elected at least one member at-large.

3. *Colegrove v. Green*, 328 U.S. 549 (1946).

4. *South v. Peters*, 339 U.S. 276 (1950).

5. Paul T. David and Ralph Eisenberg, *Evaluation of the Urban and Suburban Vote* (Charlottesville: Bureau of Public Administration, University of Virginia, 1961).

6. Nathaniel Persily, Thad Kousser, and Patrick Egan, "The Complicated Impact of One Person, One Vote on Political Competition and Representation," *North Carolina Law Review* 80 (2002): 1319–20.

7. Recency of redistricting did not prevent substantial population deviations in these two southern states. Florida had redrawn its house districts in 1955, while Georgia with its unique county unit system reallocated seats among counties in a manner somewhat akin to the reapportionment of U.S. House seats after each census.

8. Glendon Schubert and Charles Press, "Measuring Malapportionment," *American Political Science Review* 58 (June 1964): 302–27.

9. *Gomillion v. Lightfoot*, 364 U.S. 339 (1960).

10. *Baker v. Carr*, 369 U.S. 186 (1962).

11. Stephen H. Wainscott, "One Man, One Vote," in *Historic U.S. Court Cases, 1960–1990*, ed. John W. Johnson (New York: Garland, 1992), 129.

12. *Reynolds v. Sims*, 377 U.S. 533 (1964).

13. Persily, Kousser, and Egan, "Complicated Impact," 1301.

14. *Wesberry v. Sanders*, 376 U.S. 1 (1964).

15. The ideal population for a jurisdiction is the average population per district.

16. Mathew D. McCubbins and Thomas Schwartz, "Congress, the Courts, and Public Policy: Consequences of the One Man, One Vote Rule," *American Journal of Political Science* 32 (May 1998): 390.

17. *Avery v. Midland County*, 390 U.S. 474 (1968).

18. *Gray v. Sanders*, 372 U.S. 368 (1963).

19. Population figures from the 1970 Census come from *Congressional Directory, 92nd Congress, 1st Session* (Washington, DC: U.S. Government Printing Office, 1971): 94–97.

20. David Butler and Bruce Cain, *Congressional Redistricting: Comparative and Theoretical Perspectives* (New York: Macmillan, 1992), 30.

21. *Karcher v. Daggett*, 462 U.S. 725 (1983).

22. *Vieth v. Pennsylvania*, 195 F. Supp. 2d 672 (M.D. Pa. 2002).

23. If a state's population divided by the state's number of districts does not produce a whole number, then the minimum population deviation will be 1. For example, after the 2000 reapportionment, Florida had twenty-two districts with populations of 639,295 and three districts with populations of 639,296.

24. *Brown v. Thomson*, 462 U.S. 835 (1983).

25. *Larios v. Cox*, 300 F. Supp. 2d 1320 (N.D. Ga. 2004).

26. *Cox v. Larios*, 542 U.S. 947 (2004).

27. Federal cases involving redistricting are in a very limited class in which three judges hear the trial evidence. Appeals in these cases go directly to the Supreme Court.

28. In one case, the Supreme Court approved a districting plan that equalized registered voters rather than population: *Burns v. Richardson*, 384 U.S. 73 (1966). Less than twenty years later, the Supreme Court rejected Hawaii's plan based on registration because it differed too much from an alternative plan based on population. Butler and Cain, *Congressional Redistricting*, 114.

29. James E. Campbell, *Cheap Seats: The Democratic Party's Advantage in U.S. House Elections* (Columbus: Ohio State University Press, 1996).

30. Ronald E. Weber, "Race-Based Districting: Does It Help or Hinder Legislative Representation?" *Political Geography* 19 (2000): 213–47.

31. See, for example, Heather K. Gerken, "The Costs and Causes of Minimalism in Voting Cases: *Baker v. Carr* and Its Progeny," *North Carolina Law Review* 80 (2002): 1411–67.

32. Stephen Wainscott and John W. Johnson, eds., *Historic U.S. Court Cases, 1690–1900* (New York: Garland, 1992), 127.

33. David Brady and Douglas Edmonds, "One Man, One Vote—So What?" *Transaction* 4 (1967): 941–46; Thomas Dye, "Now Apportionment and Public Policy in the States," *Journal of Politics* 27 (1965): 586–601; Richard Hofferbert, "The Relationship between Public Policy and Some Structural and Environmental Variables in the American States," *American Political Science Review* 60 (March 1966): 73–82.

34. Ira Sharkansky, "Reapportionment and Roll Call Voting: The Case of the Georgia Legislature," *Social Science Quarterly* 51 (June 1970): 129–37.

35. Allan G. Pulsipher and James L. Weatherby Jr., "Malapportionment, Party Competition and Functional Distribution of Governmental Expenditures," *American Political Science Review* 62 (December 1968): 1207–19.

36. Roger A. Hanson and Robert E. Crew, "The Policy Impact of Reapportionment," *Law and Society Review* 8 (Fall 1973): 69–94.

37. Stephen Ansolabehere, Alan Gerber, and James Snyder, "Equal Votes, Equal Money: Court-Ordered Redistricting and Public Expenditures in the American States," *American Political Science Review* 96 (December 2002): 767–77.

38. Ansolabehere, Gerber, and Snyder, "Equal Votes, Equal Money," 775.

39. McCubbins and Schwartz, "Congress in the Courts," 409–12.

40. McCubbins and Schwartz, "Congress in the Courts," 411.

41. On the long court battle required to achieve single-member districts in Mississippi, see Frank R. Parker, *Black Votes Count* (Chapel Hill: University of North Carolina Press, 1990), chapter 4.

42. David T. Canon, *Race, Redistricting, and Representation* (Chicago: University of Chicago Press, 1999) shows how the concerns of black members of Congress differ even from those of white Democrats.

43. This paragraph draws on Gary W. Cox and Jonathan N. Katz, *Elbridge Gerry's Salamander* (Cambridge, UK: Cambridge University Press, 2002).

44. Persily, Kousser, and Egan, "Complicated Impact," 1333–34.

45. Persily, Kousser, and Egan, "Complicated Impact," 1337–39.

46. Persily, Kousser, and Egan, "Complicated Impact," 1340–43.

47. Charles S. Bullock III, "Reapportionment and Seat Distribution in Multi-County Districts," *Georgia Political Science Association Journal* 2 (Fall 1974): 29–42.

Chapter 3

1. John R. Dunne, assistant attorney general, Civil Rights Division, speech presented to the National Conference of State Legislators, Orlando, Florida, August 13, 1991.

2. Maurice T. Cunningham, *Maximization Whatever the Cost: Race, Redistricting, and the Department of Justice* (Westport, CN: Praeger, 2001), 142.

3. On disfranchisement see Morgan Kousser, *The Shaping of Southern Politics* (New Haven, CN: Yale University Press, 1974) and V. O. Key Jr., *Southern Politics* (New York: Knopf, 1949), chapters 25–29.

4. Key, *Southern Politics*.

5. Recall how Mississippi's heavily black Delta population was cracked, as described in chapter 1.

6. *Whitcomb v. Chavis*, 403 U.S. 124 (1971).

7. *White v. Regester*, 412 U.S. 755 (1973).

8. Harrell R. Rodgers Jr. and Charles S. Bullock III, *Law and Social Change: Civil Rights Laws and their Consequences* (New York: McGraw-Hill, 1972), 25–27.

9. Quoted in Robert Mann, *The Walls of Jericho* (New York: Harcourt Brace, 1996), 448.

10. *Allen v. State Board of Elections*, 393 U.S. 544 (1969).

11. *Georgia v. United States*, 411 U.S. 526 (1973).

12. *Beer v. United States*, 425 U.S. 130 (1976).

13. David C. Saffell, "1980s Congressional Redistricting Looks like Politics as Usual," *National Civil Review* 72 (July–August 1983): 369.

14. Charles S. Bullock III and Ronald Keith Gaddie, *The Triumph of Voting Rights in the South* (Norman: University of Oklahoma Press, 2009).

15. *City of Mobile v. Bolden*, 446 U.S. 55 (1980).

16. *Thornburg v. Gingles*, 478 U.S. 30 (1986).

17. *Holder v. Hall*, 512 U.S. 874 (1994).

18. *Growe v. Emison*, 507 U.S. 25 (1993).

19. For an enumeration of the number of multimember districts over time, see Richard G. Niemi, Jeffrey S. Hill, and Bernard Grofman, "The Impact of Multimember Districts on Party Representation in U.S. State Legislatures," *Legislative Studies Quarterly* 10 (November 1985): 446.

20. David Lublin, *The Paradox of Representation: Racial Gerrymandering and Minority Interests in Congress* (Princeton, NJ: Princeton University, 1997), 41.

21. As recently as the 102nd Congress, white Democrats held more than 60 percent of the southern districts 10–50 percent black. Republicans soon demonstrated strength in districts with more than 10 percent black populations. Charles S. Bullock III, "Partisan Changes in Southern Congressional Delegations and the Consequences," in *Continuity and Change in House Elections*, ed. David W. Brady, John F. Cogan, and Morris P. Fiorina (Stanford, CA: Stanford University Press, 2000), 45–47.

22. John R. Dunne, speaking before the National Conference of State Legislators, Orlando, Florida, August 13, 1991.

23. For an analysis of the 1992 election in Texas 29, see Douglas Abel and Bruce I. Oppenheimer, "Candidate Emergence in a Majority Hispanic District: The 29th District in Texas," in *Who Runs for Congress?* ed. Thomas Kazee (Washington, DC: Congressional Quarterly Press, 1994).

24. Mark A. Posner, "Post-1990 Redistrictings and the Preclearance Requirements of Section 5 of the Voting Rights Act," in *Race and Redistricting in the 1990s*, ed. Bernard Grofman (New York: Agathon, 1998), 88.

25. *Shaw v. Reno*, 509 U.S. 630 (1993).

26. *Miller v. Johnson*, 515 U.S. 900 (1995).

27. *Cromartie v. Hunt*, 34 F. Supp. 2d 1029 (E.D. N.C. 2000).

28. *Easley v. Cromartie*, 532 U.S. 234 (2001).

29. Quoted in Robert A. Holmes, "Reapportionment Strategies in the 1990s: The Case of Georgia," in *Race Redistricting in the 1990s*, Bernard Grofman, ed. (New York: Agathon, 1998), 211.

30. See, for example, Selwyn Carter, "The Impact of Recent Supreme Court Decisions on Racial Representation," in *Redistricting in Minority Representation*, ed. David A. Bositis (Washington, DC: University Press of America, 1998), 183–94.

31. In Louisiana's unique electoral system, all candidates, regardless of party, compete in the first round. If no one receives a majority, the top two candidates face in a runoff.

32. Charles S. Bullock III and Richard E. Dunn, "The Demise of Racial Districting and the Future of Black Representation," *Emory Law Journal* 48 (Fall 1999): 1209–53.

33. *Reno v. Bossier Parish School Board*, 528 U.S. 320 (2000).

34. *Johnson v. DeGrandy*, 512 U.S. 997 (1994).

35. *Growe v. Emison*, 507 U.S. 25 (1993).

36. Charles S. Bullock III and Susan A. MacManus, "Voting Patterns in a Tri-Ethnic Community: Conflict or Cohesion; The Case of Austin, Texas, 1975–1985," *National Civic Review* 79 (January–February 1990): 5–22.

37. Bullock and MacManus, "Voting Patterns," 839.

38. James Loewen, "Levels of Political Mobilization and Racial Bloc Voting among Latinos, Anglos, and African Americans in New York City," *Chicano-Latino Law Review* 13 (1993): 50–60.

39. The congressional district map for the Miami area in the 1990s had a Latino district that wrapped around an extension of a majority black district.

40. For a discussion of the use of 65 percent as a threshold for a minority district, see Kimball Brace, Bernard Grofman, Lisa R. Handley, and Richard G. Niemi, "Minority Equality: The 65 Percent Rule in Theory and Practice," *Law and Policy* 10 (1988): 43–62. *United Jewish Organizations of Williamsburgh v. Carey*, 430 U.S. 144 (1977).

41. *Georgia v. Ashcroft*, 539 U.S. 461 (2003).

42. *Bartlett v. Strickland*, 556 U.S. 1 (2009).

43. Mark Posner, a DOJ attorney, denies both that the department sought to maximize the number of majority-minority districts and that political considerations influenced decisions to deny preclearance. (Posner, "Post-1990s Redistrictings," 97–98.) However, the Supreme Court found that maximization drove DOJ decisions, at least in Georgia and North Carolina. *Miller v. Johnson*, 515 U.S. 900 (1995); *Shaw v. Hunt*, 517 U.S. 899 (1996).

44. Deposition of John Dunne at p. 122, *Johnson v. Miller*, 864 F. Supp. 1354 (S.D. Ga. 1994), *Aff'd*, 515 U.S. 900 (1995). There is also evidence that the Reagan Justice Department sought to promote GOP fortunes in the course of 1980s redistricting. See Matthew Cooper, "Beware of Republicans Bearing Voting Rights Suits," *Washington Monthly* (February 1987): 11–15. A very different interpretation of Dunne's motivation is that he experienced a conversion as a result of his responsibilities at DOJ and acted solely in order to increase the numbers of minority legislators. See Cunningham, *Maximization*, 123–44.

45. See, for example, David Lublin, *The Republican South* (Princeton, NJ: Princeton University Press, 2004), 104–15; Kimball Brace, Bernard Grofman, and Lisa Handley, "Does Redistricting Aimed to Helped Blacks Necessarily Help Republicans?" *Journal of Politics* 49 (February 1987): 169–185. At least some southern Republicans recognized as early as the 1970s that creating additional districts with black concentrations would likely work to the advantage of the GOP in neighboring districts. See

Engstrom and Wildgen, "Pruning Thorns from the Thicket," 473. The breakup of multimember state legislative districts into single-member districts also generally resulted in increased representation by both African Americans and Republicans at the expense of white Democrats. Charles S. Bullock III and Ronald Keith Gaddie, "Changing from Multi-Member to Single-Member Districts: Partisan, Racial, and Gender Consequences," *State and Local Government Review* 25 (Fall 1993): 155–63.

46. Quoted in Richard L. Engstrom and Jason E. Kirksey, "Race and Representational Districting in Louisiana," in *Race and Redistricting in the 1990s*, ed. Bernard Grofman (New York: Agathon Press, 1998), 247. For a discussion of the collaboration of Anglo Republicans with African Americans and Latinos in Texas, see J. Morgan Kousser, *Colorblind Injustice: Minority Voting Rights and the Undoing of the Second Reconstruction* (Chapel Hill: University of North Carolina Press, 1999), Chapter 6.

47. Two dissents to the conclusion that Democrats lost congressional seats because of the affirmative action gerrymanders are registered by Richard Engstrom and the NAACP Legal Defense and Education Fund. See Engstrom, "Voting Rights Districts: Debunking the Myths," *Campaigns and Elections* (April 1995): 24, 46; Engstrom, "Race and Southern Politics: The Special Case of Congressional Districting," in *Writing Southern Politics*, ed. Robert P. Steed and Laurence W. Moreland (Lexington: University Press of Kentucky, 2006), 91–118; NAACP Legal Defense and Education Fund, "The Effect of Section 2 of the Voting Rights Act on the 1994 Congressional Elections" (1994).

48. Charles S. Bullock III, "Winners and Losers in the Latest Round of Redistricting," *Emory Law Journal* 44 (Summer 1995): 954–55.

49. David Lublin, "Racial Redistricting and Southern Republican Congressional Gains in the 1990s," and Lisa Handley, "Drawing Effective Minority Districts: A Conceptual Model," in *Voting Rights and Minority Representation: Redistricting, 1992–2002*, ed. David A. Bositis (Lanham, MD: University Press of America, 2006), 116.

50. John R. Petrocik and Scott W. Desposato, "The Partisan Consequences of Majority-Minority Redistricting in the South, 1992 and 1994," *Journal of Politics* 60 (August 1998): 613–33.

51. Stephen Ansolabehere, James Snyder Jr., and Charles Stewart III, "Old Voters, New Voters, and the Personal Vote: Using Redistricting to Measure the Incumbency Advantage," *American Journal of Political Science* 44 (January 2002): 17–34; Seth C. McKee, *Republican Ascendancy in Southern U.S. House Elections* (Boulder, CO: Westview Press, 2010), chapter 3.

52. Lublin, *Paradox of Representation,* 96.

53. Lublin, "Racial Redistricting," and Lisa Handley, "Drawing Effective Minority Districts," 120.

54. David Lublin and D. Stephen Voss, "Racial Redistricting and Realignment in Southern State Legislatures," *American Journal of Political Science* 44 (October 2000): 805.

55. David Lublin and D. Stephen Voss, "Boll Weevil Blues: Polarized Congressional Delegations into the 21st Century," *American Review of Politics* 21 (Winter 2000): 440.

56. For a discussion of the politics involved in drawing the Frost plan for Texas, see Kousser, *Colorblind Injustice,* 292–316.

57. Donald W. Beachler, "Racial and Partisan Gerrymandering: Three States in the 1990s," *American Review of Politics* 19 (Spring 1998): 1–16.

58. Carol Swain, *Black Faces, Black Interests* (Cambridge, MA: Harvard University Press, 1993), 207.

59. Marvin Overby and Kenneth Cosgrove, "Unintended Consequences? Racial Redistricting and the Representation of Minority Interests," *Journal of Politics* 58 (1996): 540–50.

60. Christine Leveaux Sharpe and James C. Garand, "Race, Roll Calls, and Redistricting: The Impact of Race-Based Redistricting on Congressional Roll Calls," *Political Research Quarterly* 54 (March 2001): 31–51.

61. Charles S. Bullock III, "The Impact of Changing the Racial Composition of Congressional Districts on Legislators' Roll-Call Behavior," *American Politics Quarterly* 23 (April 1995): 141–58.

62. Kenneth W. Shotts, "Does Racial Redistricting Cause Conservative Policy Outcomes? Policy Preferences of Southern Representatives in the 1980s and 1990s," *Journal of Politics* 65 (February 2003): 216–26.

63. Winnet W. Hagens, "The Politics of Race: The Virginia Redistricting Experience, 1991–1997," in *Race and Redistricting in the 1990s*, ed. Bernard Grofman (New York: Agathon, 1998), 324.

64. See, for example, *Busbee v. Smith*, 549 F. Supp. 494 (D.D.C. 1982) and the discussion earlier in this chapter and in chapter 6.

65. Gregory L. Giroux, "New Twists in the Old Debate on Race and Representation," *CQ Weekly* 59 (August 11, 2001): 1972. Representative Bobby Scott (D-VA), who also has a predominantly urban district, urged Virginia legislators to reduce the black percentage in his district from 57 to 49 percent in order to beef up the black percentage in the adjoining Fourth District.

66. Charles Cameron, David Epstein, and Sharyn O'Halloran, "Do Majority-Minority Districts Maximize Substantive Black Representation in Congress?" *American Political Science Review* 90 (December 1996): 804. Also see Lisa Handley, "Drawing Effective Minority Districts," especially page 68.

67. David Epstein and Sharyn O'Halloran, "A Social Science Approach to Race, Redistricting, and Representation," *American Political Science Review* 93 (March 1999): 189.

68. Report of Dr. David Epstein in *Georgia v. Ashcroft*, 539 U.S. 461 (2003).

69. Because of large numbers of noncitizens and low turnout rates even among citizens, concentrations of Latinos need to be higher than black percentages. Leo F. Estrada, "Redistricting 2000: A Lost Opportunity for Latinos," in *Voting Rights and Minority Representation: Redistricting, 1992–2002*, ed. David A. Bositis (Lanham, MD: University Press of America, 2006), 75. Robert R. Brischetto, "Latino Voters and Redistricting in the Millennium," in *Redistricting and Minority Representation*, ed. David A. Bositis (Washington, DC: University Press of America, 1998), 50.

70. Bruce E. Cain, *The Reapportionment Puzzle* (Berkeley: University of California Press, 1984), 169.

71. *Georgia v. Ashcroft*, 539 U.S. 461 (2003).

72. Swain, *Black Faces, Black Interests*, 211–12.

73. *Sessions v. Perry*, 298 F. Supp. 2d 451 (E.D. Tex. 2004).

74. Charles S. Bullock III, "Partisan Changes in the Southern Congressional Delegation and the Consequences," in *Continuity and Change in House Elections*, ed. David W. Brady, John F. Cogan, and Morris P. Fiorina (Stanford, CA: Stanford University Press, 2000), 45–47; Charles S. Bullock III, "Georgia: The GOP Finally Takes Over," in *The New Politics of the Old South*, 3rd ed., ed. Charles S. Bullock III and Mark J. Rozell (Lanham, MD: Rowman & Littlefield, 2007), 62.

75. Thomas L. Brunell, *Redistricting and Representation: Why Competitive Elections Are Bad for America.* (New York: Routledge, 2008), 73.

76. James A. Barnes, "Minority Map Making," *National Journal* 22 (April 7, 1990): 839.

77. Bullock and Gaddie, *Triumph of Voting Rights in the South.*

78. David T. Canon, *Race, Redistricting, and Representation* (Chicago: University of Chicago Press, 1999), especially Chapter 5.

79. Swain, *Black Faces, Black Interests.*

80. Kenny J. Whitby, *The Color of Representation* (Ann Arbor: University of Michigan, 1997).

81. Claudine Gay, "Spirals of Trust? The Effect of Descriptive Representation on Relationships between Citizens and Their Government," *American Journal of Political Science* 46 (October 2002): 717–33; Susan A. Banducci, Todd Donovan, and Jeffrey A. Carp, "Minority Representation, Empowerment, and Participation," *Journal of Politics* 66 (May 2004): 534–56; Katherine Tate, "The Political Representation of Blacks in Congress: Does Race Matter?" *Legislative Studies Quarterly* 26 (November 2001): 623–638.

82. Zoltan Hajnal, "Who Loses in American Democracy? A Count of Votes Demonstrates the Limited Representation of African Americans," *American Political Science Review* 103 (February 2009): 37–57. Although not part of Hajnal's study, it is likely that most black voters also back winners in state legislative elections for the same reason that they support winners in congressional elections—they live in districts designed to be heavily minority.

83. See the testimony of Donald L. Horowitz and James F. Blumstein presented during the hearings before the Subcommittee on the Constitution of the Committee of the Judiciary, United States Senate, on the Voting Rights Act, 97th Congress, 2nd Session, vol. 2 (Washington, DC: U.S. Government Printing Office, 1993), 1307–64.

84. Bullock, "Impact of Changing the Racial Composition of Congressional Districts," 141–58.

85. Engstrom, "Voting Rights Districts."

86. Kenneth W. Shotts, "Does Racial Redistricting Cause Conservative Policy Outcomes?"

Chapter 4

1. Jason Barabas and Jennifer Jerit, "Redistricting Principles and Racial Representation," *State Politics and Policy Quarterly* 4 (Winter 2004): 418–19.

2. Michael P. McDonald, "Drawing the Line: Redistricting and Competition in Congressional Elections," *Extensions* (Fall 2004): 16.

3. Richard G. Niemi, Bernard Grofman, Carl Carlucci, and Thomas Hoffler, "Measuring Compactness and the Role of Compactness Standard in a Test for Partisan and Racial Gerrymandering," *Journal of Politics* 52 (November 1990): 1155–1181. Micah Altman, "Districting Principles and Democratic Representation" (thesis, California Institute of Technology, 1998).

4. Richard H. Pildes and Richard G. Niemi, "Expressive Harms, 'Bizarre Districts,' and Voting Rights: Evaluating Election-District Appearances after *Shaw v. Reno*," *Michigan Law Review* 92 (December 1993): 483.

5. This paragraph draws on Michael Barone with Richard E. Cohen, *The Almanac of American Politics, 2004* (Washington, DC: National Journal, 2003), 528, 529, 561, 578.

6. Laughlin McDonald, "Redistricting and Voting Rights Issues, 1992–2002: A Legal Analysis," in *Voting Rights and Minority Representation: Redistricting, 1992–2002*, ed. David A. Bositis (Lanham, MD: University Press of America, 2006), 23.

7. McDonald, "Drawing the Line," 16.

8. McDonald, "Drawing the Line," 74.

9. Bruce E. Cain, *The Reapportionment Puzzle* (Berkeley: University of California Press, 1984), 60; Charles S. Bullock III, "Reapportionment and Seat Distribution in Multi-County Districts," *Georgia Political Science Association Journal* 2 (Fall 1974), 29–42.

10. Cain, *Reapportionment Puzzle*, 63.

11. Barabas and Jerit, "Redistricting Principles."

12. *United Jewish Organizations of Williamsburgh v. Carey*, 430 U.S. 144 (1977).

13. *Easley v. Cromartie*, 532 U.S. 234 (2001).

14. Cain, *Reapportionment Puzzle*, 12.

15. McDonald, "Drawing the Line," 15.

16. Ronald Keith Gaddie, "The Texas Redistricting, Measure for Measure," *Extensions* (Fall 2004): 21.

17. Ronald Keith Gaddie and Charles S. Bullock III, "From *Ashcroft* to *Larios*: Recent Redistricting Lessons from Georgia," *Fordham Urban Law Journal* 34 (April 2007): 1014–15.

18. *Larios v. Cox*, 300 F. Supp. 2d 1320 (N.D. Ga. 2004).

19. Michael P. McDonald, "A Comparative Analysis of Redistricting Institutions in the United States, 2001–2002," *State Politics and Policy Quarterly* 4 (Winter 2004): 390.

20. Andrew Gelman and Gary King, "Enhancing Democracy through Legislative Redistricting," *American Political Science Review* 88 (September 1994): 547.

21. On the way in which Texas Democrats were divorced from their district cores, see Seth C. McKee and Daron R. Shaw, "Redistricting in Texas: Institutionalizing Republican Ascendency," in *Redistricting in the New Millennium*, ed. Peter F. Galderisi (Lanham, MD: Lexington Books, 2005): 297–99.

22. Barabas and Jerit, "Redistricting Principles."

Chapter 5

1. Alan Ehrenhalt, "Legislative Districts and Judicial Tinkering," *Congressional Quarterly Weekly Report* 43 (April 13, 1985): 703.

2. Tom Hofeller, quoted in Rhodes Cook, "Parties in High-Stakes Battle for Right to Draw Lines," *Congressional Quarterly Weekly Reports* 47 (August 12, 1989): 2138.

3. Bruce Cain, "Assessing the Partisan Effects of Redistricting," *American Political Science Review* 79 (June 1985): 326.

4. Peverill Squire, "Results of Partisan Redistricting in Seven U.S. States during the 1970s," *Legislative Studies Quarterly* 10 (May 1985): 260.

5. For an analysis that discounts the impact of computer-assisted redistricting as a major factor in producing gerrymanders, see Micah Altman, Karin Mac Donald, and Michael McDonald, "Pushbutton Gerrymanders? How Computing Has Changed Redistricting," in *Party Lines: Competition, Partisanship, and Congressional Redistricting*, ed. Thomas E. Mann and Bruce E. Cain (Washington, DC: Brookings Intuition Press, 2005), 51–66.

6. For example, Republicans spent $400,000 to win a majority in the Virginia house in anticipation of the 2001 redistricting. Greg L. Giroux, "The Hidden Election: Day of the Mapmaker," *CQ Weekly* 58 (February 19, 2000): 346. The legal problems that prompted Rep. Tom DeLay (R-TX) to resign from the House stemmed from questions about the legality of funds he funneled to win control of the Texas house. Once Republicans controlled the Texas house, they adopted a GOP gerrymander for the congressional map. See Steve Bickerstaff, *Lines in the Sand: Congressional Redistricting in Texas and the Downfall of Tom DeLay* (Austin: University of Texas Press, 2007).

7. David Butler and Bruce Cain, *Congressional Redistricting: Comparative and Theoretical Perspectives* (New York: Macmillan, 1992), 109–10.

8. Morris P. Fiorina, *Representation, Roll Calls, and Constituencies* (Lexington, MA: Lexington Books, 1974), 102–103; Charles S. Bullock III, "The Impact of Changing the Racial Composition of Congressional Districts on Legislators' Roll Call Behavior," *American Politics Quarterly* 23 (April 1995): 151–52.

9. Andrew Gelman and Gary King, "Enhancing Democracy through Legislative Redistricting," *American Political Science Review* 88 (September 1994): 541– 59.

10. David M. Farrell, *Electoral Systems* (New York: Palgrave, 2001).

11. Sam Hirsch, "The United States House of Unrepresentatives: What Went Wrong in the Latest Round of Congressional Redistricting," *Election Law Journal* 2 (2003): 206. Despite the pro-Republican bias, Democrats won an eight to seven majority of the delegation in 2008, taking 52 percent of the vote in the fourteen contested seats. John Conyers (D) ran unopposed.

12. Gelman and King, "Enhancing Democracy," 552.

13. Gelman and King, "Enhancing Democracy," 551.

14. Bryan Tyson, who drew the Georgia congressional plan adopted in 2005 and who has provided technical advice to that state's Republicans during the 2000s, devised a plan that gave his party good prospects for winning ten of the thirteen districts. The Department of Justice would have vetoed that alternative for being retrogressive,

since it reduced the number of districts in which African Americans could elect their preferred candidates from four to three. Personal communication from Bryan Tyson, August 10, 2009.

15. Fenno explains that early in their careers, legislators work to expand their base. Once they have gotten sufficient support, they simply seek to maintain that level of support. Richard F. Fenno Jr., *Home Style* (Boston: Little, Brown, 1978). For a description of how a senior, rural Democrat tried and ultimately failed to adjust to a suburbanizing, increasingly Republican constituency, see Fenno, *Congress at the Grassroots* (Chapel Hill: University of North Carolina Press, 2000), chapter 3.

16. Amihai Glazer and Marc Robbins, "Congressional Responsiveness to Constituency Change," *American Journal of Political Science* 29 (May 1985): 259–73; Christine Leveaux-Sharpe, "Congressional Responsiveness to Redistricting Induced Constituency Change: An Extension to the 1990s," *Legislative Studies Quarterly* 26 (May 2001): 275–86.

17. Carol M. Swain, *Black Faces, Black Interests: The Representation of African Americans in Congress* (Cambridge, MA: Harvard University Press, 1993), 72–73.

18. Claudine Gay, "Legislating without Constraints: The Effect of Minority Districting on Legislators' Responsiveness to Constituency Preferences," *Journal of Politics* 69 (May 2007): 442–56.

19. *Colegrove v. Green*, 328 U.S. 549 (1946).

20. *Gaffney v. Cummings*, 412 U.S. 735 (1973).

21. See, for example, Jonathan Winburn, *The Realities of Redistricting: Following the Rules and Limiting Gerrymandering and State Legislative Redistricting* (Lanham, MD: Lexington Books, 2008).

22. A partial dissent comes from Niemi and Abramowitz: "In contrast to results for the 1970s and 1980s, then, contrary to the hypothesis that mapmakers are becoming more skilled at partisan line-drawing, initial results from the 1990s indicate that, on average, partisan control of state government did little or nothing to enhance partisan gains from redistricting." Richard G. Niemi and Alan I. Abramowitz, "Partisan Redistricting in the 1992 Congressional Elections," *Journal of Politics* 56 (August 1994): 815.

23. Bruce E. Cain, Karin Mac Donald, and Michael McDonald, "From Equality to Fairness: The Path of Political Reform Since *Baker v. Carr*," in *Party Lines: Competition, Partisanship, and Congressional Redistricting*, ed. Thomas E. Mann and Bruce E. Cain (Washington, DC: Brookings Institution Press, 2005), 19.

24. *Gaffney v. Cummings*, 412 U.S. 735 (1973).

25. David Butler and Bruce Cain, *Congressional Redistricting: Comparative and Theoretical Perspectives* (New York: Macmillan, 1992), 104.

26. For a different perspective on the Frost gerrymander, see Seth C. McKee and Daron R. Shaw, "Redistricting in Texas: Institutionalizing Republican Ascendancy," in *Redistricting in the New Millennium*, ed. Peter F. Galderisi (Lanham, MD: Lexington Books, 2005), 288–92.

27. *Balderas v. Texas*, Civil Action No. 6:01CV 158 (E.D. Tex.), 2001, Slip opinion, p. 7.

28. *Balderas v. Texas*, Slip opinion, p. 9.

29. Richard E. Cohen, "The House on the Line," *National Journal* 32 (April 8, 2000): 1110.

30. Bickerstaff, *Lines in the Sand.*

31. Bernard Grofman and Thomas Brunell, "The Art of the Dummymander: The Impact of Recent Redistrictings on the Partisan Makeup of Southern House Seats," in *Redistricting in the New Millennium,* ed. Peter F. Galderisi (Lanham, MD: Lexington Books, 2005). Howard A. Scarrow describes the unsuccessful effort to produce a partisanly fair plan in Connecticut in the early 1970s and how that plan quickly ceased to reflect the partisan makeup of the electorate. Scarrow, "Partisan Gerrymandering—Invidious or Benevolent? *Gaffney v. Cummings* and Its Aftermath," *Journal of Politics* 44 (August 1982): 810–21.

32. Peverill Squire, "Results of Partisan Redistricting in Seven U. S. States during the 1970s," *Legislative Studies Quarterly* 10 (May 1985): 264.

33. Michael Barone and Grant Ujifusa, *The Almanac of American Politics, 1988* (Washington, DC: *National Journal,* 1987), 394.

34. Barone and Ujifusa, *Almanac of American Politics, 1988,* 413.

35. Michael Barone with Richard E. Cohen, *The Almanac of American Politics, 2004* (Washington, DC: National Journal, 2003), 1350.

36. The unraveling of the GOP gerrymander in Pennsylvania is but part of a broader problem with Republican plans. Hirsch notes that the Republican advantage in the House following the 2002 elections resulted largely from Republican plans adopted in Florida, Michigan, Ohio, and Pennsylvania. Half of the senators from these states were Democrats, and Al Gore won 50.7 percent of the vote in these states. Nonetheless, in 2002, Republicans won two-thirds of the House seats, increasing their numbers from forty-four to fifty-one. Hirsch, "United States House of Unrepresentatives," 201. The benefits achieved by the GOP proved short-lived. After the 2008 election, Democrats had majorities of the House delegations from all of these states except Florida and had won thirty-nine of the seats, which gave them 50.6 percent of the seats compared with Gore's 50.7 percent of the 2000 vote.

37. Cain, Mac Donald, and McDonald, "From Equality to Fairness," 23.

38. Democrats controlled both California legislative chambers and the governorship and therefore could have drawn a partisan map. They chose not to do so for fear that such a plan might endanger some of the Democrats who had taken Republican seats in 2000. Barone with Cohen, *Almanac of American Politics, 2004,* 155–57.

39. Ronald E. Weber, "Race-Based Districting: Does It Help or Hinder Legislative Representation?" *Political Geography* 19 (2000): 213–47.

40. Fiona McGillivary, *Privileging Industry: The Comparative Politics of Trade and Industrial Policy* (Princeton, NJ: Princeton University Press, 2004).

41. Robert M. Stein and Kenneth N. Bickers, "Congressional Elections and the Pork Barrel," *Journal of Politics* 56 (May 1994): 377–99.

42. Anthony Downs, *An Economic Theory of Democracy* (New York: Harper and Row, 1957).

43. Samuel Issacharoff, "Gerrymandering and Political Cartels," *Harvard Law Review* 116 (2002): 628.

44. Morris P. Fiorina, *Representatives, Roll Calls, and Constituencies* (Lexington, MA: Lexington Books, 1974).

45. Michael P. McDonald, "Drawing the Line on District Competition," *PS: Political Science and Politics* 39 (January 2, 2006): 91–94.

46. Maureen Schweers, "U.S. House Races: Republican Resurgence after Eight Lean Years," in *Midterm Madness: The Elections of 2002*, ed. Larry J. Sabato (Lanham, MD: Rowman & Littlefield, 2003), 69.

47. L. Sandy Maisel, Cherie D. Maestas, and Walter J. Stone, "The Impact of Redistricting on Candidate Emergence," in *Party Lines: Competition, Partisanship, and Congressional Redistricting*, ed. Thomas E. Mann and Bruce E. Cain (Washington, DC: Brookings Institution Press, 2005), 31.

48. Cain, Mac Donald, and McDonald, "From Equality to Fairness," 22.

49. David R. Mayhew, *Congress: The Electoral Connection* (New Haven, CN: Yale University Press, 1974), 82.

50. Norman J. Ornstein, Thomas E. Mann, and Michael J. Malbin, *Vital Statistics on Congress, 1997–1998* (Washington, DC: Congressional Quarterly, 1998), 68.

51. Rahm Emanuel, "A Big Factor in Corruption: Gerrymandering," *Roll Call* (July 25, 2006).

52. Hirsch, "United States House of Unrepresentatives," 179.

53. Editorial, "Broken Democracy," *Washington Post*, November 10, 2002, B6.

54. John A. Ferejohn, "On the Decline of Competition in Congressional Elections," *American Political Science Review* 71 (March 1977): 166–76; Albert D. Cover, "One Good Turn Deserves Another: The Advantage of Incumbency in Congressional Elections," *American Journal of Political Science* 21 (August 1977): 523–41; Charles S. Bullock III, "Redistricting and Congressional Stability, 1962–1972," *Journal of Politics* 37 (1975): 569–75.

55. Amihai Glazer, Bernard Grofman, and Marc Robbins, "Partisan and Incumbency Effects of 1970s Congressional Redistricting," *American Journal of Political Science* 31 (August 1987): 680–707.

56. Maisel, Maestas, and Stone, "Impact of Redistricting on Candidate Emergence," 36–46.

57. John R. Petrocik and Scott W. Desposato, "The Partisan Consequences of Majority-Minority Redistricting in the South, 1992 and 1994," *Journal of Politics* 60 (August 1998): 613–33.

58 Seth C. McKee, "Redistricting and Familiarity with U.S. House Candidates," *American Politics Research* 36 (November 2008): 962–79.

59. Seth C. McKee, *Republican Ascendancy in Southern U.S. House Elections* (Boulder, CO: Westview Press, 2010), chapter 3; McKee, "The Effects of Redistricting on Voting Behavior in Incumbent U.S. House Elections, 1992–1994," *Political Research Quarterly* 61 (March 2008): 122–32; M. V. Hood III and Seth C. McKee, "Trying to Thread the Needle: The Effects of Redistricting in a Georgia Congressional District," *PS: Political Science and Politics* 42 (October 2009).

60. Gary Jacobson designates as quality congressional candidates those who have office-holding experience. Jacobson, *The Electoral Origins of Divided Government:*

Competition in the U.S. House Elections, 1946–1988 (Boulder, CO: Westview Press, 1990).

61. Gary W. Cox and Jonathan N. Katz, *Elbridge Gerry's Salamander* (Cambridge, UK: Cambridge University Press, 2002), chapter 9. Also see Susan A. Banducci and Jeffery A. Carp, "Electoral Consequences of Scandal and Reapportionment in the 1992 House Elections," *American Politics Quarterly* 22 (January 1994): 3–26.

62. Thomas L. Brunell, *Redistricting and Representation: Why Competitive Elections Are Bad for America* (New York: Routledge, 2008).

63. *Davis v. Bandemer*, 478 U.S. 109 (1986).

64. *Badham v. Eu*, 695 F. Supp. 664 (N.D. Cal. 1988), affirmed in 488 U.S. 1024 (1989).

65. *Vieth v. Jubelirer*, 541 U.S. 267 (2004).

66. Samuel Issacharoff, Pamela Karlan, and Richard Pildes, *The Law of Democracy*, 2nd ed. (New York: Foundation Press, 2002), 886.

67. *Cox v. Larios*, 542 U.S. 947 (2004).

68. Some claim that California's 1982 pro-Democratic gerrymander came in reaction to what Indiana Republicans had done. Glazer, Grofman, and Robbins, "Partisan and Incumbency Effects," 696.

69. *Easley v. Cromartie*, 532 U.S. 234 (2001).

70. Donald E. Stokes, "Is There a Better Way to Redistrict?" in *Race and Redistricting in the 1990s*, ed. Bernard Grofman (New York: Agathon, 1998), 345–66; Sam Hirsch, "Unpacking *Page v. Bartels*: A Fresh Redistricting Paradigm Emerges in New Jersey," *Election Law Journal* 1 (2002): 8–11.

71. Jamie L. Carson and Michael Crespin, "The Effect of State Redistricting Methods on Electoral Competition in United States House of Representatives Races," *State Politics and Policy Quarterly* 4 (Winter 2004): 455–69.

72. Brunell, *Redistricting and Representation*.

Chapter 6

1. Kevin A. Hill, "Does the Creation of Majority Black Districts Aid Republicans? An Analysis of the 1992 Congressional Elections in Eight Southern States," *Journal of Politics* 57 (May 1995): 400.

2. John Lewis, testimony in *Georgia v. Ashcroft*, 204 F. Supp. 2d 4 (D.D.C. 2002).

3. Jonathan Winburn, *The Realities of Redistricting: Following the Rules and Limiting Gerrymandering in State Legislative Redistricting* (Lanham, MD: Lexington Books, 2008), 67.

4. The Democratic executive committee in each congressional district decided whether the outcome of the Democratic primary would be decided by popular vote or county unit vote.

5. According to McCrary and Lawson, Mississippi, Maryland, and Tennessee also used variants on the county unit system in the past. Peyton McCrary and Steven F. Lawson, "Race and Reapportionment, 1962: The Case of Georgia Senate Redistricting," *Journal of Policy History*, 12(Summer, 2000): 293-320.

6. *Baker v. Carr*, 369 U.S. 186 (1962).

7. *Gray v. Sanders*, 372 U.S. 368 (1963).

8. *Toombs v. Fortson*, 205 F. Supp. 248 (1962).

9. Carter's successful effort to thwart an attempt to steal this election is reported in Jimmy Carter, *Turning Point* (New York: Times Books, 1992).

10. *Wesberry v. Sanders*, 376 U.S. 1 (1964).

11. Scott E. Buchanan, "The Effect of the Abolition of the Georgia County Unit System on the 1962 Gubernatorial Election," *Southeastern Political Review* 25 (1997): 687–704; Albert B. Saye, "Georgia's County Unit System of Election," *Journal of Politics* 12 (February 1950): 93–106.

12. Howard Ball, Dale Krane, and Thomas Lauth, *Compromised Compliance: Implementation of the 1965 Voting Rights Act* (Westport, CN: Greenwood Press, 1982).

13. DOJ denies that it ever required 65 percent black districts. But Robert A. Holmes, a political science professor who served in the Georgia house from 1975 to 2008 wrote, "U.S. Justice Department and federal district court rulings have considered a district with a 65 percent black population as the minimum necessary to ensure the election of a black Congressman." Holmes, "Reapportionment Politics in Georgia: A Case Study," *Phylon* (1984): 180. Scholars writing later have debunked the idea that DOJ demanded 65 percent black districts. David Lublin, *The Paradox of Representation: Racial Gerrymandering and Minority Interests in Congress* (Princeton, NJ: Princeton University Press, 1997), 45–48; Kimball Brace, Bernard Grofman, Lisa Handley, and Richard G. Niemi, "Minority Voting Equality: The 65 Percent Rule in Theory and Practice," *Law and Policy* 10 (1988): 43–62. Except as noted, much of the discussion of the 1980s round of redistricting draws on Holmes.

14. Robert A. Holmes, "The Politics of Reapportionment, 1981: A Case Study of Georgia," *Urban Research Review* 8 (1982): 2.

15. Holmes writes that whites constituted 54 percent of the district's registered voters. Holmes, "Reapportionment Politics," 184.

16. See Kevin M. Kruse, *White Flight* (Princeton, NJ: Princeton University Press, 2005).

17. *Georgia v. United States*, 411 U.S. 526 (1973).

18. *Busbee v. Smith*, 549 F. Supp. 494 (D. D.C. 1982).

19. Quoted in Laughlin McDonald, *A Voting Rights Odyssey: Black Enfranchisement in Georgia* (Cambridge, UK: Cambridge University Press, 2003), 171.

20. Ladd goes on to point out that while he and McKinney are poles apart ideologically, he attended her swearing in as congresswoman when she won the Eleventh District. Personal interview with Ladd, May 21, 1998. LBC member Robert Holmes has written about the 1991–1992 redistricting from the perspective of a participant observer. Robert A. Holmes, "Reapportionment Strategies in the 1990s: The Case of Georgia," in *Race and Redistricting in the 1990s*, ed. Bernard Grofman (New York: Agathon Press, 1998). Holmes attributes the creation of the plan with three majority-black districts to Representatives Cynthia McKinney and Tyrone Brooks along with ACLU attorney Kathy Wilde (p. 193). Holmes also takes credit himself for submitting the three majority-black district congressional plan (p. 197). The opinion of the federal district court stated that "the necessary kernel of a viable three-district plan—the

Macon/Savannah trade—originated with Ms. Wilde." *Johnson v. Miller,* 864 F. Supp. 1354 (S.D. Ga., 1994).

21. Holmes attributes the "MAXBLACK" label to a state legislative plan devised by McKinney and Brooks, which provided for fifty-one majority-black house districts and fifteen majority-black senate districts. Robert A. Holmes, "Reapportionment/Redistricting Politics in Georgia in the 1990s and 2001–2002: Reflections of a Participant-Observer," in *Voting Rights and Minority Representation: Redistricting, 1992–2002,* ed. David A. Bositis (Lanham, MD: University Press of America, 2006), 88.

22. Maurice T. Cunningham, *Maximization, Whatever the Cost: Race, Redistricting, and the Department of Justice* (Westport, CN: Praeger, 2001), 142–48.

23. Deposition of John Dunne at p. 122 in *Johnson v. Miller* , 864 F. Supp. 1354 (S.D. Ga. 1994).

24. Personal interview with Rep. Bob Hanner, April 14, 1992.

25. John R. Dunne to Mark H. Cohen, January 21, 1992.

26. John R. Dunne to Mark H. Cohen, January 21, 1992.

27. John R. Dunne to Mark H. Cohen, March 20, 1992.

28. *Georgia v. Ashcroft,* 539 U.S. 461 (2003).

29. John Berendt, *Midnight in the Garden of Good and Evil* (New York: Vintage Books, 1994).

30. The creation of the new majority-black congressional districts in the early 1990s unleashed a pent-up reservoir of ambition among African American politicians. For a further discussion of this phenomenon, see David T. Canon, *Race, Redistricting, and Representation* (Chicago: University of Chicago Press, 1999), chapter 3.

31. John Alford, Holly Teeters, Daniel S. Ward, and Rick K. Wilson, "Overdraft: The Political Cost of Congressional Malfeasance," *Journal of Politics* 56 (August 1994): 788–810; Gary Jacobson and Michael A. Dimock, "Checking Out: The Effects of Overdrafts on the 1992 House Elections," *American Journal of Political Science* 38 (1994): 601–24.

32. Holmes, "Reapportionment/Redistricting Politics in Georgia," 91.

33. *Shaw v. Reno,* 509 U.S. 630 (1993).

34. *Miller v. Johnson,* 515 U.S. 900 (1995).

35. James Salzer, "Legislators Will Meet Aug. 14," *Atlanta Journal Constitution,* July 8, 1995, 13A.

36. Robert A. Holmes, "Reapportionment Strategies in the 1990s," 213.

37. *Abrams v. Johnson,* 521 U.S. 74 (1997).

38. Charles S. Bullock III and Richard E. Dunn, "The Demise of Racial Districting and the Future of Black Representation," *Emory Law Review* 48 (Fall 1999): 1209–52.

39. Holmes, "Reapportionment/Redistricting Politics in Georgia," 92.

40. Expert report of David Epstein in *Georgia v. Ashcroft.*

41. This and the next paragraph rely on Winburn, *Realities of Redistricting,* 81.

42. Ronald Keith Gaddie and Charles S. Bullock III, "From *Ashcroft* to *Larios*: Recent Redistricting Lessons from Georgia," *Fordham Urban Law Journal* 34 (April 2007): 1014–15.

43. Winburn, *Realities of Redistricting,* 76–77.

44. Gaddie and Bullock, "From *Ashcroft* to *Larios*," 1013.

45. This was one of twenty-three examples of water contiguity in the legislative plans. Expert report of Ronald Keith Gaddie, *Larios v. Cox,* 300 F. Supp. 2d 1320 (N.D. Ga. 2004).

46. Jim Galloway, "Redrawn District Takes All Day to Tour," *Atlanta Journal-Constitution,* August 11, 2001, A6.

47. Twiggs was accurate in claiming no responsibility for the senate maps. Until 2004, the norm in the Georgia General Assembly was to allow each chamber to draw its own map, which the other chamber then rubber-stamped.

48. *Georgia v. Ashcroft,* 539 U.S. 461 (2003).

49. *Georgia v. Ashcroft.*

50. Holmes, "Reapportionment/Redistricting Politics in Georgia," 107.

51. *Larios v. Cox,* 300 F. Supp. 2d. 1320 (N.D. Ga. 2004).

52. *Reynolds v. Sims,* 377 U.S. 533 (1964).

53. M. V. Hood III and Seth C. McKee, "Gerrymandering on Georgia's Mind: The Effects of Redistricting on Vote Choice in the 2006 Midterm Election," *Social Science Quarterly* 89 (March 2008): 60–77.

54. Holmes, "Reapportionment Politics," p. 180.

55. Holmes writes that the LBC "split into two factions of almost equal size over the feasibility of creating two majority-Black congressional and one 'influence' (approximately 40 percent Black) district versus three majority-Black districts" (p. 191). Later in the same chapter he reports, "In fact, the majority of its [LBC's] members actually voted to support the two-majority-Black District Congressional Plan to which Justice objected" (p. 208). Holmes, "Reapportionment Politics." The LBC chair and several other senior members supported the state plan in meetings with DOJ attorneys.

56. This difference in the relevant constituency of black legislators also occurred in Congress, with those in the House leadership more likely to support the Democratic Party position and members not incorporated into the leadership tending to be more responsive to forces outside the chamber. Nadine Cohodas, "Black House Members Striving for Influence," *Congressional Quarterly Weekly Report* 43 (April 13, 1985): 681.

57. On at least one occasion during the 2001 redistricting session, enough LBC members joined with Republicans so that Democrats had to make changes in the congressional maps. David Pendered, "Black Democrats Revolt over Murphy's Districts," *Atlanta Journal-Constitution,* September 6, 2001, C8.

58. GLBC refers to the Georgia Legislative Black Caucus. Holmes, "Reapportionment/Redistricting Politics," 107.

59. Holmes, "Reapportionment Strategies in the 1990s," 203.

60. Robert Holmes' testimony in *Georgia v. Ashcroft,* 204 F. Supp. 2d 4 (D.D.C. 2002).

61. Earl Black and Merle Black, *The Rise of Southern Republicans* (Cambridge, MA: Belknap Press, 2002); Charles S. Bullock III, Donna R. Hoffman, and Ronald K. Gaddie, "Regional Variations in the Realignment of American Politics, 1944–2004," *Social Science Quarterly* 87 (September 2006): 494–518.

Chapter 7

1. Tom Hofeller quoted in Shane D'Aprile, "The Ten-Year Storm," *Politics Magazine* (January 2010), online edition accessed at politicsmagazine.com.

2. Richard E. Cohen, "Battle Lines," *National Journal*, December 19, 2009, 28.

3. The discussion of this section draws heavily upon a press release from Election Data Services, "New Population Estimates Show Additional Changes for 2009 Congressional Apportionment, with Many States Sitting Close to the Edge for 2010," December 23, 2009.

4. For a discussion of the merits of increasing the size of the House, see Brian Frederick, *Congressional Representation and Constituents: The Case for Increasing the U.S. House of Representatives* (New York: Routledge, 2010).

5. Election Data Services, "New Population Estimates."

6. For a discussion of longitudinal trends in party strength, see Charles S. Bullock III, Donna R. Hoffman, and Ronald Keith Gaddie, "Regional Variations in the Realignment of American Politics, 1944–2004," *Social Science Quarterly* 87 (September 2006): 494–518.

7. Election Data Services, "Five States Would Gain Seats If Congress Were Reapportioned with 2005 Population Estimates," December 22, 2005.

8. D'Aprile, "The Ten-Year Storm."

9. The efforts by U.S. House Majority Leader Tom DeLay to influence Texas's state legislative elections in 2002 is chronicled in Steve Bickerstaff, *Lines in the Sand* (Austin: University of Texas Press, 2007).

10. Much of the following material is drawn from Stewart Elliott, "A Census Campaign That Speaks in Many Tongues," *New York Times*, January 14, 2010, B3.

11. Dan Chapman, "Stakes, Challenges High for Counting Every Georgian, Getting Every Dollar," *Atlanta Journal Constitution*, January 18, 2010.

12. Julia Preston, "Latino Leaders Use Churches in Census Bid," *New York Times*, December 23, 2009, A1, A4.

13. Miguel Rivera, "Should Latinos Boycott?" *Atlanta Journal Constitution*, November 29, 2009, A8.

14. Sam Roberts, "Losers and Winners in a Proposed Census Change," *New York Times*, October 28, 2009, A20.

15. Nathaniel Persily, "The Promise and Pitfalls of the New Voting Rights Act," *Yale Law Review* 117 (2007), 217.

16. Charles S. Bullock III and Richard E. Dunn, "The Demise of Racial Redistricting and the Future of Black Representation," *Emory Law Review* 48 (1999): 1210–1253; Bernard Grofman, Lisa Handley, and David Lublin, "Drawing Effective Minority Districts: A Conceptual Framework and Some Empirical Evidence," *North Carolina Law Review* 79 (2001).

17. *Georgia v. Ashcroft*, 539 U.S. 461 (2003).

18. Persily, "Promise and Pitfalls," 236. This article explores a number of issues that courts may confront when applying the 2006 Voting Rights Act to redistricting.

19. Cohen, "Battle Lines," 30.

20. Cameron Joseph, "From Black to Brown," *National Journal* (December 19, 2009): 24.

21. Assessing the likelihood that a particular minority percentage can elect its candidate of choice is subject to a number of considerations. Recent years have seen blacks fail to maintain majority-black districts they had long held. The split in the black community in the Democratic primary in 2006 opened the way for the nomination of a white candidate, who went on to win the general election and secured a second term in 2008 in the 62.8 percent black Ninth District of Tennessee. In 2008, a Vietnamese-American Republican unseated the scandal-hobbled incumbent in Louisiana's 59.5 percent black Second District. Determining the necessary concentration of Latinos for them to elect their choice is even more difficult because of the presence of noncitizens. Anglo Gene Green continues to win reelection from Houston's Twenty-Ninth congressional district, even though Latinos constitute more than 70 percent of the district's population. In 2004 Anglo Lloyd Doggett defeated Leticia Hinojosa in the Democratic primary in Texas's Twenty-Fifth District, in which more than two-thirds of the population was Hispanic.

22. *Bartlett v. Strickland*, 556 U.S. 1 (2009).

23. Ronald Brownstein, "The March of Destiny," *National Journal* 41 (December 19, 2009): 18–25.

24. Currently efforts are under way in California to place a proposition on the 2010 ballot that would give responsibility for drawing congressional districts to an independent commission. If placed on the ballot and approved by a majority of the voters, then plans like that designed by Phil Burton and described earlier in this book would no longer be crafted in the Golden State.

25. Going into the 2010 election, Republicans have a tenuous one-seat advantage in the Tennessee house that, if lost, would allow Democrats to retain a veto even if the governorship changes hands.

26. Ultimately the Supreme Court undid a portion of the DeLay plan because, in an effort to protect fellow Republican Rep. Henry Bonilla, it was guilty of retrogression when it reduced the Hispanic concentration in his district from 66.8 percent to 55.1 percent. *LULAC v. Perry*, 548 U.S. 399 (2006). The other allegation of political interference involved DOJ approval of a Georgia law requiring that voters present one of a limited number of types of photo identification in order to vote.

27. Cohen, "Battle Lines," 32.

28. The plan created two heavily Hispanic open seats. However, Gene Green ran in the Twenty-Ninth District, which he had represented since 1993 even though his home had been removed from it, and as noted elsewhere, Lloyd Doggett opted to run in a district that extended from the Rio Grande to Austin and defeated a Latina in the Democratic primary.

29.   Quoted in Cohen, "Battle Lines," 28.

Index

527 groups, 182

Abramowitz, Alan L., 205n22
Abrams v. Johnson, 155–56, 210n37
ACLU. *See* American Civil Liberties
    Union
affirmative action gerrymandering, 50,
    59, 62, 78–79, 94
African Americans, 13, 44–45, 50–53,
    55, 57, 59–60, 64, 66–67, 69–73,
    76–77, 79–84, 98–99, 113, 115,
    117–18, 132, 141–52, 159, 165,
    167–68, 170–71, 184–86, 189–90
Alabama, 7, 27, 31–34, 53, 62–64,
    73–77, 98, 141, 181; influence of, 13,
    15, 42
Alaska, 56
Albany, Ga., 149, 151
Allen v. State Board of Elections, 54, 189,
    198n10
Allgood, Tom, 144
Altman, Micah, 204n5
American Civil Liberties Union, 153–55,
    171
Annapolis, Md., 90
apportionment of seats to states, 26–28

Arizona, 7, 27, 56, 104, 114, 134–36,
    177–79, 181, 189
Arizona's Redistricting Commission,
    134–35
Arkansas, 7, 40, 61, 63
Articles of Confederation, 46
Ashcroft v. Georgia, 149, 166
Asian Americans, 69
Atlanta, Ga., 9, 50, 81, 141–42, 149,
    153–54, 160, 163, 166, 168
Atlanta's Concerned Black Clergy, 171
Augusta, Ga., 144, 146, 149
Austin, Tex., 118
Avery v. Midland County, 196n17

Badham v. Eu, 208n65
Baker v. Carr, 33–34, 36, 42, 49, 97, 140,
    195n10, 209n6
Balderas v. Texas, 205n27
Baldwin County, Ga., 148
Baltimore, Md., 90
Barnes, Roy, 158, 166, 167
Barrow, John, 168
Bartlett v. Strickland, 187, 199n43,
    213n22
Barton, Joe, 117

Beauprez, Bob, 12
Beer v. United States, 55, 68, 81, 198n12
Bexar County, Tex., 52
bias, 21, 111–12
Bickerstaff, Steve, 118, 194n11, 204n6
bipartisan gerrymanders, 122–25, 127
biracial coalitions, 68
Birmingham, Ala., 34, 50, 73
Bishop, Sanford, 151, 156, 168
black threat hypothesis, 51
bleaching of districts, 73, 77–78, 84, 128, 152, 190
Blue, Dan, 13
Blumstein, James, 202n83
Bond, Julian, 144, 171
Bonilla, Henry, 213n26
Bossier Parish, La., 68
Boston, Mass., 8
Boswell, Leonard, 133–34
Brace, Kimball, 175, 181
Brennan, William, 39
Brooks, Tyrone, 147, 153, 209–10n20
Brown v. Thomson, 196n24
Brown, Robert, 172
Brown, Scott, 189
Brown, Willie, 13
Brunell, Thomas, 22, 82–83, 129, 136
Bullock, Charles S., 79
Burns v. Richardson, 196
Burton, Philip, 114–15, 120, 130, 213n24
Busbee v. Smith, 145, 146, 201n64, 209n18
Bush v. Vera, 81, 92
Bush, George H. W., 115, 147, 154
Bush, George W., 1, 8, 94, 117, 120, 154, 165, 168, 190

Cain, Bruce E., 80, 98, 100, 126
California, 4, 22, 31–32, 56, 113–15, 121, 123, 125, 130, 134, 177–80, 184, 189, 213n24
Campbell, James, 42
Canon, David T., 13
Carmichael, James, 140

Carter, Jimmy, 1, 141, 209n9
Carter, Selwyn, 198n30
Census Bureau, 22–24, 27, 158, 175–78, 181–83
census taking, 22, 181–84
Chambliss, Saxby, 101
Chesapeake Bay, 90
Chicago, Ill., 28, 49
Civil Rights Act of 1957, 52
Civil Rights Act of 1960, 52
Civil Rights Act of 1964, 52
Clark, Tom C., 33, 36
Cleland, Max, 101
Clinton, Hillary, 69–70
Colegrove v. Green, 28–29, 33, 43, 195n3, 205n19
Collins, Mac, 151
Colorado, 7, 12, 92
Columbus, Ga., 149, 151
community of interest, 99–100, 148, 163
compactness, 58, 90–94, 104, 117, 153, 156, 163, 168–170, 188
Congressional Black Caucus, 78, 186
Congressional districts, 11–12, 15, 26, 35–40, 70, 73–78, 83, 90, 98–99, 123–26, 133–34, 141–45, 151–54, 167–71, 176–81, 187–90
Connecticut, 27, 29, 32, 114, 181, 189
contiguity, 88–90, 104, 117, 153, 188
Conyers, John, 204n11
Cook County, Ill., 28
core preservation, 102
Cosgrove, Kenneth, 79
county unit system, 140, 160, 170
court drawn plans, 12–13, 117, 167
Coverdell, Paul, 144–45
Cox v. Larios, 131, 196n26, 208n68
Cox, Gary, 12, 128
cracking, 16, 20, 51, 83
Cromartie v. Easley, 132
Cromartie v. Hunt, 198n27
crossover voting, 156
Cuban-Americans, 69

Dade County, Fla., 69
Dallas County, Tex., 52
Dallas-Fort Worth Metroplex, 118, 186
David and Eisenberg Ratios, 29–31, 42
David, Paul, 29–31, 195n5
Davis v. Bandemer, 129–131, 208n64
Deal, Nathan, 152
DeKalb County, Ga., 144, 146, 148, 151
Delaware, 3, 25
DeLay plan, 80, 82, 118, 128, 132, 190, 213n26
DeLay, Tom, 12, 118, 120, 204n6
DeLoach, George, 151, 153
Democratic districts, 23–24, 45, 67, 72–73, 75, 77, 80, 84, 86, 94, 100–101, 111–12, 114–16, 107–33, 141, 145, 159–60, 167–68, 170–72, 180, 188–89
Democratic Party, 13, 52, 55, 76, 79, 86, 101, 128, 154, 171–72; in Congress, 7, 76
Democratic Redistricting Trust, 183
Desposato, Scott, 75–76
Detroit, Mich., 49–50
Dickinson, William, 73
District of Columbia district court, 53, 55, 142, 165, 182
Doggett, Lloyd, 118–19, 213n21
Douglas, William, 36, 41
Downs, Anthony, 124
Dunne, John, 72, 147–49, 197–99, 210n27

Easley v. Cromartie, 198n28, 203n13, 208n70
Edmonds, Douglas, 196n33
Edwards, Chet, 118–20
Eisenberg, Ralph, 29–31, 195n5
Election Data Services, 175, 179, 182
Electoral College, 8, 29, 140, 178, 180–81
Engstrom, Richard L., 200n47
Epstein, David, 80, 159
Equal Protection Clause, 33, 35, 40, 66, 86–87, 129–30, 132, 153, 166
Erdreich, Ben, 73, 191

Espy, Michael, 81
Evans, Lane, 94
Everett, Robinson, 64, 66

Fields, Cleo, 67
Fifteenth Amendment, 33, 57
Florida, 4, 7, 10, 29, 43–44, 56, 62, 64, 67–69, 79, 92–94, 98, 177–79, 181, 188
Foster, Mike, 68
Fourteenth Amendment, 33, 57, 130
Frankfurter, Felix, 28–29 33, 113
Frederick, Brian, 212n4
Frost, Martin, 1–2, 77, 102, 115–16, 118–20
Fulton County, Ga., 140–41, 144, 148, 154
fund allocation, 43–44
Foundation for the Future, 183

Gaffney v. Cummings, 205n24
Garand, James C., 79
Garza, Jose, 70
Gay, Claudine, 113
Gelman, Andrew, 21, 112
Geographic Information Systems, 39–40, 158
Georgia, 3, 7, 9, 12, 16–18, 22–23, 29, 32, 35–37, 41, 48, 53, 55, 60, 62–64, 67, 70, 73, 75–77, 80–81, 83, 101, 131, 139–73, 177–78, 181
Georgia v. Ashcroft, 80–82, 165, 186, 199n41, 201n68, 210n40
Georgia v. United States, 144, 209n17
Gerry, Elbridge, 107, 191
gerrymandering, 47, 82, 85, 91, 94, 107–10, 129–31, 189, 206n36
Gingrey, Phil, 168
Gingrich, Newt, 121
Goldwater, Barry, 45
Gomillion v. Lightfoot, 32–33, 195n9
Gore, Al, 8, 12, 94, 206n36
Gray v. Sanders, 196, 209n7
Green, Gene 63, 119–20, 213n21

Hagens, Winnet W., 201
Hajnal, Zoltan, 202n82
Hall, Ralph, 118–19
Hanner, Bob, 147
Hatcher, Charles, 151
Hiler, John, 121
Hill, Jeffrey S., 198n19
Hinojosa, Leticia, 213n21
Hirsch, Sam, 127
Hispanics. *See* Latinos
Hoffler, Thomas, 183
Holmes, Robert, 172
Hopi, 134
Horowitz, Donald L., 202n83
Houston, Tex., 70, 80, 118, 186, 213n21
Hurricane Katrina, 47, 177

I–85 District, 65–66
Idaho, 27, 104
Illinois, 4, 7–8, 27–28, 32, 43, 63,
    92–94, 113, 125, 177–78, 180–81,
    184, 189
IMPACT 2000, 11
incumbency gerrymandering, 16–17
incumbents, 16–17, 41, 63, 68, 70,
    75–80, 94, 100–102, 111–23, 133–36,
    151–52, 166–68, 188, 191
independent commissions, 9
Indiana, 7, 32, 120–21, 129, 181
Indianapolis, Ind., 51–52
influence districts, 81, 149, 165, 185
Iowa, 7, 9, 32, 40, 98, 101–2, 104, 125,
    133–34, 136, 177, 181, 184
Iowa's Legislative Services Agency, 135,
    189

Jackson, Carol, 165
Jackson, Maynard, 142
Jacobson, Gary, 208n61
Jefferson County, Ala., 34
Johnson v. DeGrandy, 68, 199n34
Johnson v. Miller, 210n20
Johnson, Eddie Bernice, 103
Johnson, Lyndon, 1, 45, 52
Jordan, Barbara, 142

judge drawn plans, 154, 190
judicial challenges, 11–13

Kansas, 7
Kansas City, Mo., 38
Karcher v. Daggett, 38–40, 47, 196n21
Katz, Jonathan W., 12, 128
Katzenbach, Nicholas, 52
Kennedy, Arthur, 130
Kennedy, Ted, 189
Kentucky, 27, 181
Key, V. O., 51, 197n3
King, Gary, 21, 112
Kingston, Jack, 101, 151

Ladd, Bart, 146, 209n20
Laney, Pete, 118
Larios v. Cox, 166, 185, 203n17, 211n44
Latham, Tom, 134
Latinos, 42, 50, 52, 56–57, 60, 62–64,
    68–70, 81–82, 115, 117, 118, 120,
    135, 183–84, 186, 190
Lawson, Steven F., 208n5
Leach, Jim, 133–34
Legislative Black Caucuses, 13, 64, 80,
    143, 145–47, 152, 159, 165, 171–72,
    211n58
Legislative Redistricting Board (LBR),
    118
Lewis, John, 81, 103, 145–46, 149, 165,
    171
Linder, John, 151
Los Angeles, Calif., 31, 50, 186
Lott, Trent, 183
Louisiana, 7, 53, 61–63, 67, 72, 76, 81,
    88, 98, 181, 184, 199n31
Lublin, David, 60, 73, 76–77
LULAC v. Perry, 213n26

Macon, Ga., 141, 146, 149, 151
Maine, 32
Maisel, L. Sandy, 127
majority-minority districts, 59–61, 78,
    84, 86, 92, 94, 98, 100, 104, 113, 152,
    186, 190

Making America's Promise Secure, 183

MALDEF. *See* Mexican-American Legal Defense and Education Fund

Marion County, Ind., 51

Marshall, Jim, 168

Maryland, 89–90, 189

Massachusetts, 4, 26, 32, 177–78, 181

Matthew Principle, 21

MAXBLACK, 147, 151–54, 171–72, 210n21

Mayhew, David R., 126

McCain-Feingold campaign, 182

McClosky, Francis, 121

McDonald, Laughlin, 67, 94

McDonald, Michael P., 193n7

McIntyre, Richard, 121

McKay, Robert B., 193n1

McKee, Seth C., 128

McKinney, Cynthia, 146–47, 151, 153, 156, 172

mechanic of redistricting, 9

Meggers, Linda, 158

Mexican-American Legal Defense and Education Fund, 70

Michigan, 4, 7, 57, 88–89, 112, 131, 177–78, 180–81, 184, 189

mid-decade redistricting, 12

Miller v. Johnson, 67, 153, 156, 158, 199n43, 209n20

Miller, William, 194n15

Miller, Zell, 144

Minnesota, 27, 32, 104, 177, 179–81, 189

Mississippi, 7, 15, 45, 53–54, 61, 64, 76, 81

Missouri, 4, 27, 37, 178–79, 181

Mobile v. Bolden, 198n15

Mobile, Ala., 57

Montana, 7, 22, 27, 184

Montgomery, Ala., 73

multi-member districts, 27, 45, 51–52, 58–59, 83–84, 97, 105, 109, 160, 172

Murphy, Tom, 9, 154

NAACP. *See* National Association for the Advancement of Colored People

National Association for the Advancement of Colored People, 68

National Association of Latino Elected Officials, 183–84

National Coalition of Latino Clergy and Christian Leaders, 184

National Conference of State Legislatures, 11

National Journal, 111

National Republican Congressional Committee, 190

Navajo, 134

Nebraska, 7, 32, 104, 181

Neill Primary Act, 140

Nelson, Garrison, 8–9, 193n5

Neugebauer, Randy, 102

Nevada, 7, 32, 177, 181

New Jersey, 7, 38, 43, 133, 177–78, 181, 188–89

New Orleans, La., 47, 50, 55

New York, 3–4, 7, 27, 47, 56, 63, 68, 99, 177–78, 180–81, 184, 189

New York City, N.Y., 23, 49–50, 99

Newport News, Va., 89

Niemi, Richard G., 199n40, 203n3, 205n22, 209n13

non-retrogression. *See* retrogression

Norfolk, Va., 89

North Carolina, 3, 7, 53, 59–60, 62–67, 70, 77, 79, 88, 90, 92–94, 132, 153, 177, 179, 181, 189

Nussle, Jim, 133–34

Obama, Barack, 42–43, 70, 178, 181, 188–89

O'Connor, Sandra Day, 66, 80, 90, 113, 130, 136, 153

Ohio, 4, 7, 9, 27, 31–32, 177–78, 181, 189

Oklahoma, 22, 32, 189

Oregon, 32, 177, 179, 181

Overby, Marvin, 79

overcounting, 22

packing, 2, 17, 20, 22, 51, 187
pairing, 18, 41, 100–102, 117, 126, 133, 160, 164, 166–67
Parker, Frank R., 15
Parry, Janine A., 194n15
partisan gerrymanders, 107–37
Pastor, Ed, 135
Pennsylvania, 4, 7, 22, 26 39, 121–22, 130–31, 177–78, 181, 184, 189
Perdue, Sonny, 101
Persily, Nathaniel, 41, 45–46, 166, 185–86
Petrocik, John, 75–76
Phoenix, Ariz., 134
Posner, Mark A., 199n43
preclearance. *See* Voting Rights Act
Press, Charles, 30–32
proportional representation, 2, 3 20, 21

racial gerrymandering, 60–67, 72, 81, 85–86, 94
racially polarized voting, 58, 63, 156
Rangel, Charlie, 186
Reagan, Ronald, 120
reapportionment, 3–4, 8–12, 27, 35, 66, 90, 117, 175–81
redistricting, 101, 125, 17–18, 35–40, 54–56, 60–64, 66, 72–77, 80, 85, 97, 101, 114–25, 142–73, 184–91
redistricting commissions, 68, 132–36, 188
Reno v. Bossier Parish School Board, 135, 199n33
Renzi, Rick, 135
Republican districts, 23, 45,–46, 72–73, 75, 77, 84, 86, 94, 100–101, 111–12, 114–16 107–33, 141, 143, 145, 152, 159–60, 167–68, 170–72, 188–89
Republican Legislative Campaign Fund, 11
Republican National Committee, 11
Republican Party, 7, 79
responsiveness, 21, 110–13, 185
retrogression, 55, 59, 60, 64, 68, 80–82, 159, 168, 186, 213n26

Reyes, Ben, 63
Reynolds v. Sims, 34, 41, 46, 54–55, 166, 196n12, 211n52
Rhode Island, 25, 181
Richmond, Va., 89
Rio Grande Valley, Tex., 115, 118, 186, 213n28
Rivera, Miguel, 184, 212n13
Roosevelt, Franklin, 27
Rose Institute, 97
runoffs, 63
Rust Belt, 7

Saint Louis, Mo., 37–38
sampling, 22–24
Sanders, James, 140
Sandlin, Max, 119–20
Savannah, Ga., 141, 148–49, 151, 153, 161
Scalia, Antonin, 3, 130–31
Scarrow, Howard A., 206n31
Schubert and Press Index, 30–31
Schubert, Glendon, 30–32
Schwartz, Thomas, 44
Scott, Al, 144
Scott, Bobby, 201n65
Sharpe, Christine Leveaux, 79
Shaw v. Hunt, 199n43
Shaw v. Reno, 66–67, 69, 80, 90–91 153, 185, 187, 198n25, 210n33
Shotts, Kenneth, 79, 85
silent gerrymander, 14, 33, 43, 46
Solarz, Stephen, 63
Souter, David, 69
South Carolina, 32, 53, 62–64, 76–77, 79–80, 104, 177–79
South Dakota, 56–57
South v. Peters, 195n4
stacking, 16–17, 19, 51
Stenholm, Charles, 102
Stephens, Bill, 162
Swain, Carol M., 81, 83, 113
swing ratio, 110–11, 116, 120, 125

Talmadge, Eugene, 140,
Tennessee, 13, 33–34, 94, 189, 213n21

Texas, 1–2, 4, 7–13, 27, 52, 56–57, 62,
    64, 68, 77–81, 92, 94, 100, 102,
    115–21, 125, 128, 132–33, 168,
    177–78, 181, 183–84, 188–89
Thornburg v. Gingles, 58–59, 69, 70, 156,
    198n16
Thurmond, Michael, 147
Toombs v. Fortson, 209n8
totality-of-the-circumstances test, 58–59
traditional districting principles, 91, 104,
    153, 156, 168, 191
turnout, 42–43
Tuskegee, Ala., 32–33
Twiggs, Ralph, 164
Tyson, Bryan, 204n14

U.S. Attorney General, 53
U.S. Department of Justice, 50, 53–55,
    59–64, 66, 68, 70, 77–78, 81, 84–86,
    97, 139, 142–51, 153–54, 156,
    159, 165, 170–73, 185–87, 189–90,
    199n44, 204n14
U.S. House Leadership, 8–9
U.S. House of Representatives, 2–3,
    59–60, 63
U.S. Supreme Court, 23–24, 28 –29,
    32–36, 52, 54, 57–59, 66–68, 70–72,
    80–81, 86, 94, 113–14, 129–31,
    140–41, 145, 153, 155–56, 165, 185,
    187–91, 199n43, 213n26
undercounting, 22–23
unions, 7
*United Jewish Organizations of
    Williamsburgh v. Carey*, 199n40,
    203n12
Utah, 22, 27, 134, 177, 179, 181

Veith v. Jubelirer, 130, 193n3, 208n66
Velázquez, Nadia, 63, 68
Vermont, 29

Virginia, 3, 11, 26–27, 43, 53, 62, 67, 77,
    79, 88–89, 181, 189
Voss, Stephen, 77
vote dilution, 34, 55
Voting Rights Act, 14, 52–62, 68, 82, 84,
    87, 99–100, 109, 145, 173, 186, 190;
    Section 2, 57–60, 62, 68–69, 71–72,
    83–85, 97, 145, 187; Section 5, 50,
    52–57, 59–60, 62, 68, 70, 72, 81–85,
    98, 142, 147–48, 159, 170, 182,
    185–86, 190
VRA. *See* Voting Rights Act

Walker, Eugene, 146–47, 171
Wallace, George, Jr., 73
Warren, Earl, 34, 195n1
Washington, 7, 114, 176–79, 181, 189
Washington, Craig, 78–79
wasted votes, 17–19, 78, 160
Watt, Melvin, 80
Weber, Ronald, 42, 124
Weller, Jerry, 94
Wesberry v. Sanders, 35–37, 45, 49, 97,
    196n14, 209n10
West Virginia, 181
Westmoreland, Lynn, 190
Whitby, Kenny, 83, 202n80
Whitcomb v. Chavis, 197n6
White v. Regester, 197n7
White, Byron, 52, 114, 129
Wilde, Kathy, 153
Wildgen, John K., 193
Wilson, Joe Mack, 144–45
Winburn, Jonathan, 159
Wisconsin, 22, 181

Young, Andrew, 142–43

"Zorro" district, 61, 98